8/10

Hispanic
American
Biographies

Volume 8

Selena—Zúñiga, Martha

an imprint of

■ SCHOLASTIC

www.scholastic.com/librarypublishing

First published 2006 by Grolier,
an imprint of Scholastic Library Publishing,
Old Sherman Turnpike,
Danbury, Connecticut 06816

Set ISBN-13: 978-0-7172-6124-6
Set ISBN-10: 0-7172-6124-7
Volume ISBN-13: 978-0-7172-6132-1
Volume ISBN-10: 0-7172-6132-8

Library of Congress Cataloging-in-Publication Data
Hispanic American biographies.
     v. cm.
  Includes bibliographical references and index.
  Contents: v. 1. Acevedo-Vilá, Aníbal - Bocanegra, Carlos -- v. 2. Bonilla,
Tony - Corretjer, Juan Antonio -- v. 3. Cortés, Carlos - Gálvez, Bernardo
de -- v. 4. Gamboa, Harry, Jr. - Julia, Raul -- v. 5. Juncos, Manuel
Fernández - Montez, Maria -- v. 6. Montoya, Carlos Garcia - Ponce, Mary
Helen -- v. 7. Ponce de León, Juan - Seguín, Juan N. -- v. 8. Selena -
Zúñiga, Martha.
  ISBN-13: 978-0-7172-6124-6 (set : alk. paper) -- ISBN-10: 0-7172-6124-7
(set : alk. paper) -- ISBN-13: 978-0-7172-6125-3 (v. 1 : alk. paper) -- ISBN-
10: 0-7172-6125-5 (v. 1 : alk. paper) -- ISBN-13: 978-0-7172-6126-0 (v. 2 :
alk. paper) -- ISBN-10: 0-7172-6126-3 (v. 2 : alk. paper) -- ISBN-13: 978-0-
7172-6127-7 (v. 3 : alk. paper) -- ISBN-10: 0-7172-6127-1 (v. 3 : alk. paper)
-- ISBN-13: 978-0-7172-6128-4 (v. 4 : alk. paper) -- ISBN-10: 0-7172-6128-
X (v. 4 : alk. paper) -- ISBN-13: 978-0-7172-6129-1 (v. 5 : alk. paper) --
ISBN-10: 0-7172-6129-8 (v. 5 : alk. paper) -- ISBN-13: 978-0-7172-6130-7
(v. 6 : alk. paper) -- ISBN-10: 0-7172-6130-1 (v. 6 : alk. paper) -- ISBN-13:
978-0-7172-6131-4 (v. 7 : alk. paper) -- ISBN-10: 0-7172-6131-X (v. 7 : alk.
paper) -- ISBN-13: 978-0-7172-6132-1 (v. 8 : alk. paper) -- ISBN-10: 0-7172-
6132-8 (v. 8 : alk. paper)
  1. Hispanic Americans--Biography--Encyclopedias--Juvenile literature. I.
Grolier Publishing Company.
E184.S75H5573 2006
973'.046800922--dc22
  [B]
                                    2006012294

For information address the publisher:
Grolier, Scholastic Library Publishing,
Old Sherman Turnpike,
Danbury, Connecticut 06816

FOR THE BROWN REFERENCE GROUP PLC

Project Editor: Chris King
Editors: Henry Russell, Aruna Vasudevan,
                                  Tom Jackson, Simon Hall
Design: Q2A Solutions, Seth Grimbly,
                                  Lynne Ross
Picture Researcher: Sharon Southren
Index: Kay Ollerenshaw
Design Manager: Sarah Williams
Production Director: Alastair Gourlay
Senior Managing Editor: Tim Cooke
Editorial Director: Lindsey Lowe

ACADEMIC CONSULTANTS:

Ellen Riojas Clark,   Arnoldo de Leon,
Division of Bicultural Bilingual Department of History,
   Studies,   Angelo State University
University of Texas at San Antonio

Printed and bound in Singapore

ABOUT THIS SET

This is one of a set of eight books chronicling the lives of Hispanic Americans who have helped shape the history of the United States. The set contains biographies of more than 750 people of Hispanic origin. They range from 16th-century explorers to 21st-century musicians and movie stars. Some were born in the United States, while others immigrated there from countries such as Mexico, Cuba, or Puerto Rico. The subjects therefore come from a wide range of cultural backgrounds, historical eras, and areas of achievement.

In addition to the biographical entries, the set includes a number of guidepost articles that provide an overview of a particular aspect of the Hispanic American experience. These guidepost articles cover general areas such as civil rights and religion as well as specific historical topics such as the Treaty of Guadalupe Hidalgo. These articles serve to help place the lives of the subjects of the biographies in a wider context.

Each biographical entry contains a box listing key dates in the subject's life as well as a further reading section that gives details of books and Web sites that the reader may wish to explore. Longer biographies also include a box about the people who inspired the subject, people the subject has influenced in turn, or the legacy that the subject has left behind. Where relevant, entries also contain a "See also" section that directs the reader to related articles elsewhere in the set. A comprehensive set index is included at the end of each volume.

The entries are arranged alphabetically, mostly by surname but also by stage name. In cases where the subject has more than one surname, he or she is alphabetized under the name that is most commonly used. For example, Héctor Pérez García is usually known simply as Hector P. Garcia and is therefore alphabetized under "G." Pedro Albizu Campos, meanwhile, is generally known by his full name and is alphabetized under "A." Both variants are included in the index. Where names are commonly spelled in a variety of ways, the most widespread version is used. Similarly, the use of accents is dictated in each individual case by general usage.

Contributors: Jorge Abril Sánchez; Robert Anderson; Faisal Azam; Berta Bermúdez; Kelvin Bias; Erica Brodman; P. Scott Brown; Bec Chalkley; Anita Dalal; Zilah Deckker; Marilyn Fedewa; Stan Fedewa; Conrado Gomez; Leon Gray; Susan Green; José Angel Gutiérrez; Ted Henken; Elizabeth Juárez-Cummings; Nashieli Marcano; Luisa Moncada; Carlos Ortega; Paul Schellinger; Melissa Segura; Alberto Varon; Melina Vizcaino; Chris Wiegand; Emma Young.

CONTENTS

Selena	4	Torres, Luis Lloréns	66	Villa, Beto	110
Serra, Junípero	6	Treviño, Jacinto	67	Villanueva, Alma Luz	111
Serra, Richard	7	Treviño, Jesús	68	Villanueva, Tino	112
Serrano, José	8	Trevino, Lee	69	Villaraigosa, Antonio	113
Serrano, Samuel	9	Trinidad, Felix	71	Villarreal, José Antonio	115
Sheen, Charlie	10	Truan, Carlos	73	Villarreal, Luis	117
Sheen, Martin	11	Trujillo, Severino	74	Villaseñor, Victor	118
Sheila E.	13	Turlington, Christy	75	Viramontes, Helena Maria	119
Smits, Jimmy	14	Unanue, Joseph	76	Welch, Raquel	120
Solís Sager, Manuela	15	Urrea, Luis Alberto	77	Williams, William Carlos	122
Somohano, Arturo	16	Urrea, Teresa	78	Ximenes, Vicente	124
Sosa, Lionel	17	Valdes-Rodriguez, Alisa	79	Y'Barbo, Antonio Gil	125
Sosa, Sammy	18	Valdez, José Antonio	80	Yglesias, José	126
Soto, Gary	20	Valdez, Luis M.	81	Yzaguirre, Raúl	127
Southwest, Settlement in the	22	Valens, Ritchie	83	Zamora, Bernice	129
Suárez, Ray	28	Valentín, Bobby	85	Zapata, Carmen	130
Suárez, Xavier L.	29	Valenzuela, Fernando	86	Zaragoza, Ignacio	131
Supreme Court	31	Valenzuela, José Luis	87	Zeno Gandía, Manuel	133
Tafoya, José Piedad	35	Vallejo, Mariano Guadalupe	88	Zúñiga, Martha	134
Tanguma, Leo	36	Vargas, Elizabeth	89		
Tapia, Luis	37	Vargas, Fernando	90	Set Index	135
Tapia y Rivera, Alejandro	38	Vargas, Jay R.	91	Credits	144
Teissonnière, Gerardo	39	Vargas, Kathy	92		
Telles, Raymond	40	Vasquez, Richard	93		
Tenayuca, Emma	41	Vasquez, Tiburcio	94		
Texas, History of	42	Vasquez Villalpando, Catalina	95		
Tex-Mex Culture	48	Véa, Alfredo, Jr.	97		
Thalía	52	Vega, Bernardo	98		
Thomas, Piri	53	Vega, "Little" Louie	99		
Tiant, Luis	55	Vega Yunqué, Edgardo	100		
Tienda, Marta	56	Velasquez, Baldemar	101		
Tijerina, Felix	57	Velásquez, Willie	102		
Tijerina, Pete	58	Velazquez, Loreta Janeta	103		
Tijerina, Reies López	59	Velázquez, Nydia M.	104		
Tizol, Juan	61	Vélez, Lauren	106		
Toraño, María Elena	62	Velez, Lupe	107		
Torres, Edwin	63	Venegas, Juan E.	108		
Torres, Esteban E.	64	Vigil, Donaciano	109		
Torres, José	65				

SELENA
Singer

Selena was a Mexican American singer who became the top Tejano star of the 1990s. She was known as the "Mexican Madonna" and the "Queen of Tejano."

Selena's career was cut short when she was murdered by a business associate at the age of 23. Her life and career were immortalized in Gregory Nava's movie *Selena*. Selena was portrayed by Jennifer Lopez, in what proved to be the actor's breakthrough role. The killer was played by fellow Latina actress Lupe Ontiveros.

Learning music

Selena Quintanilla was born in Lake Jackson, Texas, in 1971. She spent most of her life in nearby Corpus Christi. The Quintanilla family was a musical one. Selena's father, Abraham, had taken a shot at the big time himself with his band Los Dinos. After only limited success in the 1950s and 1960s, the band eventually became Selena's backing group. The band also included Selena's older brother A.B. (Abraham, Jr.) on bass and sister Suzette on drums.

Abraham Quintanilla's failure in the music business drove him to transfer his dreams to his three children. He gave them music lessons after school, preventing them from playing with other children. All of the Quintanillas showed talent, but Selena was something special. By the age of six, she already possessed a clear and powerful voice. Abraham knew he had a star in the making.

In 1980 Abraham opened a restaurant named Papagallo in Lake Jackson. Each night diners were entertained by music and dancing from Selena and Los Dinos. The customers loved the music, and particularly Selena, but the

▲ *Selena performs on stage in 1994 at the height of her career. She was the number one female Spanish-language singer and was working on an English-language album at the time of her murder.*

food and service were poor. The business failed, and the Quintanillas returned to Corpus Christi in 1982. Nevertheless Selena had learned about performing while on stage at Papagallo. She continued to display her talent at weddings with Los Dinos.

At the age of 11 Selena enrolled in West Oso Junior High in Corpus Christi. Her father continued to book Los Dinos to play at many of the city's nightclubs and at weekend dances across south Texas. This caused Selena problems at school. She eventually dropped out after the

KEY DATES

1971	Born in Lake Jackson, Texas, on April 16.
1983	Releases her first recording, "Mis Primeras Grabaciones," on Freddie Records label at age 12.
1992	Selena marries Christopher Pérez, lead guitarist in her band, on April 2.
1994	Releases the album *Amor Prohibido*.
1995	Murdered by Yolanda Saldívar, Selena's fan club founder in Corpus Christi, Texas, on March 31.
1997	Release of the movie *Selena* directed by Gregory Nava and starring Jennifer Lopez.

INFLUENCES AND INSPIRATION

Tejano music is unique to south Texas and northern Mexico. It is composed of a conjunto: bass guitar, drums, and accordion. Men dominated the genre for decades with some exceptions, such as Lydia Mendoza in the 1930s.

Before Selena, the leading Latina singer was Laura Canales (1955–2005). Canales was "the Queen of Chicano Music" during the 1960s and 1970s. Selena moved her off center stage in the 1980s and took the new title as "Queen of Tejano." Selena and Los Dinos recorded hit after hit with such labels as Freddie, Cara, Manny, GP, and finally Capitol/EMI Latin Records. The list of hit albums by Selena y Los Dinos is impressive: *Alpha* (1986), *Dulce Amor* (1988), *Preciosa* (1988), *Selena y Los Dinos* (1990), *Ven Conmigo* (1991), *Entre a Mi Mundo* (1992), *Selena Live* (1993), and *Amor Prohibido* (1994). By 1992 the band had sold more than 300,000 albums, the first Tejano group to sell so many. In 1993 they won a Grammy, among several other major awards.

By this time Selena and Los Dinos were coming to the attention of the mainstream English-speaking U.S. audience. In 1994 Selena was listed as one of the 20 most influential Texans by *Texas Monthly*, a popular magazine.

eighth grade because the Quintanilla family had become reliant on Los Dinos for their income. Selena finally completed high school by correspondence course in 1989.

International star

Selena cut her first record at the age of 12. Within five years she was voted Female Vocalist of the Year at the Tejano Music Awards in San Antonio, Texas. For the next seven years Selena took home the same award, along with many others.

In 1990 Pete Astudillo and Chris Pérez joined Los Dinos. Selena married Pérez in 1992. By this time she had become the singing sensation of Latino America. Once she had perfected her Spanish, she conquered northern Mexico as well. Selena began singing in traditional Mexican styles, such as rancheras and mariachi. Her brother A.B. encouraged her to embrace his style of techno-cumbia and more international sounds, such as tropical, salsa, and merengue. Selena's album *Amor Prohibido* was her biggest hit while she was alive. It sold 400,000 copies in less than a year, and knocked Gloria Estefan's *Mi Tierra* off the number one spot in the Mexican charts.

Had her life not been cut short, Selena undoubtedly would have become an international star with hits in both English and Spanish. In 1994 she began to record a series of English-language songs and signed to release them as an album. She only managed to record four English songs before her death, and the album *Dreaming of You* became her first posthumous release. The rest of the album's songs were remixes of her most popular Spanish tracks. The album has sold 5 million copies. On its first day on sale alone, 300,000 copies were purchased. This makes *Dreaming of You* the fastest selling Hispanic American album of all time. Mariah Carey had previously held the record, but after her death Selena sold more in one day than Carey did in a week.

Selena Etc.

Selena was known for her sexy clothing as much as her singing. In 1994 the singer opened her first fashion boutique and salon in Corpus Christi. The enterprise was named Selena Etc. Selena appointed the president and founder of her fan club, Yolanda Saldívar (1960–), as the boutique's manager.

A second shop was opened in San Antonio the following year. However, Selena and Saldívar began to quarrel over money that was missing from the business. Selena fired Saldívar in early March and demanded the money back by the end of the month. The pair met again on the last day of March in a room at the Days Inn Motel in Corpus Christi. The exact course of that meeting is uncertain, but when Selena attempted to leave, Saldívar shot her in the back. Selena managed to reach the motel lobby and tell staff what Saldívar had done before collapsing. She died in a hospital one hour later. Saldívar was apprehended after a seven-hour standoff with police, broadcast live on television. Saldívar was sentenced to life imprisonment in October 1995.

See also: Canales, Laura; Carey, Mariah; Estefan, Gloria; Lopez, Jennifer; Mendoza, Lydia; Nava, Gregory; Ontiveros, Lupe

Further reading: Arrarás, Mariá Celeste. *Selena's Secret: The Revealing Story behind Her Tragic Death*. New York, NY: Simon & Schuster, 1997.
http://www.selenaetc.com/selena.html (official Web site).

SERRA, Junípero
Missionary

Called the "Father of California" for his pioneering work in founding missions along the length of California, Junípero Serra is considered by historians to be one of the leading forces in the settlement of the American West.

Early life
Miguel José Serra was born on the Spanish island of Mallorca on November 24, 1713, to Antonio Serra and Margarita Ferrer, who were poor farmers. Although too frail to work the family's farm, Serra was very good at his studies. He went on to attend Luliana University in Palma, Mallorca, a college that did not charge the poor for tuition.

A religious calling
In 1731 Serra joined the Franciscan religious order, adopting the name Junípero. Seven years later he earned his doctorate in theology; he was also ordained a priest. Serra taught philosophy at Luliana, and preached in local parishes. Serra had a deep and powerful voice and was a compelling orator.

In 1749, inspired by the writings of the Spanish mystic María de Ágreda, Serra set sail for the Americas with his friend and later biographer Father Francisco Palóu.

"King's Highway" missions
After journeying overseas, Serra walked several hundred miles to reach Mexico City on January 1, 1750. Serra and Palóu dedicated their time to preaching to the Pame Indians in the Sierra Gorda Mountains; they worked alongside the native people, providing them with livestock and tools for farming. In 1758 Serra returned to Mexico City to supervise mission operations and to oversee the College of San Fernando in the city.

▲ *Junípero Serra traveled from the island of Mallorca to Mexico to help convert the native people to Christianity.*

In 1767 the king of Spain expelled the Jesuits from Spanish colonies. He appointed Serra president of California missions; he directed the 14 existing missions that had been taken from the Jesuits.

In 1769 Serra established the San Diego Mission, the first of 21 new missions founded throughout California, nine of which Serra developed personally. The sites of these missions became the locations of many of California's principal cities; the route between them, "El Camino Real," or "The King's Highway," is followed today by California's spectacular Highway 1.

A devout man who dedicated his life to God, Serra has been criticized by some Native American Catholics for the effect his work had on the erosion of local tribal culture and life. Serra is generally regarded as one of the main forces in California's colonization.

Further reading: DeNevi, Don. *Juníper Serra: The Illustrated Story of the Franciscan Founder of California's Missions.* San Francisco, CA: Harper & Row, 1985.
http://www.sandiegohistory.org/bio/serra/serra.htm (San Diego Historical Society's page on Serra).

KEY DATES	
1713	Born in Petra, Mallorca, on November 24.
1749	Arrives in Vera Cruz, Mexico, on December 6.
1767	Becomes president of California missions, until 1784.
1769	Founds first of many California missions in San Diego.
1784	Dies at San Carlos Mission, California, on August 28.

SERRA, Richard
Sculptor

Displaying massive steel sculptures in virtually every major contemporary art museum in the world, Mexican American Richard Serra is considered one of the most important sculptors of the 20th century.

Early life

Serra was born in 1939 in San Francisco, California. His father was a pipe fitter in a shipyard. This job involved bending steel with immense forces, a process that was later echoed in Serra's work. As a young man, Serra was inspired by the structural design of the Bay Area bridges, and by the marvel of ships being launched into the sea. He explained: "The ship went through a transformation from obdurate weight to a buoyant structure ... my awe and wonder at that moment remained ... and has become a recurring dream."

Between 1957 and 1961 Serra studied English literature at the University of California at Berkeley and at the University of California at Santa Barbara. He supported himself through college by working in steel mills, a phase of his life that would have a lasting impact on his artwork.

From 1961 to 1964 Serra studied fine art at Yale University in Connecticut, completing both a bachelor's and a master of fine arts degree. After winning a Yale Traveling Fellowship and a Fulbright grant, he studied in Paris, France, and Florence, Italy, for the next two years. In 1966 Serra moved to New York City, where he befriended several well-known artists and gained entry into the art world.

Professional artist

Serra's first sculptures, created in 1966, were composed of nontraditional materials like fiberglass and rubber. In the late 1960s he explored the sculpting process through a series of pieces called *Splash*. These involved literally

▲ *Richard Serra is best known for his immense minimalist structures of rolled steel. His sculptures are intended to rust, thus enhancing their appearance.*

splashing molten lead onto floors and walls. Serra's sculptures then evolved into large free-standing sheets of metal. Serra's work was a new kind of sculpture that required public interaction. "The biggest break in the history of 20th-century sculpture," Serra observed, "occurred when the pedestal was removed."

In 1981 Serra installed *Tilted Arc*, a curving 12-foot (3.6 m) wall of steel that ran 120 feet (36 m) through Federal Plaza in New York City. It caused an uproar when pedestrians complained that the wall obstructed passage through the plaza. A public hearing in 1985 voted that the piece should be moved, but Serra argued that changing the location would destroy the meaning of the work. In 1989 the sculpture was sold as scrap. The controversial incident raised numerous questions about public art, but has not prevented Serra's work from appearing in public spaces around the world.

KEY DATES

1939	Born in San Francisco, California, on November 2.
1966	Moves to New York and creates his first sculptures.
1989	His controversial sculpture, *Tilted Arc*, is removed from New York's Federal Plaza.
2005	His sculpture, *Ballast*, is installed on the campus of the University of California, San Francisco.

Further reading: Serra, Richard. *Writings, Interviews.* Chicago, IL: University of Chicago Press, 1994.
http://www.pbs.org/art21/artists/serra (biography).

SERRANO, José
Politician

José Serrano is a U.S. congressman representing New York's 16th Congressional District. This is a densely populated area in the South Bronx where Hispanic Americans form the majority. Serrano is the most senior congressman of Puerto Rican origin.

Serrano was born in 1943 in Mayagüez, Puerto Rico, and moved to the Bronx, New York, aged seven. After attending local public schools, Serrano studied at Lehman College of the City University of New York. He then served in the U.S. Army Medical Corps for two years, receiving an honorable discharge in 1966. Serrano went on to work in a bank and as a school administrator.

Political career

Serrano's political career began as chairman of the South Bronx Community Corporation in 1969. He also served on the New York City Board of Education. In 1974 Serrano was elected as a Democrat to the New York State Assembly. He became the chair of the Committee on Consumer Affairs and Protection. Later becoming the chair of the state's Committee on Education, Serrano was also responsible for doubling state funding for bilingual education programs. He also passed legislation that provided $50 million to improve New York's problems with school attendance.

Serrano was first elected to the U.S. House of Representatives in 1990 after winning 92 percent of the vote in a special election. In the following year he was reelected for a full term.

Serrano's liberal values were immediately evident. He argued that government must help society's most vulnerable members, and sought to increase equality of opportunity in education, housing, and health care.

KEY DATES	
1943	Born in Mayagüez, Puerto Rico, on October 24.
1969	Becomes chairman of the South Bronx Community Corporation, and serves on the New York City Board of Education.
1974	Elected to the New York State Assembly.
1990	Elected to U.S. House of Representatives.
1993	Becomes chair of the Congressional Hispanic Caucus.

▲ *José Serrano takes part in a debate on MTV as part of the Voto Latino campaign, which aimed to encourage young Hispanic Americans to vote in 2004.*

In 1992 Serrano introduced legislation guaranteeing that voting materials would continue to be offered in different languages. He also introduced the Classroom Safety Act to reduce violent crime in schools.

Hispanic issues

Serrano was appointed chair of the Congressional Hispanic Caucus during the 103rd Congress (1993–1995). One of his achievements was to prevent the establishment of English as the official U.S. language, which he considered a threat to cultural diversity. Instead he supports a program encouraging Americans to become bilingual.

While serving on the Appropriations Committee from 1993, Serrano ensured investment for the Bronx, directed into education, the environment, the arts, and programs to develop small businesses. Serrano has a son, also named José, who is a member of the New York State Senate.

Further reading: http://www.house.gov/serrano (Serrano's Web site).

SERRANO, Samuel
Boxer

Samuel Serrano was twice world junior lightweight champion (122 pounds; 55kg). His career spanned four decades, with a final record of 51 wins, 17 by knockout, four defeats, and one draw. Known as "El Torbellino," meaning "the Whirlwind," Serrano darted around his opponents, using a powerful counterpunch to great effect.

Local champion

Serrano was born in 1952 in Toa Alta, Puerto Rico. He fought his first 23 professional bouts in Puerto Rico. In the first, against Ramon Laureano in 1969, Serrano won in four rounds. His opponent was too hurt to continue.

In 1971 Serrano won the Puerto Rican featherweight title by defeating Francisco Villegas, only to lose the title to him a year later. This defeat marked the end of a 16-match winning streak.

World champion

Serrano's first attempt at a world title ended in controversy. In Honolulu, Hawaii, in 1976, Serrano faced the World Boxing Association (WBA) world junior lightweight champion, Ben Villaflor. The referee announced a draw, but many watching believed Serrano had won. In a rematch that year, Serrano won 12 out of 15 rounds and was crowned world junior lightweight champion.

Serrano lost his title in 1980 to Japanese Yasutsune Uehara in a fight in Detroit, Michigan. After establishing a good lead, Serrano was knocked out in round six. When

▲ *Samuel Serrano after a successful defense of his junior lightweight title in 1982. Serrano eventually lost his title the following year.*

the pair met again in 1981, the Puerto Rican employed more cautious tactics that paid off. Serrano was declared the winner after 15 rounds.

He successfully made two further title defenses before losing to Chilean Benedicto Villablanca in 1982. Serrano was in the lead when he sustained a cut above an eye, which eventually forced an end to the fight. Serrano complained that the cut had not been caused by a punch but by a clash of heads, making the defeat invalid. The WBA agreed, and Serrano was restored as the champion.

Defeat

Serrano succumbed to Roger Mayweather in his next bout in 1983. He retired after winning one more fight in 1984. Serrano settled in Bayamon, Puerto Rico, and tried various enterprises, including opening a gym. However, he was also drawn into drug trafficking and was sentenced to 15 years in jail in 1987.

Released early, Serrano returned to boxing in 1996. He won the Puerto Rican lightweight title and defended the the title a year later. Serrano has since made a beer commercial and also worked as an electrician for a Puerto Rican telephone company.

Further reading: http://www.cyberboxingzone.com/boxing/serrano.htm (Serrano's boxing statistics).

KEY DATES	
1952	Born in Toa Alta, Puerto Rico, on November 7.
1969	Wins first professional fight.
1971	Wins Puerto Rican featherweight title.
1976	Wins World Boxing Association junior lightweight title.
1980	Defeated by Yasutsune Uehara.
1981	Regains world title.
1984	Retires for the first time.
1987	Sentenced to jail for drug trafficking.
1996	Wins Puerto Rican lightweight title.

SHEEN, Charlie
Actor

Like his older brother Emilio Estevez, Charlie Sheen followed in the footsteps of his famous father, the actor Martin Sheen (*Apocalypse Now*; *West Wing*). He became a bankable movie star, but his talent has sometimes been compromised by poor project choices.

Early life
Charlie Sheen was born Carlos Irwin Estevez in 1965 in New York. He was raised in southern California, where he developed a passion for films and made home movies with his brother Emilio and their friends. While studying at Santa Monica High School, he was offered a college baseball scholarship but did not achieve the required academic grades.

He then tried to find work as an actor using a stage name that combined the English form of Carlos and the professional surname of his famous father. After an uncertain start in the movie business, Charlie Sheen's breakthrough came in the role of a sensitive raw recruit fighting in Vietnam in Oliver Stone's *Platoon* (1986). The part had originally been offered to Emilio Estevez. Sheen endured an exhausting two-week training program before filming began in the Philippines.

Keeping it in the family
As his fame increased, Sheen gained a reputation for partying, and allegations about substance dependency appeared in newspapers and magazines. His next major movie was Stone's *Wall Street* (1987), in which he played Bud Fox, an ambitious young Manhattan stock trader. The character's father, Carl, was played by Martin Sheen.

Charlie Sheen enjoyed another hit with *Young Guns* (1988), a Western starring Emilio Estevez as Billy the Kid. Estevez also directed his brother in the movies *Wisdom*

▲ *Actor Charlie Sheen first found fame when he appeared in the Vietnam War movie,* **Platoon.**

(1986) and *Men at Work* (1990). On completing the latter movie, Sheen then played opposite one of his idols, Clint Eastwood, in the cop thriller *The Rookie* (1990). He later appeared in two action spoofs, *Hot Shots!* (1991) and *Hot Shots! Part Deux* (1993). Meanwhile, he turned down a role in *Indecent Proposal* (1993), which became a box-office hit, in order to star in the less successful *The Chase* (1994), of which he was also the executive producer. He later set up a production company with rock singer Bret Michaels.

In 2003, Sheen took a starring role in the TV sitcom *Two and a Half Men*. Sheen's more recent movie appearances have included *Scary Movie 3* (2003), *The Big Bounce* (2004), and *Scary Movie 4* (2006).

See also: Estevez, Emilio; Sheen, Martin

Further reading: Riley, Lee, and David Schumacher. *The Sheens: Martin, Charlie, and Emilio Estevez*. New York, NY: St. Martin's Press, 1989.
http://www.imdb.com/name/nm0000221 (full television and movie credits).

KEY DATES	
1965	Born in New York on September 3.
1986	Stars in *Platoon*.
1987	Stars in *Wall Street*.
1990	Costars with Clint Eastwood in *The Rookie*.
2000	Begins two-year role in TV series *Spin City*.

SHEEN, Martin
Actor

Over the course of a lengthy acting career that began in the late 1950s, Martin Sheen earned a formidable reputation for prolific output and powerful performances. His most famous role was that of Captain Benjamin L. Willard in Francis Ford Coppola's epic Vietnam War movie *Apocalypse Now* (1979).

Early life

Sheen was born Ramón Gerard Antonio Estévez in 1940 in Dayton, Ohio. He was one of 10 children of a Spanish-born father, Francisco Estévez, and an Irish American mother, Mary Anne Phelan. He attended Chaminade High School, where he was regarded as a gifted pupil, but his educational opportunities were limited by his family's modest means and by his own overwhelming ambition to act. He was inspired by James Dean, his early hero, and discouraged by his father, who thought that acting was too risky a career. The young Estévez worked weekends and vacations as a golf caddy until age 18, when he left school, moved to New York City, and became involved with a pacifist drama group, the Living Theater. His stage name—adopted in order to avoid anti-Hispanic prejudice and ethnic stereotyping—was inspired in part by Catholic archbishop Fulton J. Sheen, one of the United States's first television preachers.

In 1961 Sheen earned favorable reviews for his role in *The Subject Was Roses*, a play by Frank D. Gilroy that later transferred to Broadway and won its author a Pulitzer Prize. In the same year he married art student Janet Templeton. The couple had four children who all became actors: Emilio Estevez (born 1962), Ramón Luis Estevez (born 1963), Charlie Sheen (born 1965), and Renée Estevez (born 1967).

Struggle and triumph

Although Sheen reprised his stage performance in Ulu Grosbard's movie version of *The Subject Was Roses* (1968), he struggled for the greater part of the 1960s. He worked sporadically in various television drama series, but did not land another important screen role until *Catch-22* (1970). He then costarred with Sissy Spacek in the crime drama *Badlands* (1973).

In 1974 Sheen was nominated for an Emmy Award for his portrayal of the hero in *The Execution of Private Slovik*,

▲ *Martin Sheen starred as President Josiah Bartlet in hit TV series* **The West Wing.**

a made-for-television movie about the last U.S. soldier to be executed for desertion in World War II (1939–1945). Although he lost out at the awards to Hal Holbrook in *Pueblo*, the attendant publicity brought him to the attention of Francis Ford Coppola. When the director fell out with Harvey Keitel, whom he had originally cast in the role of Benjamin Willard in *Apocalypse Now*, he hired Sheen to replace him. The movie became famous for its behind-the-scenes story when Sheen suffered a heart attack on set. He was so sick that he even received the last rites. Despite the difficulties, the completed movie was acclaimed as a masterpiece, and Sheen's status rose from that of a dependable character actor into a major Hollywood star.

INFLUENCES AND INSPIRATION

Martin Sheen was raised in a devoutly Roman Catholic home, and priests at the local church helped finance his 1958 move to New York City.

While Sheen works and campaigns politically to further the interests of Hispanic Americans, he also has a strong affinity with his Irish heritage. His maternal grandfather had links with the Irish Republican Army (IRA)—a revolutionary group that demanded liberation from British rule in Ireland—and was forced to emigrate to the United States from his native County Galway after the Easter Rising in 1916.

Sheen's earliest inspiration as an actor was James Dean (1931–1955), the star of movies such as *Rebel without a Cause* and *East of Eden* (both 1955). Another role model was the method actor Marlon Brando (1924–2004). Sheen studied Brando's acting technique. For years he admired his work from a distance, but finally, in 1979, he starred with his idol in *Apocalypse Now*.

Sheen has, in turn, inspired and influenced his own children, all four of whom have followed him into movies. Only one of them, Charlie Sheen, has retained his stage name, however; the other three have reverted to the family name of Estevez.

After *Apocalypse Now*, Sheen was free to choose his work. He took a small part as a reporter in Richard Attenborough's *Gandhi* (1982), starring Ben Kingsley as the Indian spiritual leader, and donated his salary to charity. A committed activist and high-profile advocate on social justice issues such as homelessness, Sheen has taken part in numerous marches and protests, and has been arrested several times. He was particularly outspoken in his criticism of the U.S. response to the terrorist attacks on New York and Washington, D.C., on September 11, 2001, and vigorously opposed the 2003 invasion of Iraq by the United States and its allies. His public utterances and appearances at demonstrations have attracted greater media attention than his movies. Nevertheless, Sheen has racked up more than 150 credits in TV and film, often appearing in average fare but usually providing interesting performances.

Family affairs

Sheen starred opposite his third son, Charlie, in *Wall Street* (1987), then directed him in a military drama, *Cadence* (1990). He played Confederate general Robert E. Lee in *Gettysburg* (1993) and 1930s' bank robber John Dillinger in *Dillinger and Capone* (1995). The latter movie also featured Joe Estevez, one of Martin Sheen's younger brothers. In 1999 Sheen landed a prominent role in the TV political drama *The West Wing*. His portrayal of President Josiah Bartlet won him an American Latino Media Arts (ALMA) award and a Golden Globe. In 2006 he acted in *Bobby*—a movie about the assassination of Robert F. Kennedy, directed by his eldest son, Emilio—and *Bordertown*, a crime thriller with Antonio Banderas and Jennifer Lopez.

See also: Estevez, Emilio; Lopez, Jennifer; Sheen, Charlie

Further reading: Riley, Lee, and David Schumacher. *The Sheens: Martin, Charlie, and Emilio Estevez*. New York, NY: St. Martin's Press, 1989.
http://www.nbc.com/The_West_Wing/bios/Martin_Sheen.html (biography at official Web site for *The West Wing*).

KEY DATES

1940	Born in Dayton, Ohio, on August 3.
1958	Moves to New York City to pursue an acting career.
1961	Stars on stage in *The Subject Was Roses*.
1968	Reprises stage role in movie version of *The Subject Was Roses*.
1970	Appears in Mike Nichols's movie version of Joseph Heller's novel *Catch-22*.
1973	Stars opposite Sissy Spacek in *Badlands*.
1974	Lead role in *The Execution of Private Slovik* wins Emmy Award nomination.
1979	Stars in *Apocalypse Now*.
1987	Plays the father of his real-life son Charlie Sheen in *Wall Street*, directed by Oliver Stone.
1993	Stars as Robert E. Lee in *Gettysburg*.
1995	Stars with F. Murray Abraham in *Dillinger and Capone*.
1999	Stars in acclaimed TV series *The West Wing*.

SHEILA E.
Musician

Sheila E. is an acclaimed percussionist, composer, and record producer. Best known for her work with pop star Prince, she has performed and recorded with many of the world's other top musical artists, including Marvin Gaye, Jennifer Lopez, Lionel Richie, Gloria Estefan, Diana Ross, Tito Puente, and Placido Domingo. She has received several honors for her work, including a Grammy nomination for her first album, *The Glamorous Life*.

Early life

Sheila E. was born Sheila Escovedo in 1957 in Oakland, California. Her parents, Pete and Juanita Escovedo, were of African American and Mexican heritage. Her father, an accomplished Latin jazz musician, encouraged her from an early age, and she began playing music at age three. Her first public appearance came at age five, when she performed on stage with her father in front of an audience of 3,000. By age 17, she had become a professional musician and performed regularly with Azteca, her father's Latin jazz band.

▼ *Percussionist Sheila E. is best known for her musical relationship with Prince, which has lasted more than 20 years.*

KEY DATES	
1957	Born in Oakland, California, on December 12.
1963	Makes first live appearance, at age five.
1984	Releases her first album, *The Glamorous Life*.
1985	Plays herself in the movie *Krush Groove*.
2001	Releases her sixth album, *Heaven*.

Becoming Sheila E.

In 1983 Escovedo met Prince and changed her name to Sheila E. She sang on "Erotic City," the B-side of Prince's number one record "Let's Go Crazy." Prince then helped Sheila record and release her critically acclaimed debut solo album, *The Glamorous Life* (1984). Her first single, also titled "The Glamorous Life," won the MTV Best Video Award and received Grammy and American Music award nominations. Sheila opened for Prince on his Purple Rain tour in 1984 and 1985.

In 1985 Sheila's second album, *Romance 1600*, and subsequent single, "A Love Bizarre," were both hits, and she played herself in the feature film *Krush Groove*. Another single, "Hold Me," reached number one on the *Billboard* chart. In 1986, she supported Lionel Richie on tour. In 1987 Sheila released her third album, *Sheila E.*, and joined Prince's Sign O' the Times tour. She appeared with Prince again in 1988 on his Lovesexy tour. In 1990 Sheila released her fourth album, *Sex Cymbal*. After a period of poor health, she resumed live performances and studio recordings in 1994 with her new group, The E-Train. In 1998 she released her *Writes of Passage* album, and became the first female bandleader on the television show *The Magic Hour*. In 2001, she released another album, *Heaven*.

Sheila E. has performed at the Grammy Awards with Placido Domingo, toured with Jennifer Lopez and Ringo Starr, and in 2004 joined Prince on his Musicology tour.

See also: Estefan, Gloria; Lopez, Jennifer; Puente, Tito

Further reading: Granados, Christine. *Sheila E*. Childs, MD: Mitchell Lane, 1999.
http://www.sheilae.com (official Web site).

SMITS, Jimmy
Actor

Jimmy Smits is a U.S. actor of mixed Puerto Rican–Surinamese heritage. He has appeared in several movies and starred in the TV series *L.A. Law* and *NYPD Blue*.

Early life
Smits was born in 1955 in Brooklyn, New York. He was the eldest child and only son of a nurse and a former merchant seaman. He first visited Puerto Rico at age five, and his mother later took him to live there for a short time. Smits attended high school and college in Brooklyn, then went on to Cornell University, where he received an MFA in 1982. Meanwhile he had fathered a daughter at age 19. He later married the mother, and they had another child, a son, but the couple divorced in 1987.

As a student, Smits became increasingly involved in theater. His inspiration was the Puerto Rican actor Raul Julia. On graduating, he was determined to become a professional actor. Success did not come quickly, however. Although Smits appeared in several off-Broadway productions, he endured some lean times. He later recalled taking money from his daughter's piggy bank to pay to travel to one audition.

Television stardom
After a few small roles on television, including a short turn in *Miami Vice* in 1984, Smits rose to fame as an idealistic lawyer on *L.A. Law*, despite failing his initial reading for the part. Smits settled into a new life in California, and as his career blossomed so did a lasting romance with actress Wanda De Jesus. After leaving *L.A. Law* in 1991, he appeared in several TV films, including *The Cisco Kid* (1994), in which he played the title role. Later that year he joined the top-rated TV show *NYPD Blue*, in which he was

▲ *Jimmy Smits is best known for his performances as policeman Bobby Simone in the TV series* **NYPD Blue.**

cast as Bobby Simone, a French-Portuguese, Brooklyn-born detective. Simone's relationship with his partner Andy Sipowicz (played by Dennis Franz), and his romance with another officer, Diane Russell (Kim Delaney), became central to the storyline. Smits's perceptive portrayal earned him two American Latino Media Arts (ALMA) awards. More than 20 million people watched his final appearance on the show in 1998. Since leaving *NYPD Blue*, Smits has appeared in two *Star Wars* movies—*Episode II: Attack of the Clones* (2002), and *Episode III: Revenge of the Sith* (2005)—and became a regular in the celebrated TV series *The West Wing* from 2004 until 2006.

Campaigning work
In 1997 Smits and fellow actor Esai Morales cofounded the National Hispanic Foundation for the Arts. The organization aims to increase Latino and Latina involvement in film and television, and to reduce the negative stereotyping of Hispanic Americans.

See also: Julia, Raul; Morales, Esai

Further reading: Cole, Melanie. *Jimmy Smits*. Childs, MD: Mitchell Lane, 1998.
http://www.gale.com/free_resources/chh/bio/smits_j.htm (biography).

KEY DATES	
1955	Born in Brooklyn, New York, on July 9.
1986	Wins role in long-running TV series *L.A. Law*.
1991	Quits *L.A. Law*.
1994	Joins *NYPD Blue*.
1998	Quits *NYPD Blue* after four seasons.
2004	Takes regular role in *The West Wing*.

SOLÍS SAGER, Manuela
Activist

Manuela Solís Sager was highly influential in the civil rights struggle of Mexican Americans in Texas. She came to prominence as a labor activist who led a campaign for better conditions for Chicano workers in the 1930s. Solís Sager was a founding member of the South Texas Agricultural Workers' Union (STAWU) and, alongside fellow Chicano activists Emma Tenayuca and Luisa Moreno, played a key role in the 1938 pecan shellers' strike in San Antonio, Texas.

Seeds of unrest

Solís was born in 1912, and first became involved in labor activism in the early 1930s. At this time Mexicans and Mexican Americans were among the worst paid workers in the United States. Most of them were unskilled and worked on farms and in factories in Texas and California. They generally had to work long hours and in hazardous conditions. They were also often denied membership in the labor unions used by their Anglo-American neighbors.

One of the results of the Great Depression that followed the Wall Street Crash of 1929 was that the cost of unskilled labor was reduced. This deepened the economic hardship of Hispanic American workers. They also began to experience more prejudice and resentment as they competed with Anglo-American workers for the few jobs available. These factors combined to radicalize an entire generation of Hispanic Americans and led to widespread unrest and militant activism.

Organizing labor

Solís Sager was at the forefront of this activism. She had married James Sager and added his name to hers. The couple often worked together to represent Mexican American workers.

Solís Sager initially worked among garment and farmworkers in and around the Texas border city of Laredo. In 1934 she won a one-year scholarship from the Hispanic labor union La Asociación de Jornaleros (The Journeymen's Association) to study at the Universidad Obrera de México (Workers' University of Mexico) in Mexico City, where she received training as a union leader. On her return in 1935, she and her husband helped to organize a conference in Corpus Christi, Texas. This was attended by representatives from across the state and led to the foundation of the South Texas Agricultural Workers' Union (STAWU).

KEY DATES	
1912	Born in Texas on April 19.
1934	Wins scholarship to Universidad Obrera de México, Mexico City.
1935	Becomes a founding member of the South Texas Agricultural Workers' Union (STAWU).
1938	Helps organize the landmark pecan shellers' strike, San Antonio, Texas.
1984	Honored along with Emma Tenayuca by the National Association for Chicano Studies.

The Pecan Shellers' Strike

As STAWU organizers, Solís Sager and her husband initially worked among the farm workers of the Lower Rio Grande Valley. Despite fierce opposition from local landowners and growers, they succeeded in unionizing more than 1,000 Hispanic American workers. However, the growers remained intransigent in the face of their workers' demands for change.

In 1938 Solís Sager turned her attention to activity in San Antonio, Texas, where she helped Emma Tenayuca organize the mass strike among the city's mostly female pecan-shelling workers. Although the strike ended with only a partial victory for the workers, it became a landmark event in Mexican American labor history.

Inspirational figure

Solís Sager has continued to be active in the labor movement. In 1984 the National Association for Chicano Studies (NACS) honored both her and Tenayuca for their lifetimes of service to Mexican workers. Solís Sager's pioneering work remains an inspiration to Chicana union activists across the United States today.

See also: Moreno, Luisa; Tenayuca, Emma

Further reading: Marable, Manning, Immanuel Ness, and Joseph Wilson, eds. *Race and Labor Matters in the United States.* Lanham, MD: Rowman & Littlefield, 2006.
http://ucsub.colorado.edu/~bruningr (biography.)
http://www.tsha.utexas.edu/handbook/online/articles/PP/oep1.html (history of pecan shellers' strike).

SOMOHANO, Arturo
Composer

Arturo Somohano was an influential composer and famed classical conductor from Puerto Rico. He founded the San Juan Symphony Orchestra, and helped popularize Puerto Rican forms of classical music.

Early life

Born in 1910 in San Juan, Puerto Rico, Somohano was a musically precocious child. He acquired a taste for classical music and learned to play the piano at an early age. As a young man, Somohano was inspired to write his own music during his studies at a Franciscan chapel on the island. While there, he learned about musical composition and harmony, as well as developing a deep appreciation for the classical style.

From entertainer to impresario

Somohano entered the world of professional music playing the piano for U.S. Army troops and directing concerts at various military bases during World War II (1939–1945). During this period, he composed "Canciones de las Américas" (Songs of the Americas), which became a favorite song for Army personnel.

After the war, Somohano returned to Puerto Rico. He founded the San Juan Symphony Orchestra in 1950, and became its first director. He spent the next decade developing an internationally respected philharmonic orchestra. He also oversaw the restoration of the Tapia Theater, a historic performing arts center built in San Juan's Old Town in 1832, and named for Alejandro Tapia y Rivera, a popular Puerto Rican playwright.

By the end of the 1950s, Somohano had become a world-renowned conductor. In response to increased demand for his performances in Europe, he embarked on two concert tours that included appearances in Spain, Switzerland, and Germany, as well as the United States. Celebrating his 100th concert as a director in Madrid in the mid-1960s, Somohano was awarded the Cross of Isabel the Catholic, and named honorary conductor of the Madrid Symphony Orchestra by the Spanish parliament. At the close of a fruitful decade, Somohano was honored in his native Puerto Rico by being sworn in as an assembly member of the city of San Juan in 1969.

Music for the people

During his lifetime, Arturo Somohano helped popularize Puerto Rican classical music by publishing numerous works of danza, the rich—sometimes romantic, sometimes melancholic—form of indigenous Puerto Rican classical music. Among the danza composers he championed was Juan Morel Campos, the uncle of one of Puerto Rico's greatest nationalist heroes, Pedro Albizu Campos.

Somohano also composed musical accompaniments for five plays in collaboration with his friend, Manuel Méndez Ballester (1909–2002). Several of Somohano's compositions have earned a secure place in the canon of Puerto Rican classical music.

Well remembered

On Somohano's death in 1977, the San Juan Symphony Orchestra he had founded was renamed the Arturo Somohano Symphony Orchestra, and the city of San Juan named both a school and a plaza in his honor.

The Puerto Rico Conservatoire pays annual tribute to this eminent figure in classical music by awarding the outstanding student with the Arturo Somohano Medal for excellence in international musical achievement.

See also: Albizu Campos, Pedro; Campos, Juan Morel; Tapia y Rivera, Alejandro

Further reading: http://www.musicofpuertorico.com/en/arturo_somohano.html (Music of Puerto Rico Web site).

KEY DATES

1910   Born in San Juan, Puerto Rico, on September 1.

1942   Becomes an entertainer for U.S Army after the United States enters World War II.

1950   Founds the San Juan Symphony Orchestra and becomes its first director.

1958   Achieves worldwide recognition and begins to make tours to Europe and the United States.

1969   Sworn in as a member of the legislative assembly of the city of San Juan.

1977   Dies in Hato Rey, Puerto Rico, on March 23; the San Juan Symphony Orchestra is renamed the Arturo Somohano Symphony Orchestra.

SOSA, Lionel
Advertising Magnate

Lionel Sosa has been a leading figure in Hispanic American advertising and marketing for four decades. His ability to connect with Latinos and Latinas across the country has also been employed by the Republican Party. Hispanic Americans traditionally vote Democratic, but thanks to Sosa more have come to vote Republican than ever before. Sosa has been an adviser to every Republican presidential hopeful since Ronald Reagan, whom he helped take the White House in 1980.

Advertising career
Sosa was born in San Antonio, Texas, in 1939. He is reputed to have become a Republican at the age of 13, after watching Dwight Eisenhower speak on the family's new TV set. He trained as a graphic artist in school and became a sign painter as a young adult, soon founding his own business. In 1974, however, Sosa changed direction and joined the advertising firm of Ed Yardang. He was soon a success and moved up the ranks to associate. In 1981 he founded his own firm, Sosa and Associates.

Money and votes
When Sosa began in advertising, the Fortune 500 (the 500 largest U.S. companies) spent just $3 million a year on advertising aimed at Latinos. The spending power of Latinos has grown considerably. In 2004, Latinos spent $700 billion. Today $60 million is spent each year to target products at them.

Hispanic American voters have also become a political force. They provided 5.3 percent of the total votes cast in the 2000 presidential election, more than enough to swing

▲ *Lionel Sosa changed the face of U.S. advertising by targeting products directly at Hispanic Americans.*

the result. Sosa has been involved in political campaigns since 1978. He helped to reelect Texas Republican John Tower to the U.S. Senate in 1978. Thanks in part to Sosa, Tower won 37 percent of the Tejano vote. No previous Republican candidate had polled more than 8 percent in Texas. Sosa's skill was put to use again during Ronald Reagan's 1980 presidential campaign. Reagan secured Sosa's services by saying: "Latinos are Republican. They just don't know it yet." Sosa has been very effective in letting them know. He has headed the Hispanic advertising campaigns for all six Republican presidential candidates since 1980. In 1996 Bob Dole's failed campaign won 21 percent of the Hispanic vote. In 2004 George W. Bush won 40 percent. Now in semiretirement, Sosa writes motivational books but still works on election campaigns.

Further reading: Sosa, Lionel. *Think and Grow Rich: A Latino Choice*. New York, NY: Ballantine Books, 2006.

KEY DATES	
1939	Born in San Antonio, Texas, on May 27.
1974	Joins Ed Yardang and Associates.
1978	Becomes Hispanic media consultant for Texas Republican Senator John Tower.
1981	Founds Sosa and Associates.
1996	Joins Garcia LKS, the largest independent Hispanic American advertising agency.
2004	Works on his seventh Republican presidential campaign, helping to reelect George W. Bush.

SOSA, Sammy
Baseball Player

One of the great sluggers in the history of baseball, Sammy Sosa emerged in 1998 as a hero to fans in the United States, in his native Dominican Republic, and throughout the baseball world as he chased the single-season home-run record. For six seasons after that magical year, Sosa continued to amass some of the most impressive power statistics in the history of the game. Yet his accomplishments were tarnished with suspicions that he had used steroids.

Early life

Sammy Sosa was born in San Pedro de Macoris, Dominican Republic, on November 12, 1968. With his mother and six siblings, Sosa lived in poverty in a two-room apartment. With no father to support the family (he had died when Sammy was seven years old), Sosa sold fruit and shined shoes to provide income.

Sosa's first baseball games were played using a milk carton for a glove, wadded socks for a baseball, and a stick for a bat. When he was 16, Sosa caught the eye of a scout

▼ *One of the most successful hitters in baseball, Sosa spent most of his career with the Chicago Cubs.*

from the Texas Rangers. The scout signed him up and gave him a $3,500 bonus, which Sosa gave to his mother.

Sosa made his major league debut with the Rangers on June 16, 1989, when he was 20 years old. After playing in 25 games with the Rangers, he was traded to the Chicago White Sox to fill out an unremarkable 1989 season. The following season, however, Sosa showed more promise. He appeared in 153 games for the White Sox in 1990, hitting 15 home runs and driving in 70 runs. But with a subpar batting average of .233, followed the next season with an average of .203, Sosa's future still did not look so bright.

Just prior to the start of the 1992 season, Sosa was traded across town to the Chicago Cubs, the team with which he would be associated during his climb to become one of the greats of the game. He began that season playing center field for the Cubs, but appeared in only 67 games owing to injury. Then, in 1993, Sosa played right field, and began to emerge as the star-caliber player that many scouts had suspected he could be. Sosa finished that season with 33 home runs, a batting average of .261, and a slugging percentage of .485. He also stole 36 bases to become the first Chicago Cub ever to hit at least 30 home runs and steal at least 30 bases in the same season. Cubs fans began to identify with this smiling, enthusiastic player who went all-out on every play.

Rise to greatness

In 1995 Sosa hit 36 home runs, and then in 1996 he set a personal best of 40 home runs, followed again in 1997 with 36—very impressive numbers indeed. But no one could have imagined the great power—and the even greater drama—that would emerge during the 1998 season when Sosa, along with the St. Louis Cardinals' first baseman Mark McGwire, captivated the baseball world. The players were on course to reach one of the most sacrosanct records in the game: the single-season home run mark of 61, set in 1961 by Roger Maris of the New York Yankees.

The "great home run race" of 1998 was a blessing for baseball. Since the strike-shortened 1994 season, many baseball fans had soured on the national pastime. That season had ended on September 14 after teams had played approximately 115 out of the 162 games scheduled. The postseason games, including the World Series, were all canceled—for the first time since 1904. For the next three years attendance at games was down.

INFLUENCES AND INSPIRATION

Along with many Latin players in the major leagues, Sammy Sosa idolized the great Roberto Clemente. He wore Clemente's number 21 on his jersey as a sign of his respect and tried to fashion his game after Clemente's. Although no one would maintain that Sosa fielded his position in right field as well as Clemente did (many claim that the graceful Clemente had the best outfield arm in the history of baseball), his all-out passion for the game certainly bore Clemente's stamp.

Clemente was one of the greatest baseball players of all time. He entered the Baseball Hall of Fame after an 18–year career in which he posted a lifetime batting average of .317 and led the Pittsburgh Pirates to two World Series. But Clemente was also a tireless humanitarian, putting great store in helping people in whatever way possible. Clemente died in a plane crash on New Year's Eve in 1972 while flying to Nicaragua to help victims there of a recent earthquake.

In the heat of the "great home run chase" of 1998, Sammy Sosa turned his attention to his native Dominican Republic, when Hurricane George struck on September 22. By that time, both Sosa and Mark McGwire had surpassed Roger Maris's single-season record of 61, and the entire baseball world was focused on who would edge out the other. Yet for the rest of the season, Sosa turned interviews into pleas for assistance to go to victims of the hurricane.

Sosa's and McGwire's pursuit of Maris's record gave fans something to come back to. Although McGwire would be the first to surpass Maris's mark of 61 home runs, ending the season with 70 to Sosa's 66, Sosa arguably played a more important role because of the enthusiasm he exuded—something that baseball fans responded to in kind. He was voted the Most Valuable Player in the National League that year.

The home-run race of 1998 is perhaps Sammy Sosa's finest legacy to the game. However, Sosa's best baseball was ahead of him. After hitting 66 home runs in 1998, he followed up with 63 the following year, then hit 50 in 2000, and in 2001 he posted his best overall year as a hitter. Along with 64 home runs that year, Sosa finished with a career-high batting average of .328 and a staggering .737 slugging percentage. He remains the only player in baseball history to hit 60 or more home runs in three seasons.

Decline and controversy

Sosa's 2002 campaign, while still strong (49 home runs; .288 batting average), represented the start of a decline in his overall performance. His numbers fell off every year after his peak season of 2001. His image took a considerable hit when, during a game in June 2003, he broke his bat. It was revealed to contain cork—a clear violation of league policy. That event, which led to an eight-game suspension, along with widespread suspicion of Sosa's use of steroids (in March 2005 he was subpoenaed to appear before a congressional committee, where he denied steroid use), have considerably tarnished Sosa's reputation. After a controversial finish to the 2004 season, in which the Chicago Cubs maintained that Sosa walked

out on the team before the final game of the season, Sosa was traded to the Baltimore Orioles. His 2005 performance with the Orioles ranked among the worst of his career. Whatever happens to his image as a result of the controversies that marked the late stage of his career, however, Sosa will be remembered as one of the greatest sluggers in baseball history. By the end of the 2005 season, he had made 588 home runs, the fifth highest total of all time.

KEY DATES	
1968	Born in the Dominican Republic on November 12.
1989	Makes major league debut on June 16.
1992	Traded to the Chicago Cubs.
1998	Voted Most Valuable Player in the National League.
2001	Best overall season, and a record third season hitting over 60 home runs.
2003	Suspended for eight games after caught using a corked bat on June 3.

See also: Clemente, Roberto

Further reading: Sosa, Sammy (with Marcos Breton). *Sammy Sosa: An Autobiography.* New York, NY: Warner, 2000.
http://www.latinosportslegends.com/sosa.htm (biographies of Latino athletes).
http://espn.go.com/classic/biography/s/Sosa_Sammy.html (ESPN page and links).

SOTO, Gary
Writer

As one of the most critically acclaimed Latino poets, Gary Soto has written more than 50 books, including award-winning novels, short stories, plays, biographies, and picture books.

Early life

The grandson of Mexican immigrants, Gary Soto was born in 1952, in Fresno, California. Both of his parents worked in food-processing plants. Money was tight, and Soto and his brother Rick entertained themselves by playing in the alleyways near their house. The everyday pleasures of kicking cans and climbing fences would later become fertile material for Soto's poems and young-adult novels.

When Soto was five, his father died in an accident at work. His mother remarried, and the family moved to a better neighborhood. After graduating from high school, Soto enrolled in community college, partly to avoid being drafted into the Vietnam War. He lived with his brother and several artists in a crowded house, an experience fictionalized in the novel *Jesse* (1994) and in the poetry collection *Junior College* (1997).

One day when Soto should have been researching a paper, he pulled a poetry anthology off a shelf in the library and started reading. He credits the work of Beat poets like Allen Ginsberg and Gregory Corso, and particularly a poem entitled "Unwanted" by Edward Field, for inspiring him to write.

Passion for poetry

Soto transferred to Fresno State, where he met other Chicano writers such as Luis Omar Salinas and Leonard Adame. He studied under the renowned poet Philip Levine, who taught him "how to handle language with care," a lesson Soto took to heart when crafting his early poems, which were often grim and sometimes surreal.

The best of his work at Fresno State appeared in his first book, *The Elements of San Joaquin*, in 1977. Soto wrote the remainder of the poems in that collection at the University of California, Irvine, where he earned a master of fine arts degree in creative writing in 1976.

Young talent

Aged 25, fresh out of college and newly married, Soto was one of the most celebrated young U.S. poets. He won several important awards, and his poems frequently

▲ *Writer Gary Soto is known for his poetry and novels. He writes for both adults and children.*

appeared in the influential journal *Poetry*. His next books—*The Tale of Sunlight* (1978), *Where Sparrows Work Hard* (1981), and *Black Hair* (1985)—set a new standard for literary quality in Chicano poetry. Some Chicanos, however, criticized Soto for not writing more overtly political poetry.

By the time he completed *Black Hair*, Soto was a parent and a teacher at the University of California, Berkeley. His poems reflected these changes in his life. At first Soto's work was marked by short, hard lines, but it now grew more expansive and narrative. He began looking back at the joys of childhood. In *Black Hair*, Soto turns a barrio baseball game into an expression of ethnic pride as the poem's narrator imagines himself scoring, crossing the plate cheered by his teammates—"Coming home to the arms of brown people."

Producing prose

In the mid-1980s Soto wrote his first prose pieces, which he called "narrative recollections" of his youth. The first of these books, *Living Up the Street* (1985), won the American

INFLUENCES AND INSPIRATION

Gary Soto's poetic influences have changed over time. His early poems have magical-realist elements inspired by the work of Latin American writers such as Chilean Pablo Neruda and Colombian Gabriel García Márquez. His later work is more narrative, similar to the stories in Philip Levine's poems and the humor of Billy Collins.

Soto's greatest inspiration, however, has been his childhood. He suffered from the effects of poverty, an industrial accident killed his father, and he watched the lingering death of an uncle from terminal cancer. As a result Soto's work is often haunted by violence. The poem "The Morning They Shot Tony López, Barber, and Pusher Who Went Too Far, 1958," for example, imagines the final moments of a murder victim and relies on metaphors, describing López's burial as "The earth you would slip into like a shirt."

Nevertheless Soto also finds joy and hope in small events. In doing so he captures the wonder and discovery of childhood as well as any other writer working today. In one of his most beloved poems, "Oranges," Soto marvels at a the simplicity of a piece of fruit: "I peeled my orange / That was so bright against / The gray of December / That, from some distance, / Someone might have thought / I was making a fire in my hands."

Book Award. In 1990 Soto's first collection of short stories, *Baseball in April*, won praise from book reviewers and went on to sell more than 100,000 copies. The success of the book, and the books for young adults that followed, enabled Soto to quit his job at the university to write full time. It also marked the beginning of a second period of intense creativity.

Courting controversy

Soto began experimenting with filmmaking, writing three short movies. *The Pool Party* (1992), a film based on one of Soto's novels, won an Andrew Carnegie medal. His 1995 book, *New and Selected Poems*, was a finalist for the National Book Award. In 1996 a picture book for children, *Chato's Kitchen*, won a Pura Belpré Award. The book's controversial subject—Chato is a cool, streetwise alley cat—led to it being banned from some school libraries in Soto's native Fresno.

Soto's aversion to stereotyping the Mexican American experience has generated controversy on other occasions.

KEY DATES

1952	Born in Fresno, California, on April 12.
1973	Begins to study under poet Philip Levine.
1977	Publishes first book, *The Elements of San Joaquin*.
1985	Wins American Book Award for *Living Up the Street*.
1995	Finalist for National Book Award.
2007	Publishes *Mercy on These Teenage Chimps*.

Marisol (2004) drew protest in Illinois. In the story a Latino family moves from a "dangerous" Chicago barrio to a nearby suburb. Activists complained that the book was an attack on a proud Latino neighborhood. However, the story did reflect reality. Even in Chicago, Latinos are moving from the inner city to the suburbs.

Many critics believe that Soto's finest recent work is found in *Buried Onions* (1997), *Petty Crimes* (1998), and *The Afterlife* (2003), three loosely related books about teenagers affected by death and violence in Fresno. *Buried Onions* opens with a heart-wrenching list of people the young narrator knows who are dead—killed at work or by disease, or who have been murdered. A powerful story in *Petty Crimes* describes a girl who buys back her late mother's clothes from a thrift store, and *The Afterlife* is told from the point of view of a murdered teenager.

Publisher

Soto is also a publisher, and has produced more than 30 collections of poems by young Chicano writers. In the 1980s he published Sandra Cisneros's first book, along with early works by important writers, such as Luis Omar Salinas, Jimmy Santiago Baca, and Alberto Rios. In the 1990s Soto printed poems by up-and-coming writers like Francisco Aragón, Rigoberto González, and Richard Yáñez.

See also: Baca, Jimmy Santiago; Cisneros, Sandra; Rios, Alberto; Salinas, Luis Omar

Further reading: Orr, Tamra. *Gary Soto.* New York, NY: Rosen Publishing Group, 2005.
http://www.garysoto.com (Soto's Web site).

SOUTHWEST, SETTLEMENT IN THE

The American Southwest, which includes the states of New Mexico, Arizona, Texas, California, Nevada, Utah, and Colorado, is a region of great beauty and culture. Natural wonders such as the Grand Canyon (Arizona), Monument Valley (Utah/Arizona border), and the Carlsbad Caverns (New Mexico) lie in this region.

In the Southwest states Spanish American, Native American, and Anglo-American cultures coexist. When the Spanish arrived in the early 16th century, the region was inhabited by Native American peoples such as the Apache, Navajo, and Hopi. Spanish and Native American people lived in the region from the 16th century until the early 19th century, when large-scale Anglo-American settlement began.

The 1848 Treaty of Guadalupe Hidalgo, by which more more than 55 percent of Mexican territory was ceded to the United States, brought even greater Anglo-American settlement to the region, changing both its demographic makeup and economic basis. The Anglo-American population brought technological advances in agriculture, mining, and rail transport, for example, which greatly affected the lives of all resident groups. Over the years the U.S. government also introduced a series of laws to control such issues as immigration into the Southwest, which restricted nonwhite settlement in the area.

Today, according to the U.S. State Department, one in four people living in the Southwest is of Hispanic origin and one person in 100 is Native American; the remaining majority is Anglo-American. Both minority cultures have had a long-lasting impact on the area, however. This is illustrated by the abundance of Hispanic and Native American placenames in the Southwest and by the development of a unique culture in the border region that draws on Spanish, Native American, and Anglo cultures.

Early settlers and explorers

The Southwest's native population was made up of several different peoples, including the Hohokam, an ancient people in the area that is now Arizona, the Navajo in the Four Corners area (where Colorado, Utah, Arizona, and New Mexico meet), and several Apache groups in New Mexico and Arizona. There is evidence that settlement in what is now New Mexico began 10,000

One of the Southwest's most beautiful sites, Monument Valley is situated on the Utah/Arizona border toward the southeast corner of Utah.

years ago. Stone spearheads found near the New Mexico town of Folsom indicate that native peoples hunted in the northeast part of the state at about that time.

Spanish occupation of the area began in the early 16th century. In the 1500s, Spain was the leading world colonial power. The Spanish Empire reached as far as Mexico and well into South America.

By the 1530s, the Spanish in Mexico began to hear stories of great riches in the so-called Seven Cities of Cíbola to the north. In 1539, a Franciscan priest named Marcos de Niza became the first white person known to have entered the Arizona region. One year later, the Spanish explorer

Francisco Vásquez de Coronado led an expedition to find the Seven Cities of Cíbola. Although Coronado was unsuccessful in his quest, he did make it as far as modern-day Kansas.

The Pueblo Revolt

Coronado's expedition pushed Spanish control farther into North America. By the latter half of the 1600s, the Spanish had conquered more than 100 pueblos (villages) in what is now the Southwest.

Spanish soldiers and missionary priests imposed a forced-labor system on the Pueblo, the native peoples who occupied the lands around what is today Santa Fe, New Mexico (founded in 1610). The Spanish refused to allow the Pueblo to practice their long-held beliefs or worship ancient gods. Eventually, the Pueblos revolted. In August 1680, warriors attacked several Spanish settlements. Led by Popé, a tribal leader, the Pueblos killed more than 400 Spanish and held approximately 1,000 more under siege in Santa Fe. The Spanish went several days without water, but finally escaped to El Paso del Norte (today El Paso, Texas).

Popé set himself up as leader of all of New Mexico, residing in the Governor's Palace in Santa Fe. Under Popé, the Pueblos ruled New Mexico for 12 years, destroying most of the Roman Catholic icons and artifacts left behind by the Spanish. The Pueblos erased virtually all vestiges of the Roman Catholic church, the religion of their oppressors. After Popé's death in approximately 1688, Spanish soldiers, led by Diego de Vargas, reclaimed the territory without much resistance.

By 1700, the Spanish had a firm grip on New Mexico. However, the Pueblo Revolt was the first major taste of a repeated pattern of antagonism between white settlers and the Native Americans, whose lands the colonial powers were taking. The Spanish were the first; soon Mexico and then the United States took military action against the native peoples, most of whom just wanted to maintain control of their land. Over the ensuing 200 years, Native Americans lost most of their territory. Today, the majority live on reservations, several centered around the Four Corners and California. More than 300,000 Native Americans also occupy reservations in New Mexico and Arizona.

Missionaries

From the early 16th century, missionaries in the Southwest played a vital role in sustaining Spanish rule. They converted the native peoples to Christianity through the Roman Catholic church and also enforced their own customs and culture on native groups.

After the Pueblo Revolt, Spanish missionaries began to spread farther westward into what are present-day Arizona and California. Between 1691 and 1711 an Italian-born Jesuit missionary named Eusebio Francisco Kino led several expeditions into Arizona. Kino explored as far west as California. Kino also introduced grain, cattle, sheep, and mules to the region. The Franciscan order took control of the Arizona area in 1768 and moved westward.

Into California

Spanish claims to California began in earnest in 1769, when soldiers and missionaries, including the Franciscan priest Junípero Serra, claimed the area around modern-day San Diego. The Franciscans founded missions along the California coast, stretching north

KEY DATES	
1521	Spanish conquest of Mexico City.
1610	Sante Fe founded.
1700	Spanish expand their dominion north as far as modern New Mexico.
1821	Mexico becomes independent; first major Anglo settlement in 1823.
1836	Texas becomes a republic.
1848	Treaty of Guadalupe Hidalgo ends U.S.–Mexico War; by passing 55 percent of Mexican territory (the American Southwest) to the United States, it affects about 100,000 Mexicans living in the area. Gold discovered on John S. Sutter's land in California and major settlement follows in the Southwest.
1942	Bracero Program introduced between Mexico and the United States to bring temporary Mexican labor into the United States.
1945	After end of World War II, mass migration to Southwest states begins.
1965	Immigration Act introduces quotas.
2000	U.S. Census shows one in four people living in Southwest is of Hispanic origin and one in 100 is Native American.

all the way to Sonoma County, just above San Francisco. The missions housed several thousand native people and helped bring European settlers to California's Central Valley and Pacific Coast.

Mexican Independence

By the early 1800s Spain was having trouble maintaining control over its Mexican colony.

In 1820 two factions emerged in Mexico, the first led by a military officer named Agustín de Iturbide, and the second by Vicente Guerrero, a rebel leader whom Iturbide was sent to defeat. In 1821 Iturbide wrote Guerrero a letter proposing that they join forces to achieve Mexico's independence. In 1821 the last Spanish officials withdrew from Mexico and the region became independent from Spain. Mexico

The original Mission San Xavier de Bac, Arizona, was built in 1700 by Father Eusebio Francisco Kino; the existing church (below) was built between 1783 and 1797.

claimed Spain's former territory, which included Alta California (modern-day California) and the vast New Mexico territory. In 1824 Mexico established a constitution; for most of the next three decades, the new republic suffered political unrest.

Early Anglo migration

New Mexico had developed trade links with French traders from Illinois and Louisiana from the mid-18th century. By the early 19th century, traders such as William Becknell and Stephen Cooper had established successful trade operations in Sante Fe, opening the way for other U.S. traders to follow. In that period U.S. settlers also petitioned to establish colonies in Texas, supported by members of the Mexican elite such as Erasmo Seguín and his son, Juan. Seguín helped Stephen Fuller Austin acquire a land contract from the Mexican government in the early 1820s. Austin went on to found the city of San Felipe de Austin.

The Mexican government also authorized further colonization through agents. The Anglo population grew substantially in Texas, leading to numerous conflicts between existing Mexican landowners and new settlers.

After Mexican president Antonio López de Santa Anna abrogated the 1824 Constitution and pushed for centralized power in Mexico, many Texan settlers in the northern part of the Mexican state of Coahuila–Tejas (Texas) began to revolt.

In 1836 Texas declared itself a republic. It opened up diplomatic relations with Britain and the United States, but Mexico did not recognize the new republic's sovereignty. The border of Texas and Mexico, along the Rio Grande, was also disputed territory.

Manifest Destiny

In the first half of the 19th century many Americans began to discuss the idea of Manifest Destiny to justify territorial expansion. The phrase was coined by John L. O'Sullivan, editor of the *Democratic Review*, in 1839, and the concept became significant in directing the U.S. government's policy toward Mexico and its northern territories.

Manifest Destiny promoted the notion that the United States was destined to rule the continent from the Atlantic to the Pacific oceans. Based on ideas such as Anglo-American supremacy over nonwhite people, and the belief that God had ordained Anglo-Americans the chosen people, Manifest Destiny also promoted the idea that nonwhite people were incapable of self-government and democracy.

THE SOUTHEASTERN STATES

Unlike the largely arid Southwest, the southeastern United States is a fertile area with a great deal of natural farmland. Settlement of the southeastern states—Alabama, Florida, Georgia, Kentucky, Mississippi, North Carolina, South Carolina, Tennessee, Virginia, and West Virginia—was founded on an agrarian, slave-based economy. The population of these states is today predominantly white, with African Americans making up the largest minority group. In Alabama, for example, the population in 2000 was 71.1 percent white, followed by African Americans (26 percent), while Hispanics made up 1.7 percent of the population.

That is in striking contrast to Florida, where in the same year whites made up 78 percent of the population, but people of Hispanic origin (16.8 percent) were the largest minority, followed by African Americans (14.6 percent).

The development of Florida differs from that of its neighboring states, partly because of its historic links with Spain. In the early 1500s, the Spanish explorer Juan Ponce de León searched for the fabled fountain of youth in the region. Britain later controlled Florida, after which it experienced a second period of Spanish rule. The state was eventually incorporated into the Union in 1821.

Another contributory factor to the difference between the demographics of Florida and those of the Southwest is the state's proximity to the Caribbean. There has long been steady immigration from the mainly Spanish-speaking neighboring islands, and the stream has periodically turned into a tide during political upheavals. One of the most significant crises was the takeover of Cuba by Fidel Castro in 1959. The communist regime that he established sent thousands of Cubans into exile. Their immigration was encouraged by the U.S. government, and there is now a prosperous Cuban American community based in, but not confined to, Florida.

In 1845, as part of its territorial expansion, the United States offered Texas the opportunity to join the Union; Texas accepted and became the United States's 28th state. The Mexican government felt that the United States had taken sovereign Mexican territory. It was further provoked by the United States's assertion that the Texas–Mexico border lay along the Rio Grande rather than at the Rio Nueces, 20 miles (32 km) to the north, as Mexico argued.

The Polk administration
Newly elected U.S. president James K. Polk (1845–1849) wanted to annex the Mexican provinces of California and New Mexico for $30 million, and sent diplomat John Slidell to Mexico to negotiate the sale. After Slidell was refused entry to Mexico, Polk sent General Zachary Taylor and his troops to take up position at a fort near the Rio Grande.

On May 13, 1846, the United States declared war on Mexico. The war raged for two years, with General Winfield Scott ultimately leading U.S. troops into Mexico City.

In 1848, the two powers signed the Treaty of Guadalupe Hidalgo. The Mexican Cession (part of the treaty) handed over 55 percent of its territory (present-day Arizona, California, New Mexico, and parts of Colorado, Nevada, and Utah) to the United States in exchange for $15 million in compensation for war-related damage to Mexican property. At the time, approximately 100,000 Mexicans lived in the area.

The Gadsden Purchase
Border issues remained a problem between the United States and Mexico. Although the Treaty of Guadalupe Hidalgo gave the United States control of most of what is now Arizona and New Mexico, the U.S. government wanted to construct a route for a transcontinental railroad south of the land ceded by Mexico in the treaty.

U.S. Secretary of War Jefferson Davis, who later became president of the Confederacy that fought the North in the Civil War (1861–1865), convinced President Franklin Pierce to acquire the desert land. President Pierce dispatched James Gadsden, who had business interests in the railroad, to Mexico to negotiate a land purchase with the Mexican

COLONIAS

Colonias (neighborhoods) is the term used to describe the low-income, unincorporated subdivision housing that exists along the United States–Mexico border. Although *colonias* can be found in Arizona and California, most (nearly 1,500) are located in Texas on the low-lying areas of the Rio Grande near El Paso or in Las Cruces, New Mexico. The residents are predominantly of Hispanic origin, the majority born in the United States.

Built in the 1950s, when developers sold small plots of land to low-income families, *colonias* are often little more than shacks and exist without even basic services such as electricity or safe drinking water.

The inhabitants of *colonias* often have to deal with a lack of solid-waste-disposal units or water treatment plants and substandard plumbing. As a result of these poor conditions, hepatitis and gastrointestinal diseases are prevalent.

Texas counties did not have the authority to make it mandatory for new developments to have water and sewage systems until 1989. In practice, it has often proved extremely difficult to make builders comply with the law requiring that these systems be put in place or upgraded. Despite such problems of enforcement, since 1996 the Texas attorney general has filed nearly 45 lawsuits against *colonia* developers.

president Antonio López de Santa Anna.

On December 30, 1853, the United States paid Mexico $10 million for what is termed the Gadsden Purchase. The purchase constituted the final boundaries of the continental United States. The Arizona cities of Tucson, Yuma, and Sierra Vista lie within the land area acquired at the time.

The shifting balance

In California, news came in 1848 that gold had been discovered on John S. Sutter's land. The prospect of quick riches and mineral speculation brought large numbers of settlers and prospectors to the Southwest, all dreaming of achieving wealth and success.

The growing number of Anglo-American settlers in the region led to conflicts with Native Americans and Hispanic Californios, who found their lands increasingly encroached on by the new migrants. Many Anglos abused the rights of the original settlers, squatting on private lands, challenging land grants, and stealing the mine claims of non-Anglos.

Although Californios received a degree of protection for their language and culture under the 1848 state constitution, after California joined the United States in 1850 they found themselves increasingly marginalized and discriminated against in every sector of society.

Native Americans tried to fight back. The Apaches, for example, led famously by Geronimo, resisted the westward encroachment by white settlers until 1886. As the rights and laws of Anglo settlers prevailed, however, many Southwest Native American tribes were relocated to reservations by force.

In the courts minority groups often found their rights were not protected and were even undermined. The 1897 case of *United States v. Sandoval,* for example, rejected New Mexico Pueblo claims to common lands

that had been held by them for more than 250 years.

Increasingly non-Anglos found that, as the white populations became more successful, the poverty rates in their communities increased, while the economic opportunities available to them declined.

Appalled by the treatment meted out to them, many Hispanic and non-Anglo groups formed societies to fight for their rights: *Mutualistas* (mutual-aid groups), for example, led the way for the formation of later Latino activist groups such as the League of United Latin American Citizens (LULAC).

The 20th century

In the last two decades of the 19th century extensive construction of roads in the Southwest resulted in an increase in immigration. By the 1920s most of this labor was Mexican, leading some Anglo-Americans to complain about immigrant groups taking white jobs.

Phoenix, Arizona, is one of the three fastest growing cities in the country and the nation's fifth-largest city, with a population of nearly 1.4 million.

In the 1930s the United States suffered the Great Depression, and the government forcibly repatriated Mexicans back to Mexico, even those who were legitimate U.S. citizens.

World War II (1939–1945) brought another population boom to the Southwest. Short of labor, the U.S. government encouraged the temporary migration of Mexican agricultural labor to the United States from 1942 onward through the Bracero Program.

In practice, the amount of labor legally allowed into the United States to work on farms was not adequate, and illegal immigrants increasingly crossed the Rio Grande to find work. In the first half of the 1950s, the U.S. Immigration and Naturalization Service forcibly repatriated more than one million Mexicans back to Mexico through the highly contentious Operation Wetback.

Hispanic immigrants for the most part lived in much poorer conditions than their Anglo-American neighbors. From the 1950s onward, many lived in *colonias,* low-income housing that arose in several states along the border (see *box on page 26*).

After 1945 other regions in the Southwest also experienced population growth. Many military personnel who trained in the Arizona desert returned to the area. Phoenix and Tucson became popular destinations for these war veterans. Los Angeles, California, similarly became a metropolitan area, attractive to settlers.

Immigration issues

The last half of the 20th century brought increasing debate about the merits and problems of immigration, particularly illegal immigration in the Southwest. Laws such as the Immigration Act of 1965 were introduced to regulate immigration from specific nations. Illegal immigration from Latin American countries in particular became an increasingly sensitive matter, particularly in states with high Hispanic populations. In 2000, California had a Latino population of more than 32 percent (the white population made up 59 percent), and problems such as bilingual education and welfare to illegal immigrants became vexed topics.

In 2006 illegal immigration across the long U.S.–Mexico border became politically controversial. Some U.S. politicians proposed building a concrete barrier along the border to keep out illegal immigrants who brave the treacherous desert conditions to reach the United States.

By the early 21st century the population of the Southwest had ballooned to approximately 70 million. Apart from immigration, some commentators are concerned about the negative effects of this growth on the environment. Housing developments are springing up in what were once rural areas of Utah, and in 2006 the Utah Geological Survey warned that Salt Lake City's rapid population growth was increasing the probability of landslides. Water pollution and water rights issues continue to be concerns in the arid Southwest. Nevertheless, thousands of people move to the region each year.

See also: Coronado, Francisco Vázquez de; De Niza, Marcos; Galán, Héctor; Guadalupe Hidalgo, Treaty of; Ponce de Léon, Juan; Serra, Junípero; Texas, History of

Further reading: Sheridan, Thomas E. *A History of the Southwest: The Land and Its People.* Tucson, AZ: Southwestern Parks and Monuments Association, 1998.
http://www.census.gov (Official U.S. government site of the Census Bureau).

SUÁREZ, Ray
Journalist

Ray Suárez is a radio and television news journalist who is also a prolific author, essayist, and critic for leading newspapers. His broadcasting career has followed that of Rubén Salazar, whose memorial award Suárez received in 1996 from the National Council of La Raza (NCLR).

Early life
Suárez was born in 1957 in Brooklyn, New York, to Puerto Rican parents. He graduated from New York University with a bachelor's degree in African history, and then took a master's degree in social sciences at the University of Chicago, where he specialized in urban affairs. He later received the former school's Alumni Achievement Award, and the latter's Professional Achievement Award.

Suárez's career began at the National Broadcast Corporation (NBC) in Chicago, where he was active in the local community, working to combat gangs. He also joined the National Association of Hispanic Journalists (NAHJ). After NBC, he worked for the Cable News Network (CNN) in Los Angeles, California, the American Broadcasting Corporation (ABC) in New York, and various other U.S. news services, as well as for broadcasting stations in Britain and Germany.

Into public broadcasting
In 1993 Suárez moved to National Public Radio (NPR), where he hosted the nationwide call-in program *Talk of the Nation*. In 1999 he took a job in Washington, D.C., as a senior TV correspondent for *The NewsHour* on the Public Broadcasting Service (PBS). In 2005 Suárez joined the NPR and Public Radio International (PRI) program *America Abroad* as an anchor, bringing listeners one-hour international affairs programs.

KEY DATES	
1957	Born in Brooklyn, New York.
1993	Hosts *Talk of the Nation* for NPR.
1996	Receives Rubén Salazar Award from the National Council of La Raza.
1999	Becomes correspondent for PBS's *The NewsHour*.
2005	Joins *America Abroad* public radio program as an anchor.

▲ **Ray Suárez has said that he prefers public broadcasting, which is audience-directed, to commercial stations, which are driven by advertisers.**

Suárez has since narrated, anchored, and reported for public radio and television programs such as *Follow the Money*, *The Execution Tapes*, *State of the Union*, and *Growing Up Scared*. Suárez is also the author of several books, including *The Old Neighborhood: What We Lost in the Great Suburban Migration 1966–1999* (1999).

During the course of a distinguished career, Suárez has received many accolades. His work for NPR on the first multiracial elections in South Africa and the first 100 days of the 104th U.S. Congress earned him two duPont-Columbia Silver Baton Awards in 1993–1994 and 1994–1995. In 1995 *Current History Magazine* presented him with its Global Awareness Award. He also received a Chicago Emmy Award. Several universities and colleges have bestowed honorary doctorates on him.

See also: Salazar, Rubén

Further reading: Díaz, Katherine A. "Rey of Public Broadcasting." *Hispanic*. October 1999.
http://www.ctforum.org/popups/bio.asp?event_bio_image_id=2586 (biography).

SUÁREZ, Xavier L.
Politician

Xavier L. Suárez was the first Cuban-born mayor of Miami, Florida. Suárez served as mayor from 1985 to 1993, and was reelected to office in 1997. He was subsequently removed from the post in 1998, after a judge ruled that his election had involved an abuse of absentee-ballot laws.

Early life
Born in Cuba in 1948, Suárez went to Belen Jesuit Preparatory School. After graduating he studied at Villanova University in Pennsylvania, earning an engineering degree in 1971. Suárez went on to study at the law and government schools at Harvard.

A man of the people
After gaining his law degree, Suárez moved to Miami, Florida, where he began practicing. He emerged as a prominent member of Miami's Cuban community, working with several community groups and campaigning on mental health, crime, and education-related issues.

A popular man, Suárez decided to stand for the mayoral elections in 1984. Backed by several important people, including Cuban political activist Ivon Fuente (*see box on page 30*), the Republican Suárez was elected

▼ *Lawyer and activist Xavier Suárez was the first Cuban American to become mayor of Miami, Florida. He won election in 1985.*

KEY DATES	
1948	Born in Cuba.
1971	Earns a degree in engineering from Villanova University, Pennsylvania.
1985	Becomes the first Cuban American mayor of Miami, Florida.
1993	First term as mayor ends; returns to practice law.
1997	Runs for mayoral office again.
1998	Removed from office after 111 days following absentee-ballot fraud scandal.
2004	Stands for post of representative of District 7 of Miami–Dade County Commission; fails to win election.

to power, replacing Puerto Rican-born Democrat Maurice Ferre, who in 1973 had become the first Latino to be elected mayor of a major U.S. city. Suárez was sworn into office on November 13, 1985.

The first Cuban American mayor of Miami
Suárez was mayor from 1985 to 1993. During his time in office, he attracted a lot of attention. He ordered the firing of 70 city officials, an action that was overturned by the state's attorney who concluded that Suárez had acted beyond his powers.

Suárez's critics accused him of behaving erratically because of such actions as his declaration of October 7, 1990, as "Yahweh ben Yahweh Day," after the leader of the black supremacist group the Nation of Yahweh. A high-profile figure in the Miami community, Yahweh raised money for numerous charities in the city. He was also suspected of criminal activity, however, and, just weeks after Suárez's controversial announcement, the religious leader was arrested on charges of conspiracy to murder and extortion. Hounded by news reporters, who wanted to know his reaction to Yahweh's arrest, Suárez commented that he had obviously been mistaken in his opinion of Yahweh.

In 1993 Suárez chose not to run again in the mayoral elections, returning to practice law instead. At the time Miami faced financial ruin, had the United State's highest murder rate, and suffered from an extremely high rate of poverty.

INFLUENCES AND INSPIRATION

Xavier Suárez's political career was launched by die-hard Republican Ivon Fuente (1914–2006). Cuban-born Fuente, whose real name was Estrella Rubio, was one of the grandes dames of Miami politics. Rubio adopted her new name following her arrival in the United States from Cuba in the 1960s, taking "Ivon" to honor the Russian leader Ivan the Terrible (1530–1584) and "Fuente" because it was the surname of her husband, Judge José de la Fuente Hernández.

A Cuban patriot who hated Communism, Ivon Fuente left her native country after Fidel Castro's rise to power.

In the 1960s, she set up a business bringing Cubans to the United States via Mexico for $100 a person. She is also reported to have used her own money to send a boat full of weapons to anti-Castro forces in Cuba.

Fuente became involved in Miami politics through the mayoral campaign of Maurice Ferre, but she lost faith in him.

Fuente sometimes broke the law in her efforts to get her political candidates elected. Following Xavier Suárez's 1997 mayoral campaign, she was accused of committing vote fraud. Fuente had helped the city commissioner Humberto Hernández get Suárez elected

mayor. She signed as a witness to the vote of a woman named María Padrón. Interviewed by investigators looking into vote fraud, Padrón told them that two men representing Commissioner Hernández had picked up her ballot and that she had never even met Fuente.

One of 19 people arrested in a vote-fraud investigation that eventually led a judge to remove Suárez from office and reinstate Joe Carollo, Fuente had just had open-heart surgery when police came to arrest her. She collapsed and was taken to the hospital. Hernández was later given a year sentence for the electoral fraud. Fuente died in 2006.

An unfortunate election

Suárez campaigned to become the city mayor again in 1997, running against Joe Carollo, the sitting mayor. He won the election on November 4, 1997, by a narrow margin. However, Carollo soon brought a lawsuit challenging the legitimacy of Suárez's win.

In addition to the subsequent investigation into absentee-ballot fraud, Suárez also began to attract attention for his sometimes inexplicable and seemingly erratic behavior. He reportedly referred to state senator Ron Silver as "Santa Claus," and insisted that a $68 million budget deficit did not really exist. He attracted most attention after he turned up late at night uninvited on the doorstep of Edna Benson, a 68-year-old woman, who had written to Suárez, taking him to task for Miami's civic mess. The woman initially thought that Suárez was an intruder and got her gun, only putting it away when she realized who he was.

Mayor Loco

In December 1997, Suárez became extremely upset with the best-selling novelist Carl Hiaasen, a columnist for the *Miami Herald*. Hiaasen wrote that: "Another chaotic week ends, leaving Miamians to wonder how long before the white-suited men with butterfly nets come to take the mayor away." Hiaasen coined the nickname "Mayor Loco"

for Suárez, who subsequently threatened to sue both the novelist and the paper. Suárez is reported to have told the paper's advertising manager that the *Miami Herald* should be nicer to him and to his people, since Suárez was subsidizing it financially through advertisements relating to official notices.

In March 1998, circuit judge Thomas Wilson ruled after a month-long trial in favor of Carollo, concluding that there was evidence of "fraud and abuse of the absentee-ballot laws" in Suárez's election. Judge Wilson insisted on a new election. Joe Carollo declared: "It's a great day for Miami. We live in a great country and I'm proud to be American."

Return

In 2004, Xavier Suárez ran for public office again, this time as the representative for District 7 of the Miami-Dade County Commission, a position that had fallen vacant when Jimmy Morales announced that he was running in the Miami mayoral elections. Suárez lost the ensuing vote, however, and former Miami city manager Carlos Gimenez became commissioner for the area.

Further reading: http://www.firn.edu/civiced/games/faces/suarez.html (short biography).

SUPREME COURT

The Supreme Court has played a key role in helping Latinos achieve better and more equal rights, allowing them to challenge unfair legal decisions and to assert their rights as protected by the U.S. Constitution.

The role of the court

The U.S. Supreme Court is the highest court in the nation. It is the most important part of the judicial branch of the government, and was created to act as a check and a balance on both the legislature (Congress) and the executive (the president). The Supreme Court hears cases that have a direct bearing on the interpretation of the U.S. Constitution, legislative acts, or international treaties in which the United States is involved.

Justices sit on the Supreme Court for life after having been nominated by the U.S. president and confirmed through the Senate. Nine justices serve on the court in total.

Latino judges

The Latino population of the United States grew enormously in the late 20th and early 21st centuries: By 2004 Latinos made up about 14 percent of the total U.S. population. Yet very few Latinos have been nominated to serve as Supreme Court judges. Critics regard the underrepresentation of such a large ethnic minority as racist. There is a broad consensus that more people of Hispanic origin are needed on the bench to represent

and defend the rights of the Latino population and ensure that justice is properly served under the law.

Even when Latinos are nominated, the choices have sometimes been controversial. In 2001, for example, President George W. Bush put forward the name of Honduran-born Miguel Estrada for appointment to the U.S. Circuit Court of Appeals in Washington, D.C. Estrada was a respected and prominent lawyer, but his nomination divided the Latino community. The Puerto Rican Legal Defense and Education Fund and the Congressional Hispanic Caucus both opposed it on the grounds that, in their view, Estrada had not demonstrated an adequate commitment to

The Supreme Court has played a major part in the Latino struggle for fairer representation and greater involvement in U.S. society. Several of the court's decisions have been landmarks on the road to full civil rights.

protecting the rights of the Hispanic community. Two years later Estrada withdrew his nomination after he failed to gain a Senate vote on the nomination.

Second-class citizens

Hispanics have historically been treated as second-class citizens in the United States and, like African Americans, were seen by many Anglo-Americans as racially inferior. As a result, they often experienced discrimination on a day-to-day basis, in school, work, and in matters relating to ownership and occupancy of land and property.

At the end of the U.S.–Mexico War (1846–1848), the northern half of Mexico was annexed by the United States under the terms of the Treaty of Guadalupe Hidalgo (1848). Approximately 100,000 Mexicans were living in the affected region at the time. Although the treaty granted them all U.S. citizenship and full constitutional rights, in practice those people now described as Mexican Americans found themselves increasingly marginalized and discriminated against. As Anglo-American migration to the Southwest increased rapidly from the mid-19th century, Mexican Americans had to struggle to keep their land, despite the treaty stating that private property rights would be "inviolably respected."

Land and property

In the 19th century, several land-related cases reached the Supreme Court. In the 1850s Mariano G. Vallejo—a Mexican who had supported the U.S. annexation of California, where he owned large tracts of land—petitioned the U.S. Supreme Court for recognition of his title to property in the northern part of the state. Although his ownership had been undisputed before 1848, and should therefore have been protected under the Treaty of Guadalupe Hidalgo, he lost his application, and died a virtual pauper on his small remaining parcel of land.

Similarly, in 1899 in *Botiller v. Dominguez*, a Mexican land grantee brought an action to recover possession of land from settlers who claimed that, under the 1862 Homestead Act, it was theirs because they had lived on it for five years.

The Supreme Court decided that, although Dominguez's land grant was seen to be perfect under Mexican law, it had not been presented to the U.S. land claims commission for confirmation. The justices ruled "that no title to land in California dependent upon Spanish or Mexican land grants can be of any validity" unless presented to and confirmed by the board of land commissioners within the time prescribed by the statute. The Court therefore invalidated a perfect title that had been granted by Mexico 20 years earlier. Some commentators believe that the decision reflected the role of the Supreme Court as part of a conquering U.S. government in the Southwest after the U.S.–Mexico War.

Education

Such cases were symptomatic of the growing marginalization of Mexican Americans. While their property was being expropriated, they were further victimized through segregation. The provision of separate schools on the grounds of race became a key issue for both Hispanic and African American activists, particularly after the 1896 Supreme Court ruling in *Plessy v. Ferguson* that the practice was constitutional if "separate but equal" conditions were maintained for whites and blacks or other nonwhites.

Nonwhite children generally received substandard education, and the children of Spanish-speaking parents were often punished for speaking their native language at school. Hispanic activists wanted to bring an end to segregation and also to protect their children's language rights.

KEY DATES

1850s   Supreme Court rules against Mariano G. Vallejo's petition to claim his considerable land holdings.

1896   Supreme Court rules segregation is constitutional if "separate but equal" in *Plessy v. Ferguson*.

1931   Mexican Americans challenge segregation in Lemon Grove, California.

1946   The Supreme Court rules in the Lemon Grove case that the segregation of Mexican children in schools is unconstitutional.

1954   Court rules in *Brown v. Board of Education*, based in part on *Méndez v. Westminster*.

1954   Court rules on jury discrimination in *Hernández v. Texas*.

1966   Supreme Court rules on rights of arrested individuals in *Miranda v. Arizona*.

1968   Mexican American Legal Defense and Educational Fund formed.

1976   Court rules in *Regents of the University of California v. Bakke*, based on 1964 Civil Rights Act.

1982   MALDEF involved in bringing action in *Plyler v. Doe*.

In 1954 the U.S. Supreme Court overturned the conviction for murder of Mexican American Pete Hernández (center) on the grounds that the case had been inspired by prejudice. On the left is the accused's attorney, Gus García.

Organizations such as the League of United Latin American Citizens (LULAC) and the American GI Forum, the predecessors of legal organizations such as the Mexican American Legal Defense and Educational Fund (MALDEF) (*see box on page 34*), took their struggle against injustice to the Supreme Court.

One of the most famous Supreme Court decisions during the civil rights era was that in *Brown v. Board of Education* (1954), which paved the way for the end of segregation in schools. The case hinged on the exclusion from school of an African American pupil, but many commentators believe that its success was facilitated by several previous cases involving Latinos and Latinas.

Landmarks in education

One of the most important of these was the Lemon Grove case. In January 1931 the principal of the Lemon Grove Grammar School, California, prevented more than 70 children of Mexican descent from entering school. The students were directed to a separate school that had been set up specially for them in a nearby barn. The Mexican American community subsequently sued the Lemon Grove School Board and the case reached the California Supreme Court. Although San Diego Supreme Court judge Claude Chambers ruled that the school board's action was wrong, his judgment was itself based on the racist premise that Mexicans were officially Caucasians who could not legally be segregated from other Caucasians.

Méndez v. Westminster was another significant case in segregation history. In 1943 the children of Gonzalo and Felicitas Méndez were denied access to the school that Gonzalo Méndez had himself attended as a child. With the backing of LULAC, the Méndez family and others challenged segregation in four local school districts. In 1946 federal judge Paul J. McCormick ruled that the schools were in breach of the equal protection clause of the Fourteenth Amendment.

The Méndez family's victory led to the desegregation of public schools in Orange County. In 1947, following the success of the appeal in the Ninth Circuit Court, Governor Earl Warren stopped segregation in all California public schools. In 1954 Warren, as chief justice of the U.S. Supreme Court, wrote the majority opinion in *Brown v. Board of Education*.

Although legislation such as the 1964 Civil Rights Act and the 1965 Voting Rights Act provided Latinos with a greater degree of protection under the law, many were still victims of discrimination. Several important cases were ruled on in the Supreme Court. *Lau v. Nichols*, for example, a case involving Chinese students, had a direct effect on the Latino community. In 1974 the Court ruled that Chinese-speaking students in San Francisco who had not been provided with English-language instruction had been denied equal protection under the Constitution and the protections provided for under the Civil Rights Act of 1964. That paved the way for a more meaningful implementation of bilingual education, although it was later challenged under Proposition 227 in California (1998).

MALDEF

In 1968 the Mexican American Legal Defense and Educational Fund was established. Known more commonly by its acronym, MALDEF, the organization was modeled on the Legal Defense Fund established by the National Association for the Advancement of Colored People (NAACP).

Based in San Antonio, Texas, MALDEF was formed with a $2 million grant from the Ford Foundation. MALDEF promotes and protects the civil rights of the more than 40 million Hispanics living in the United States, primarily through litigation and test cases in the areas of education, housing, employment, immigration, and voting rights, but also through funding scholarships for Chicano law students.

MALDEF has won a number of important cases in the Supreme Court, including the 1982 case *Plyler v. Doe,* which challenged a Texas statute that denied children of undocumented aliens access to public education. The Court ruled that undocumented children have the same right to a free public education as U.S. citizens and permanent residents and that they must attend school until they reach the age mandated by state law.

On criminal justice

Many commentators believe that nonwhite Americans are treated unfairly by the legal system. There have been numerous accounts of Hispanics and people from other ethnic minorities being arrested and tried for crimes that they did not commit. Similarly, some critics claim that minority groups often suffer much harsher sentencing because of unequal ethnic representation on juries and within the judiciary.

In 1954 the case of *Hernández v. Texas* highlighted inadequate Mexican American representation on juries and its effects on sentencing. In 1950 an all-white jury had found cotton-picker Pete Hernández guilty of murder. LULAC and the American GI Forum lawyer Gus García challenged the verdict, taking the case all the way to the Supreme Court. Chief Justice Warren ruled that the conviction could not stand since it taxed his "credulity to say that mere chance resulted in there being no members of [Mexican American] class among the over 6,000 jurors called in the past 25 years [in that Texas county]. The result bespeaks discrimination."

Miranda v. Arizona (1966) was another key case in providing ethnic minorities with greater protection under the law. The Supreme Court ruled that law enforcement agencies had to inform suspects of their Fifth Amendment right against self-incrimination and their Sixth Amendment right to the assistance of an attorney before their statements could be used as evidence in a court of law.

Affirmative action

One of the most controversial policies, introduced by Executive Order 11246 in 1965, was affirmative action (positive discrimination). Through the introduction of affirmative policies, such as employment and education quotas, many Latinos were able to enter professions or attend colleges previously closed to them. However, their legality was soon challenged in discrimination cases brought by white Americans. For example, in 1973 and 1974 Alan Bakke sued the University of California at Davis because it set aside places in the medical school for minority candidates who, he claimed, were less qualified than himself. In June 1978 the Supreme Court ruled that race could not be used as the sole criterion for admission.

The U.S. Supreme Court is no champion of Latino interests: That is not its role. Nevertheless, some of its rulings have helped protect the often threatened rights of Hispanic Americans.

See also: Civil Rights; García, Gustavo C.; Herrera, John J.; National Organizations; Vallejo, Mariano G.

Further reading: López, Ian F. Haney. *Racism on Trial: The Chicano Fight for Justice.* Cambridge, MA: Harvard University Press, 2003.
Soltero, Carlos. *Latinos and American Law: Landmark Supreme Court Cases.* Austin, TX: University of Texas Press, 2006.
http://www.maldef.org (Web site for the Mexican American Legal Defense and Education Fund).
www.aclu.org (American Civil Liberties Union site).

TAFOYA, José Piedad
Comanchero

José Piedad Tafoya was one of the most celebrated, and perhaps notorious, of the comancheros. Comancheros were Mexican traders who acted as middle men between the Comanche and European farmers and merchants.

Most of the comancheros worked on the Llano Estacado, meaning "staked plain." This is a vast tableland that forms the southern end of the Great Plains region. It straddles northwestern Texas, northern New Mexico, and western Oklahoma. This arid region was named by the conquistador Francisco Vásquez de Coronado, who thought the tall rock formations around the high plain looked like a stockade made from wooden stakes.

The Comanche who lived in this area and elsewhere on the plains were Native American Shoshone people who had adopted a nomadic lifestyle from about 1600 onward. This life revolved around horses, which had been introduced to North America by Spanish explorers. The Comanche lived by hunting buffalo, but by the mid-19th century they increasingly used their expert horsemanship to steal cattle from farmers. Comancheros then traded the rustled livestock for guns and ammunition.

Early life
José Piedad Tafoya was born in about 1830 in northern New Mexico. At that time this land was a part of Mexico, but in 1845 the territory was annexed by the United States. Tafoya spent his early life running a sheep ranch in what is today San Miguel County.

In 1860 Tafoya began working for the U.S. Army, taking part in some of the campaigns against the Navajo people, who lived in western New Mexico, Arizona, and southern Utah. The military actions against the Navajo throughout the 19th century are known collectively as the Navajo Wars. Tafoya was able to speak and write in both English and Spanish. This skill, combined with the contacts he had among army officers and frontier merchants, enabled him to establish himself as a successful comanchero.

Originally the comancheros had been legitimate traders, but through the 19th century they increasingly used their position as middlemen to deal in stolen goods. By 1865 Tafoya had established himself as a leader in this illicit trade, spending long periods traveling through the Llano Estacado.

Tafoya's base was a simple adobe house near the present-day town of Quitaque in Briscoe County, Texas, but he was undoubtedly a very wealthy man. One contemporary estimated that in his heyday in the 1860s and early 1870s, Tafoya was running more than 250 wagons across the Llano Estacado at any one time.

The scout
In the late 1860s the U.S. authorities began to crack down on the comancheros' trade as they consolidated their control of the New Mexico Territory. Some reports suggest that Tafoya was briefly captured in 1874 by the Civil-War hero Colonel Ranald Slidell Mackenzie. Certainly, at about this time his career as a comanchero came to an end and, together with his wife and family, he settled down once more to live on his ranch in New Mexico.

During his years of trading in the wilds of the high plains, Tafoya built up an intimate knowledge of the Llano Estacado. From time to time he returned to this region not as an outlaw comanchero, but acting as a scout for the U.S. Army. In 1877 Tafoya assisted Captain Nicholas Nolan in an expedition to pursue a group of Comanche cattle raiders across the Llano Estacado. Although the raiders were eventually tracked down, several of their pursuers died of thirst. Tafoya's later life is not well known. He was certainly still alive in 1893, when he was called to testify before a U.S. court about the activities of the comancheros, but the date of his death is unknown.

See also: Coronado, Francisco Vásquez de

Further reading: Kenner, Charles L. *The Comanchero Frontier: A History of New Mexican Plains Indian Relations.* Norman, OK: University of Oklahoma Press, 1994.
http://www.tsha.utexas.edu/handbook/online/articles/TT/fta47.html (biography).

KEY DATES	
1830	Born in northern New Mexico at about this time.
1845	New Mexico becomes U.S. territory.
1860	Joins U.S. Army's campaign against the Navajos.
1865	Established as a comanchero in present-day Briscoe County, Texas.
1877	Takes part in the Nolan Expedition.

TANGUMA, Leo
Artist

Leo Tanguma is a Chicano painter who has a reputation for producing vast, colorful murals that address powerful political and multicultural themes. He often works in collaboration with other muralists, notably his daughter Leticia, as well as with self-taught artists drawn from local communities. Tanguma's public work has roused strong feelings owing to its politically and emotionally charged content. As a result, several of his murals have been painted over.

Artistic talent
The son of Mexican immigrant farmworkers, Tanguma was born in Texas in 1941. He started painting at the age of eight when his older sister bought him a set of paints as a present. Despite his obvious talent, Tanguma's parents were too poor to pay for him to go to art college, and he was largely self-taught.

Tanguma began painting murals in the 1960s. At the same time, he became involved in the Chicano civil rights movement. Murals were an integral part of the Chicano movement. The murals were often sited in public, highly visible places, such as on the walls of prominent buildings, and were used to proclaim Chicano pride.

Continuing tradition
Tanguma took much of the inspiration for his work from the great Mexican muralists Diego Rivera (1886–1957), José Clemente Orozco (1883–1949), and David Alfaro Siqueiros (1896–1974), who had also used their work to proclaim revolutionary, left-wing ideas and messages. In his first important work, *The Rebirth of Our Nationality* (1972), Tanguma depicted the struggle for Mexican American rights on the wall of the Continental Can Company in Houston, Texas. At the center of the 260-foot (79m) mural was the banner of the United Farm Workers, the Mexican American labor union led by César Chávez.

Leaving Texas
Sometimes Tanguma used his work to respond to specific events. For example, in the early 1980s Houston police officers killed a Mexican American Vietnam war veteran, provoking a wave of unrest in the city's Chicano community. Tanguma set about creating a wood-based mural protesting police brutality, but to his dismay the work vanished from his studio before he could finish it.

KEY DATES	
1941	Born in Texas on November 5.
1972	Paints mural *The Rebirth of Our Nationality* on the wall of the Continental Can Company in Houston, Texas.
1995	Completes controversial murals in the concourses of Denver International Airport.
1996	Creates mural at the University of Wisconsin at Madison.
2000	Paints mural in Candelaria Hall at the University of Northern Colorado at Greeley.

The incident deeply upset Tanguma and led him to leave Texas for Denver, Colorado, where he continues to live and work today.

Controversial work
In Denver Tanguma was able to win a number of prestigious commissions. In 1995 he completed three large murals for the main terminal of the new Denver International Airport. The murals addressed political themes such as war, discrimination, injustice, and the destruction of the environment. They attracted controversy because of the unsettling nature of some of the images. In one mural, for instance, a Nazi-like soldier in a gas mask stabs a dove with a giant sword. This image in particular has fed a conspiracy theory that Denver International Airport is the location of a secret base run by aliens or a fascist elite set on genocide.

Tanguma has also carried out other, far less controversial works, such as his murals for the Memorial Union at the University of Wisconsin at Madison (1996) and for Candelaria Hall at the University of Northern Colorado (2000).

See also: Chávez, César

Further reading: Dempsey, Paul Stephen. *Denver International Airport: Lessons Learned.* New York, NY: McGraw-Hill, 1997. psych.colorado.edu/~dciarlo/trans5.html (images and discussion of the Denver International Airport murals). http://www.tsha.utexas.edu/handbook/online/articles/CC/kjc3.html (history of Chicano murals).

TAPIA, Luis
Artist

Luis Tapia is an artist of Mexican American origin who has been categorized as both a naïve and a Chicano artist. He differs from other naïve artists in consciously including a sophisticated social commentary in his work (naïve art is usually known for its simplicity, especially in form and color). As a Chicano artist, Tapia belongs to a particular trend that looks to renew the traditional Latino handicraft of *santeros*—wood-carvers of *santos* (saints images). Santeros reflect one of the oldest traditions of religious devotion practiced by Hispanic Americans.

Early life
Luis Eligio Tapia was born in Santa Fe, New Mexico, in 1950, to a family of early settlers of the region. Tapia attended schools in Santa Fe and studied for one year at New Mexico State University, but did not receive any art education. His interest in art occurred through his general interest in the Chicano civil rights movement in the early 1970s, which led him to rediscover the Hispanic tradition of carving santos. The Spanish colonial tradition of wood carving had remained alive in the Southwest and had been revived in the 1930s as part of the general interest in

▼ *Luis Tapia revived the old Latino religious art of carving* **santos** *(images of saints), but with a modern interpretation relevant to a contemporary audience.*

KEY DATES

1950	Born in Santa Fe, New Mexico, on July 6.
1970	Starts to make *santos*.
1978	Cofounds La Cofradía de Artes y Artesanos Hispánicos.
1991	Stages first major solo exhibition.

American "folk" art. It had decayed, however, into the production of monochrome or falsely aged colored sculptures for the tourist market.

Tapia studied Spanish colonial art in churches and in the Museum of International Folk Art in Santa Fe and led the return to authentic polychrome santos, but without sticking to strict traditional conventions. In 1976 and 1977 Tapia's santos were well received at the Festival of American Folklife at the Smithsonian Institution, Washington, D.C., which encouraged him to continue developing his style. In 1978 Tapia cofounded La Cofradía de Artes y Artesanos Hispánicos, which presented four shows before closing in 1982. The group's most influential show was at the Museum of Fine Arts in Santa Fe.

Later work
In the 1990s Tapia diversified his subject matter, creating nonreligious figures, and intensified the social commentary within his work. *Pieta* (1999) shows the dead Christ in modern clothing, alluding to contemporary violence.

Tapia's work became accepted in the art world when he was included in the seminal exhibition and catalog "Hispanic Art in the United States: 30 Contemporary Painters and Sculptors" (Houston Fine Art Museum, 1987). He had his first major solo exhibition in 1991 at Owing-Dewey Fine Art, Santa Fe, and received the "Distinguished Artist of the Year Award" from the Santa Fe Rotary Foundation in 1994. Tapia is also a restorer and maker of church retablos (altar paintings) and has made devotional images for several churches in the Southwest.

Further reading: Kalb, Larie Beth. *Crafting Devotions: Tradition in Contemporary New Mexico Santos.* Albuquerque, NM: University of New Mexico Press, 1994.
http://www.owingsdewey.com/artists/luistapia/index.html

TAPIA Y RIVERA, Alejandro
Writer

A poet, essayist, and dramatist, Alejandro Tapia y Rivera is considered the father of Puerto Rican literature. As well as making a huge contribution to Puerto Rican writing, Tapia y Rivera was also a political activist. He campaigned for the abolition of slavery in the Americas and was an advocate of equal rights for women.

Early life
Tapia y Rivera was born in Puerto Rico's capital city, San Juan, on November 12, 1826. He completed primary school in San Juan under the tutelage of the distinguished educator Rafael Cordero (1790–1868). Cordero was a Puerto Rican of African descent. Although born into poverty, Cordero educated himself and started a free school in his house.

As the years passed, Tapia y Rivera proved to be an avid reader. However, because of his family's financial difficulties, he could not continue with his formal education. He began his working life at Puerto Rico's Department of Housing. After being involved in an illegal duel with an artillery officer in 1850, Tapia was forced to leave his native island.

KEY DATES

1826	Born in San Juan, Puerto Rico, on November 12.
1848	Writes his first book, *El Heliotropo* (The Heliotrope).
1850	Goes into exile in Spain.
1852	Returns to Puerto Rico from exile
1854	Publishes *Biblioteca Histórica de Puerto Rico* (Historical Library of Puerto Rico).
1856	Writes first play, *Robert D'Evreux*.
1873	Publishes biography of Puerto Rican social rights advocate Rámon Power.
1874	Composes the poetry collection *La Sataniada*.
1882	Dies in San Juan, Puerto Rico, on July 19.
1927	Tapia y Rivera's unfinished autobiography, *Mis Memorias (My Memories),* is published.
1937	Teatro Municipal in San Juan is renamed Teatro Tapia in honor of the writer.

Further education
Tapia went into exile in Spain, and there resumed his studies. He learned French, English, and Arabic, as well as being tutored in math, chemistry, and physics. Along with other expatriate Puerto Ricans, he established the Sociedad Recolectora de Documentos Históricos de la Isla de San Juan Bautista de Puerto Rico. The organization aimed to collect and organize historical documents about the island.

After being pardoned by the newly elected governor of Puerto Rico, General Fernando de Norzagaray, Tapia returned home in 1852. He soon founded the Sociedad Filarmónica de Puerto Rico (Philharmonic Society of Puerto Rico), a body devoted to the arts.

Written word
Among Tapia y Rivera's most acclaimed novels are: *El Heliotropo* (The Heliotrope; 1848), *La Palma del Cacique* (The Boss's Palm, 1852), *La Antigua Sirena* (The Old Siren, 1862), *Póstumo el Transmigrado* (Reincarnation, 1872) and its sequel, *Póstumo el Envirginado* (1882), *La Leyenda de los Veinte Años* (The Legend of the Twenty Years; 1874), and *Cofresí* (1876).

Tapia y Rivera's repertoire of plays includes *Roberto D'Evreux* (1856), *Bernardo de Palyssy* (1857), *La Cuarterona* (1867), *Camoens* (1868), and *Vasco Núñez de Balboa* (1872). In 1854 Tapia also wrote a biography of the Puerto Rican painter José Campeche y Jordán (1751–1809) and in 1873 another of the Puerto Rican social-rights advocates Ramón Power (1775–1813).

In the poetry genre, Tapia y Rivera composed the collections of poems *La Sataniada* in 1874 and *Misceláneas* in 1880. His incomplete autobiography was published in 1927 after his death.

Tapia y Rivera received several awards, among them the Medal of the Royal Knight and the Distinguished Order of Carlos III from the government of Spain. He was a member of the Puerto Rican Intellectual Society and founder and first president of the Ateneo Puertorriqueño (Athenaeum of Puerto Rico). While giving a speech at the Ateneo in 1882, Tapia y Rivera collapsed and died from a stroke.

See also: Campeche y Jordán, José

Further reading: http://www.puertorico-herald.org/issues/2002/vol6n23/TapiaTheater-en.shtml (history of the Tapia Theater).

TEISSONNIÈRE, Gerardo
Pianist

Gerardo Teissonnière is a prominent classical pianist. He was born in Puerto Rico and established himself in the United States, where he now enjoys a distinguished career both as a performer and teacher. He is best known for his interpretations of the 20th century repertoire, having given the premiere performance of several contemporary works.

Early career

Teissonnière was born in Ponce, Puerto Rico, in 1961, and started musical studies at an early age in San Juan, Puerto Rico. Teissonnière continued at the Conservatory of Music there, where he studied piano with the celebrated Puerto Rican pianist Jesús Maria Sanromá (1902–1984). In 1980 Teissonnière was the winner of the first Jesús Maria Sanromá Piano Competition, and made his debut as soloist with the Orquestra Sinfónica de Puerto Rico. Teissonnière went to the United States to participate in the Aspen Music Festival in 1981, and subsequently enrolled at the Cleveland Institute of Music, where he studied with Vitya Vronsky (1909–1992). Following his graduation, Teissonnière advanced his studies in Europe with Dmitri Bashkirov (b 1931) and Joaquín Achúcarro (b 1931). He was appointed to the Cleveland Institute of Music faculty in 1989 and settled in the United States.

Critical success

Teissonnière first came to critical attention in the United States during a series of highly regarded recitals as part of the Bicentennial Celebrations of Franz Schubert in 1997. A celebrated solo recital at the prestigious National Gallery of Art in Washington, D.C., in 1999 established his professional career as a performer. Since the 2000–2001 season Teissonnière has concentrated on interpreting the

▲ *Puerto Rican Gerardo Teissonnière is an internationally renowned contemporary pianist.*

work of 20th-century composers and new music by living composers. He has given the premiere of the music of such composers as Pablo Casals (1876–1973), Darius Milhaud (1892–1974), Aaron Copland (1900–1990), Alberto Ginastera (1916–1983), Arvo Pärt (b. 1935), and Lowell Liebermann (b. 1961).

As a faculty member of the Cleveland Institute of Music, Teissonnière is very active in education and is in great demand as a teacher. He has been highly praised for his work with young musicians. Teissonnière is the recipient of the Arthur Loesser Memorial Award and the Pi Kappa Lambda Award of the Cleveland Institute of Music and is an artist in residence at the Amati Music Festival in New York. As a performer, Teissonnière has a busy schedule with solo recitals and as a soloist with orchestras in the United States, Europe, and Latin America; he has also appeared on radio and television in the United States.

Further reading: http://www.gerardoteissonniere.com (official site).
http://www.musicofpuertorico.com/en/gerardo_teissonniere.html (Puerto Rican music site).

KEY DATES	
1961	Born in Ponce, Puerto Rico, on March 29.
1980	Wins the first Jesús Maria Sanromá Piano Competition; makes first solo debut with the Orquestra Sinfónica de Puerto Rico.
1989	Appointed to the Cleveland Institute of Music.
1999	Acclaimed solo recital at the National Gallery of Art, Washington D.C.

TELLES, Raymond
Politician

Raymond Telles was the first Latino to be elected mayor of a major U.S. city. His political career in El Paso, Texas, set an example for subsequent generations of Hispanic Americans.

Early life

Telles was born in El Paso in 1915. His father was a Tejano bricklayer, while his mother had been born in Chihuahua, Mexico. Telles's parents plowed all their money into their three sons' education. Raymond, Richard, and José, attended private schools, not segregated public schools.

Telles graduated from high school in 1933 and got a job as a civil servant and then as a clerk at a federal prison. These jobs helped keep the Telles family afloat during the Depression era.

In 1941, when the United States entered World War II (1939–1945), Telles was drafted into the U.S. Army in the officer program. In the following year he reached the rank

▼ *Raymond Telles during the election for clerk of El Paso County in 1951. He later served two terms as the city's mayor, and planned a third before being appointed ambassador to Costa Rica.*

KEY DATES	
1915	Born in El Paso, Texas, on September 15.
1941	Drafted into U.S. Army.
1948	Elected county clerk of El Paso County.
1957	Elected mayor of El Paso.
1959	Reelected as mayor.
1961	Appointed as U.S. ambassador to Costa Rica. He serves in this role until 1967.
1971	Appointed as chair of the Equal Employment Opportunity Commission.

of lieutenant, and transferred to the Army Air Corps. Also in 1942, he married his sweetheart, Delfina Navarro. Telles then served in the U.S. Air Force, where he became chief of the Lend-Lease Program for Central and South America, an organization set up to enable the United States to supply weapons to its wartime allies. Telles then became the military liaison between the U.S. president and Latin American governments.

Politics

On his return to El Paso in 1948, Telles ran for county clerk. He focused on getting Hispanic Americans to pay the $1.75 poll tax required so they could register to vote. The tactic worked, and Telles held the position until 1957, when he ran for mayor of El Paso and won easily. He was reelected in 1959. Telles and his brothers had become a powerful political force. Telles supported John F. Kennedy when he came to Texas looking for votes in the presidential election. Telles's backing helped Kennedy win the state.

The newly elected President Kennedy repaid Telles by appointing him as U.S. Ambassador to Costa Rica. President Lyndon Johnson appointed him chair of the U.S.–Mexico Border Commission, and in 1971 President Richard Nixon named him chairman of the Equal Employment Opportunity Commission.

Further reading: Garciá, Mario T. *The Making of a Mexican American Mayor: Raymond L. Telles of El Paso.* El Paso, TX: Texas Western Press, University of Texas at El Paso, 1998. http://www.epcc.edu/nwlibrary/borderlands/14_first_hispanic_mayor.htm (biography).

TENAYUCA, Emma
Activist

Union activist Emma Tenayuca is best known for her involvement in the San Antonio pecan shellers' strike of 1938, where she campaigned alongside fellow activist Manuela Solís Sager. Tenayuca's commitment to the cause earned her the nickname "La Pasionaria" (passionflower).

Early political activity

Tenayuca was born on December 21, 1916, in San Antonio, Texas. From her father, she learned to value social justice and have concern for the needs of working people. A strike against the Finck Cigar Company in 1932 initiated Tenayuca's political life. By 1937 Tenayuca had organized two local groups of the International Ladies Garment Workers Union and was a member of the executive committee of the Workers Alliance, a national federation of unemployed workers' organizations that was affiliated with the Communist Party.

On January 31, 1938, 12,000 San Antonio pecan shellers, mostly Mexican women, walked off their jobs protesting a wage cut. Wages for pecan shellers averaged just $2.73 per week, and entire families had to work at pecan shelling in order to meet their most basic needs. The owners of pecan factories acknowledged these conditions as less than perfect, but also believed that Mexican

▼ *Emma Tenayuca was a determined socialist who fought for the rights of Mexican workers in her native San Antonio, Texas.*

KEY DATES

1916   Born in San Antonio, Texas, on December 21.

1938   Involved in strike of Mexican pecan shellers; earns nickname "La Pasionaria" (passionflower) for her commitment to the working classes.

1984   Honored by the National Association of Chicana/o Studies for her political contributions to the Mexican community in the United States.

1999   Dies in San Antonio, Texas, on July 23.

workers were happy to work in such conditions since they did not have aspirations for a better life. With these beliefs, owners went ahead and reduced wages.

Support for the strike came from the United Cannery, Agricultural, Packing, and Allied Workers of America (UCAPAWA) union, part of the Congress of Industrial Organizations (CIO). Tenayuca was slated to lead the strike, but the CIO, uncomfortable with her Communist Party membership, replaced her. However, she was named as honorary strike leader in recognition of her previous union work. In March 1938 both sides of the strike agreed to arbitration and reached an agreement on hourly wages. Pecan factory owners, however, installed cracking machines and replaced more than 10,000 workers.

Later life

Owing to harassment and threats to her life because of her union work, Tenayuca left San Antonio in 1939. During World War II (1939–1945) her enlistment in the Women's Army Corps was rejected, Tenayuca believed, because of her association with the Communist Party. She ultimately found work sewing military uniforms. After the war Tenayuca moved to San Francisco, enrolled in college, and in 1952 earned a state teaching license. Returning to San Antonio in 1960, Tenayuca taught in the Harlandale School District. She died in 1999.

See also: Solís Sager, Manuela

Further reading: Rodolfo, Acuña. *Occupied America*, 3rd Edition. New York, NY: Harper and Row, 1988.
http://www.texancultures.utsa.edu/memories/htms/Tenayuca_transcript.htm (interview with Tenayuca).

TEXAS, HISTORY OF

Since it was first settled by Europeans in the 18th century, Texas has belonged to five countries, and was also for a time an independent nation. Spain, France, Mexico, the Confederacy, and the United States have all claimed Texas as part of their territory.

From Spain to Mexico

Texas was part of New Spain until 1821, when the Spanish colony achieved independence from European rule and became the Republic of Mexico. From 1821 to 1835, Texas was part of the Mexican state of Coahuila y Tejas. The name Tejas (pronounced TAY-has) derives from the Spanish understanding of a Caddo (east Texas Native American) word meaning "friend."

Influx of settlers

During the 1820s, many pioneers set out from the United States for Texas. In 1824, the Mexican government entered a historic contract with Stephen F. Austin (1793–1836), a prominent U.S. settler and the so-called "Father of Texas." The agreement allowed large numbers of American families to immigrate to Texas on the conditions that they took Mexican citizenship and converted to Catholicism. Before long, thousands of U.S. settlers had immigrated, mostly to eastern Texas. They were welcomed for a time, but later they came into conflict with the Mexican government over a range of contentious matters. Tension

Texas president Sam Houston (1793–1863) led the struggle to free the state from Mexican control.

was exacerbated by cultural and political differences. By the end of the 1820s, Mexico had become alarmed at the rising level of immigration. In 1829, the government attempted to discourage further settlers in Texas by abolishing slavery, which most incoming Anglo-Americans regarded as their right. When that failed to produce the desired effect, in the following year Mexico banned immigration completely. Both measures proved futile, however: The American settlement of Texas was already an accomplished fact.

The political situation was further complicated by disagreements over immigration policy between the central government in Mexico City and local authorities in Texas. While the former feared that the state might be swamped by foreigners, the latter continued to welcome new arrivals from the United States because they contributed significantly to a great boom in the state economy. The American population in Texas, often referred to as the Texians, grew from 300 in 1823 to an estimated 25,000 to 50,000 by 1833. Meanwhile, the Mexican population of the state was almost unchanged, remaining at just 4,000 throughout the period.

In 1833, Mexican president Antonio López de Santa Anna (c. 1795–1876) repealed the anti-immigration law. That served the interests of the settlers and pro-immigration Texas residents, but it did not resolve the conflict. On the contrary, it sowed the seeds of the U.S.–Mexico War (1846–1848).

Independence from Mexico

In 1835, Santa Anna abolished the 1824 Mexican Constitution. He used his increased power to crack down on the relative autonomy of the provincial governments, especially those of Yucatán and Texas. In December of that year, an attack on San Antonio acted as a catalyst for the Texas independence movement, which had support from American settlers and Tejanos (Texas Mexicans) alike. The most memorable battle in the ensuing war took place at the Alamo, a former Spanish mission. It was there that Texan forces held out for 13 days against the besieging Mexican army, which eventually stormed the fort on March 6, 1836.

Remember the Alamo

After that defeat, "Remember the Alamo" became the battle cry of Texas rebels for the remainder of what became known as the Texas Revolution. In the meantime, the Texans defiantly enacted their declaration of independence at Washington-on-Brazos on March 2, 1836. On April 21, 1836, at the Battle of San Jacinto, Texas general Sam Houston defeated Santa Anna's forces and captured the president himself the next day. The Republic of Texas was free from Mexican control.

In May 1836, the Treaties of Velasco were signed between Texas and Mexico, temporarily

The Battle of San Jacinto *was completed in 1895 by the painter Henry Arthur McArdle (1836–1908).*

ending hostilities. Although Santa Anna thereby recognized Texas independence, the Mexican government still refused to acknowledge Texas as a republic, and made numerous attempts to recapture its lost Texas territories, all of which ended in failure. During the nine years of the existence of the Republic of Texas, four Tejanos served in the Texas Congress: José Antonio Navarro, José Francisco Ruíz, Juan N. Seguín, and Rafael de la Garza.

Annexation to the United States

From its inception, the Republic of Texas had lobbied to become part of the United States. Initially, the federal government refused to accept another slave state into the Union. Its attitude changed, however, as the United States became more expansionist, and attempted to take over California and other parts of northern Mexico. On February 28, 1845, the U.S. Congress passed a bill authorizing the annexation of the

Republic of Texas as a slave state. On March 3, 1845, President James K. Polk signed the bill into law. Texas voted overwhelmingly to accept the proposed annexation.

By the end of the year, Texas was formally admitted into the Union, ceding its entire territory to the U.S. government. The Mexican government viewed the move as an act of open hostility.

The U.S.–Mexico War

As U.S.–Mexico relations deteriorated, Polk sent diplomat John Slidell to Mexico City to negotiate. However, Mexican president Mariano Paredes y Arrillaga, who had recently overthrown the moderate administration of José Joaquín Herrera, refused to negotiate, heightening tension between the two countries. Fulfilling a previous agreement with Texas, Polk then sent the U.S. Army to the north bank of the Rio Grande. The territory occupied by the troops was disputed: The United States

claimed that the river was the frontier; Mexico insisted that the border ran along the Nueces River, about 100 miles (160km) to the north, and therefore that the armed incursion was an act of war.

On April 24, 1846, General Mariano Arista led Mexican troops across the Rio Grande and attacked a U.S. cavalry company under Seth Thornton. Polk urged the U.S. Congress to pass a war resolution in response to "Mexican aggression." The United States declared war on Mexico on May 13, 1846.

The initial battles of the conflict were fought on Texas soil, at Palo Alto and Resaca de la Palma. By the late summer of 1847, however, U.S. troops had advanced as far as Mexico City, routing a demoralized Mexican resistance force at Chapultepec Hill. The last-ditch defenders, mainly young Mexican cadets, became known in Mexico as "*los niños héroes*" (the heroic children). With victory in sight, the U.S. Army marched into the Mexican National Palace and raised the U.S. flag. The triumph has since been immortalized in the Marine Corps anthem "The Halls of Montezuma."

The Treaty of Guadalupe Hidalgo
On February 2, 1848, U.S. State Department official Nicholas Trist negotiated the Treaty of Guadalupe Hidalgo, which ended a war that had cost the lives of 13,000 Americans and an estimated 25,000 Mexicans. The United States agreed to pay Mexico $15 million in reparations, and gained all Mexican territory west of Texas, including California and Nevada. As a result, approximately 100,000 Mexicans were now living in the United States; the treaty guaranteed their property rights and citizenship. Only a few thousand Mexicans opted to remain in Mexico by moving south of the Rio Grande.

Repercussions in Texas
Although the territory that Mexico lost in 1848 was approximately one-half of its former land area, it had been home to only about 1 percent of its population. The central government in Mexico City had neither made full use of its resources, nor protected them adequately from foreign plundering. Even if Mexico had been able to rule Texas effectively, Mexican opinion had always been divided over the best way to deal

with its remote outpost. Many opposed the state's independence, but recognized that annexation was impossible. When the United States annexed Texas, making it the 28th state of the Union, the Mexican elite urged military action. The rationale for the call to arms was an 1828 border treaty in which the United States had agreed to respect the integrity of Mexican territory. Likewise, the Monroe Doctrine of 1823 had purportedly committed the United States to oppose the transfer of territories, and recognized the political sovereignty of the new Latin American republics. In a last-ditch effort to prevent U.S. annexation of Texas, Mexico offered to recognize Texas independence. The offer was summarily rejected in 1875 both in Austin, Texas, and in Washington, D.C.

In the years following the U.S.–Mexico War, tensions between Anglo-Americans and Mexican Americans in Texas again rose significantly. There were violent clashes after Tejanos were accused of helping slaves escape to Mexico. Mexicans found themselves in a "new" land, with new laws and institutions over

THE SAN PATRICIOS

During the U.S.–Mexico War, a group of Irish Catholic immigrants grew tired of their ill-treatment by mainly Protestant Anglo-American officers. They were increasingly puzzled about why they were fighting against their coreligionists. So they deserted the U.S. Army under General Zachary Taylor, and joined the Mexican side. The renegades, led by Captain John Riley from County Galway, called themselves Los San Patricios, or St. Patrick's Battalion, after the patron saint of their native country. They were joined by Germans and other disaffected ethnic minorities.

At the Battle of Churubsco, 83 San Patricios were captured, and 72 were court martialed. Of this number, 50 were sentenced to be hanged and 16 were flogged and branded on their cheeks with the letter "D" for deserter. Today, however, many Mexicans and Tejanos hail them as heroes.

MANIFEST DESTINY IN TEXAS HISTORY

The U.S.–Mexico War was a confrontation between Mexico, the Republic of Texas, and the United States's fulfillment of Manifest Destiny. President Polk was a firm believer in Manifest Destiny, a pervasive ideology that equated North American continental expansion with a divine plan. During the 1840s, while perhaps a majority of U.S. citizens agreed with Polk, there was nevertheless a vociferous antiwar movement made up mostly of abolitionists opposed to the expansion of slavery. The best known of them was the poet and philosopher Henry David Thoreau (1817–1862), who famously spent a night in jail for refusing to pay his war tax.

The outcome of the war sent shock waves throughout Latin America, tarnishing the United States's image as a beacon of freedom and defender of sovereignty. In Mexico and much of Latin America, the conflict became known as the "War of American Aggression." One lingering question is whether the United States provoked the war as a pretext to further its pursuit of Manifest Destiny.

While Mexico suffered a great loss of life and territory, its defeat in 1848 forced the country to rethink its national identity, and to rebuild its infrastructure and political system. In the wake of defeat, Mexico endured a long period of instability, invasion, and civil strife during the 1860s. The war also created a close, if often tense, relationship between Mexico and the United States. Years later, President Porfirio Díaz made the wry comment: "Poor Mexico, so far from God, and so close to the United States!"

which they had limited control, and a language that they did not fully understand. Despite undertakings in the Treaty of Guadalupe Hidalgo that guaranteed the property rights of Mexican Americans, many Tejanos had their homes expropriated and their lands illegally confiscated.

The new state government of Texas made no effort to assimilate non-English-speaking inhabitants, and its failure to do so contributed significantly to the development of a Mexican American underclass in the state. Throughout Texas, as elsewhere in the U.S. Southwest, U.S. individualism vied with—and generally prevailed over—the Mexican tradition of collectivism.

Texas in the Civil War

On the outbreak of the Civil War, Texas voted to secede from the Union on February 1, 1861. Texas president Sam Houston refused to take an oath to the Confederacy, however, and a new government was formed. The war divided Texans, Anglo Americans, and Tejanos alike. Initially, 2,500 Mexican Americans took up arms for the Confederacy, while 950 joined the Union forces. Colonel Santos Benavides led the rebel Confederate 33rd Texas Cavalry, and was the highest-ranking Mexican American in the Confederate Army. Tejanos such as Benavides were among the first to take up arms for Texas and the Confederacy and among the last to surrender. At the end of the Civil War, Texas was readmitted into the Union.

During the postbellum Reconstruction period, Tejanos dominated politics in most of the state's southwestern border towns, where they represented the majority. For decades following the annexation of Texas, border clashes continued. The 1870s were particularly violent, with intense conflicts between Anglo-Americans, Tejanos, and Mexican citizens.

Mexican outlaw Juan Cortina led raids on several south Texas ranches, stealing or slaughtering cattle, and wreaking havoc over wide areas. By the turn of the century, however, the struggle for Mexican American rights was maintained by predominantly peaceful means under the leadership of *sociedades mutualistas* (voluntary associations).

20th-century immigration

Although Mexican immigration to the United States between 1850 and 1900 averaged just 1,000 per year, after the turn of the 20th century arrivals began to increase. That was partly a result of new immigration laws that placed outright bars on Asian immigration and strict quotas on other national groups, but exempted the inhabitants of the Western Hemisphere. The growth in Mexican immigration after 1900 was also fueled by the corrupt presidency of Porfirio Díaz and

the subsequent Mexican Revolution (1910–1920), both of which disrupted traditional land tenancy arrangements and the lives of many Mexicans.

Advocacy groups

The early-20th century also saw the emergence of numerous Mexican, Tejano, and Latin American advocacy groups in the United States. Many such organizations were founded in Texas. For example, in 1929 the League of United Latin American Citizens (LULAC) held its first meeting in Corpus Christi. LULAC aimed to achieve the assimilation of Mexican American citizens nationwide and their acceptance as equal citizens. To those ends, LULAC stressed the importance to Spanish-speakers of learning and mastering the English language. At the start of the 21st century, LULAC remained one of the leading pan-Latino organizations in the United States.

Economic downturn

The Mexican American community of Texas was particularly hard hit by the Great Depression (1929–1939). Millions of U.S. citizens and Mexican guest-workers lost their jobs during the period, and more than 130,000 Mexicans were deported from Texas alone. In response to the economic crisis, LULAC turned its attention away from immigration toward U.S. domestic issues, such as education and the registration of ethnic-minority voters.

In 1941, the United States entered World War II (1939–1945), and thousands of Anglo-American workers enlisted in the armed forces to fight in Europe and the Pacific. In order to fill the jobs thus vacated, the U.S. and Mexican governments reached a bilateral agreement, known as the Bracero program, which encouraged Mexicans to cross the border for work. Notably, Texas did not directly participate in the scheme at

A yucca blooms on the hills overlooking the Rio Grande, the modern U.S.–Mexico border.

its inception in 1942, partly because ranchers and farmers in the state preferred an open border policy that made Mexican labor readily accessible. At the same time, the Mexican government lobbied against Texas's participation in the program because the state had a history of worker abuse.

Abiding hostility

Anti-Tejano sentiment in Texas persisted. In 1941, the U.S. government responded by forming the Office of the Coordinator of Inter-American Affairs to foster good relations among Texans of all ethnic backgrounds. In 1943, as part of President Franklin D. Roosevelt's efforts to improve U.S.–Latin American relations, the Texas governor established the Good Neighbor Commission, which proposed (but never implemented) a series of antidiscrimination policies in the state. Claims of abuse and mistreatment were so extensive that, in 1944, the Mexican government barred its citizens from working in Texas. The Texas state legislature then passed the Caucasian Race Resolution, declaring all Mexican Americans "white" in an attempt to ensure their equal treatment in a segregated society.

Postwar developments

Many Mexican Americans served in the U.S. military during World War II. Five Tejanos were awarded the Congressional Medal of Honor.

After the conflict, Tejanos and Anglo-Americans strove to improve community relations. In 1947, middle-class Chicanos in San Antonio established the Mexican American Chamber of Commerce. The Texas Council on Human Relations was founded in 1950 to facilitate good relations among Texas's diverse population. Tejanos now began to see an improvement in their educational attainment. However, the achievement gap between Mexican Americans and Anglo-Americans remained wide. One influential group that arose during the 1960s' civil rights movement was the Mexican American Youth Organization (MAYO), founded in San Antonio by Willie Velásquez and the pragmatic, moderate José Ángel Gutiérrez.

The 1960s saw the formation of numerous militant groups within the Tejano and Mexican American communities, most famously the Raza Unida Party. The radicalization of Mexican American politics was shortlived, however, and in the following decade moderation returned to center stage. Pete Tijerina founded the Mexican American Legal Defense and Education Fund (MALDEF), which won numerous legal battles for social and economic rights for Mexican Americans in Texas and across the nation.

Latest trends

The number of elected Tejano officials increased during the 1970s and 1980s. The new political leadership was accompanied by a surge in social mobility for Mexican Americans. In Texas, the number of Tejano voters increased by 41 percent between 1978 and 1982. By the 1990s, 40 percent of Tejano workers had skilled, white-collar, professional jobs, a great increase from the 15 percent who were middle-class in the 1930s.

At the start of the 21st century, 7.3 million Texans were Hispanic (32 percent of the population). Of them, 76 percent are of Mexican descent.

See also: Border, Mexico–U.S.; Cortina, Juan Nepomuceno; Guadalupe Hidalgo, Treaty of; Gutiérrez, José Ángel; Navarro, José Antonio; Seguín, Juan N.; Tijerina, Pete; Velásquez, Willie

---

Further reading: Arreola, Daniel. *Tejano South Texas: A Mexican American Cultural Province*. Austin, TX: University of Texas Press, 2002.
Novas, Himilce. *Everything You Need to Know about Latino History*. New York, NY: Plume, 1994.
Thompson, Jerry D. *Vaqueros in Blue and Gray*. Austin, TX: State House Press, 2000.
http://www.pbs.org/kera/usmexicanwar (chronicle of the U.S.–Mexico War through multiple perspectives from both sides of the conflict).
http://www.tsha.utexas.edu/handbook/online (Handbook of Texas Online).

KEY DATES

1821	Texas, previously a province of New Spain, becomes part of Mexico.
1829	Mexico abolishes slavery to discourage U.S. immigration to Texas.
1830	Mexico bans all immigration.
1833	Mexico president Snata Anna repeals anti-immigration legislation.
1836	Texas declares independence from Mexico.
1836	The Texas Revolution ends in victory for the republic.
1845	Texas becomes the 28th state of the United States.
1846	U.S.–Mexico War breaks out after a skirmish on the Texas frontier.
1861	Texas secedes from Union at start of Civil War.
1865	Texas readmitted into the Union.
1929	LULAC founded in Corpus Christi, Texas.
1944	Texas state legislature passes Caucasian Race Resolution, which gives Latinos equal status with Anglo-Americans in the still-segregated state.
1947	Mexican-American Chamber of Commerce founded in San Antonio.
1950	Texas Council on Human Relations established.

TEX-MEX CULTURE

Texans of Mexican ancestry (Tejanos) have developed their own unique "Tex-Mex" (Texas-Mexican) culture based on their borderland experience. Also known as Tejano culture, Tex-Mex encompasses folklore, music, food, dress, and the arts, and expresses a unique cultural nationalism. Tejano culture is distinct from that of Californios (California Mexicans) or Hispanos from New Mexico. Tex-Mex music and food in particular have both become part of mainstream U.S. popular culture.

As early as the 1850s, a few years after Mexico ceded more than half of its territory to the United States under the 1848 Treaty of Guadalupe Hidalgo, Tex-Mex culture was being documented in *corridos* (songs) and in articles in Spanish-language newspapers.

Some commentators claim that the name Tex-Mex came from the Texas–Mexican railroad built in the 1870s, during the heyday of railroad construction in the West. The railroad not only moved products out of the Southwest in refrigerated boxcars but also moved Anglo-American settlers into the region. The majority of workers were Mexican, but the bosses were mostly white, leading to a dynamic exchange of ideas, experiences, and cultures. A hybrid language known as "Spanglish" or "Tex-Mex" arose among workers; it was made up of Spanish and English. Boxcar communities sprang up in Texas and in other places in the United States where Mexicans worked on the railroads.

History
After Mexico acquired its independence from Spain in 1821, the border regions became more heavily populated. This was particularly the case in Texas.

As early as 1822, the Mexican government encouraged Mexicans to move north, and Anglo-Americans began petitioning to move west from the United States into Texas, leading to an intermingling of people and cultures, but increasingly also a clash between them.

Texas eventually separated from Mexico in 1836, after the battles of the Alamo, Goliad, and San Jacinto. Texas remained a republic for nine years until its annexation by the United States in 1845. This contributed to the outbreak of war between Mexico and the United States, which lasted from 1846 to 1848.

At the time of the 1848 Treaty of Guadalupe Hidalgo, about 100,000 Mexicans resided in areas that passed to the United States. The treaty promised legal protection to allow them to maintain their land, religion, language, and culture, but in practice Tejano rights were rarely respected in U.S. courts and on the

On March 31, 2005, fans gathered to pay tribute to the Mexican American singer and cultural icon Selena on the 10th anniversary of her murder.

streets. Tejanos were largely left to look after themselves in a situation where the U.S. government largely ignored them, and the Mexican government lacked the power to enforce the treaty to protect their civil and human rights. Organizations such as the Texas Rangers often terrorized Mexicans, as did other vigilante groups.

Texas Mexicans adopted several strategies to cope with increasing Anglo encroachment into their region and on their way of life. Some people resisted, while others tried accommodation, merging old and new ways of life. Some Tejanos tried to assimilate into Anglo-American society as a means of protecting their families and livelihoods. However they reacted, Tejanos living in the region were forced to interact with Anglos on a day-to-day basis, and the subsequent blending of cultures, music, food, and language resulted in the development of a unique culture that became known as Tex-Mex.

Music
Music became one of the most recognizable features of Tex-Mex culture. *Corridos*, songs based on the Spanish romance tradition, were common in Mexico. They also became popular in the U.S. Southwest in the late 19th century. As Tejanos found themselves increasingly marginalized by Anglo-American settlers, the songs became a way for them both to complain about injustices and to maintain their Hispanic culture. *Corridos* usually featured a Mexican hero who triumphed over a marauding Anglo. From the 1920s, such songs were recorded with great popular success.

KEY DATES	
1820s	Mexican government encourages Anglo-American settlement in Texas.
1836	Texas becomes a republic.
1845	Texas annexed to the United States; Mexican–American War breaks out in the next year, lasting until 1848, when 55 percent of Mexico is ceded to the United States.
1875	Construction begins on the Texas–Mexican railroad.
1930s	Narciso Martínez begins playing; his records help popularize *conjunto* music.
1972	Diana Kennedy begins documenting Tex-Mex cuisine.
1982	First Tejano-Conjunto Festival held in San Antonio, Texas.
1994	Selena y Los Dinos win Grammy for best Mexican American artist; Selena voted one of top 20 most influential Texans.

Probably the most popular music style of Tejano culture is conjunto or *norteño* music. Conjunto music is based around the accordion, introduced by German immigrants into northeastern Mexico from the mid-19th century onward. The accordion quickly became a popular instrument at workers' dances, both in northern Mexico and south Texas. Conjunto music combined elements of traditional Mexican music and the salon music introduced by European migrants to the region, such as the polka, mazurka, and waltz.

Until the 1920s conjunto was mainly performed by a solo accordionist, a *bajo sexto* (12-string guitar) player, and a *tambora de rancho* (ranch drum) player. In the 1930s Narciso Martínez revolutionized the conjunto sound, neglecting the left-hand, bass-chord keys on the accordion almost entirely to concentrate instead on the treble, melodic buttons. He left the bass and harmonic accompaniment to the *bajo sexto*, played by Santiago Almeida.

Martínez's style of music influenced later conjunto stars, including Valerio Longoria and Paulino Bernal. Although most Anglo-Americans may not recognize those names, they are likely to be familiar with their musical descendants, such as Los Lobos, Selena, or Flaco Jiménez.

Conjunto, Tejano, or Tex-Mex music is about more than just the instruments and styles, however. It is a reflection of a merging of two cultures, lives, and shared experiences. It is also an expression of the mixing of several immigrant groups.

Tex-Mex music is also an expression of cultural nationalism and identification. Lyrics, for example, frequently express the unique cultural experience of Tejanos. In Flaco Jiménez's "Un Mojado sin Licensia," the lyrics express the frustration of being an undocumented immigrant in the humorous fashion typical of the self-stereotyping found in Chicano popular culture.

By the 1970s, Tex-Mex music had moved from the margins to the mainstream. Music that had

Since 1982 the Guadalupe Cultural Arts Center has sponsored an annual May festival of conjunto, *norteño,* and Tex-Mex music in San Antonio, Texas. The festival started off small and was originally held over the course of a weekend, but it now lasts for a full week and features the music of South Texas.

Conjunto or *norteño* music features the push-button accordion and the *bajo sexto* as its primary instruments. This type of music draws not only on the music traditions of the Tejanos of South Texas and Norteños of northern Mexico but also on influences from Anglo-American, African American, Czech, Bohemian, German, and Italian music.

Each year the conjunto festival includes the best performers in the country. In addition to the concerts, an annual poster competition and student recitals are also held.

Every year artists are inducted into the Conjunto Hall of Fame, also established in 1982. Inductees include Narciso Martínez, the "father of conjunto music," Valerio Longoria, and Esteban Jordan. Each year the Tex-Mex festival draws in excess of 30,000 people.

previously been played at outdoor dances held in fields and markets in the early 1900s, was recorded in the 1920s and 1930s. Regional record labels, such as Ideal and Falcon records, emerged to cater to Tejano audiences. Spanish-language radio stations played the music on both sides of the border. During the Great Depression, the WPA (Works Progress Administration) also recorded many local artists as part of its project to chronicle the regional cultures of the United States.

By 1982 there were not only many recording labels and artists specializing in Tex-Mex music, but also an entire festival dedicated to Tejano conjunto (*see box*). Musicians such as Flaco Jiménez, the Texas Tornados, and Los Lobos became popular with audiences as they mixed Tex-Mex with rock, jazz, country, and other popular musical styles.

By the 1990s Tex-Mex music had crossed over to appeal to more mainstream audiences through the songs of the popular young singer Selena. Murdered by the president of her fan club, Yolanda Saldívar, Selena became a cultural icon. The posthumously released album, *Dreaming of You,* was the fastest-selling album by any Hispanic American. In 2003, Selena's life was turned into a major motion picture starring Jennifer Lopez.

Food

Most people are familiar with Tex-Mex cuisine, which blends northern Mexican and Southwest U.S. cooking. Typical dishes include tortillas, enchiladas, fajitas, burritos, and salsas. Diana Kennedy helped draw attention to Tex-Mex cuisine, writing several best-selling books on the subject, and making Tex-Mex recipes accessible to wider audiences. Kennedy noted in her 1972 book *The Cuisines of Mexico* that there was a radical difference between Mexican food served in Mexico and Mexican food served in the United States.

In 1973 the *Mexico City News* used the term Tex-Mex in a derogatory fashion to distinguish between what Mexicans served in Mexico versus what Tejanos and Anglo-Americans served on the other side of the Rio Grande. Mexican derision for Latinos in the United States went far beyond food. Tejanos were often referred to as "*pochos,*" meaning that they were not true or real Mexicans. Similarly, people of Mexican ancestry were not viewed as being properly American, and neither was their food.

In 1998, Robb Walsh, a journalist for the *Houston Press,* wrote a ground-breaking six-part series in which he traced the roots of Tex-Mex cuisine back to the contact between Anglo-Americans and Mexicans in Texas in the early 1800s. Walsh states that traditional Mexican cooking began to change in Texas on the arrival of Anglo-Americans, whose different tastes led Mexicans to adapt their cooking style. Tejanos altered their traditional dishes to suit different tastes, cooking Mexican cuisine with the utensils and food brought by white settlers to the region. Some Mexicans became entrepreneurs: From being cooks for Anglo-Americans, they progressed to selling food in the markets, or from street pushcarts, and eventually to opening their own restaurants.

The resulting cuisine was marketed to Anglo-Americans in the form of Tex-Mex restaurant chains, such as Taco Bell, Chili's, Chi-Chi's, El Torrito, Taco Time, Chipotle, Baja Fresh, and other fast-food franchises. Non-Hispanic diners thus became familiar with Tex-Mex regional food. Among the dishes that became widely popular in the United States were tacos with iceberg lettuce and cheese, salsa, and chili con carne.

Today Tex-Mex cuisine is known well beyond the border regions, and is even eaten in areas outside of the United States and Mexico.

A food vendor serves a line of hungry customers with fajitas from her skillet at the Fiesta Tejano in San Antonio, Texas.

Tex-Mex restaurants are found all over the world, even in countries such as Japan and Thailand that already had strong gastronomic traditions of their own.

An important culture

Among other practices common in Tex-Mex culture are those influenced by the Roman Catholic Church. For example, *compadrazgo* is a system of ritual coparenthood that closely links the godparents and parents of a child; the *quinceañera,* which celebrates the transition to womanhood of a 15-year-old Tejana, is still common practice.

Language remains on the fault line of the cultural divide: Tejanos tend to speak English in society and Spanish in the home.

Tex-Mex culture is a mixture of American and Hispanic cultures. Tex-Mex music and food have

gradually become accepted parts of mainstream U.S. life. They are now familiar not only to U.S. citizens who have no Hispanic heritage of their own but also to non-Latinos throughout the world.

See also: Hispanic Culture and Identity; Jimenez, Flaco; Lopez, Jennifer; Los Lobos; Martínez, Narciso; Selena

Further reading: Tejeda, Juan, and Avelardo Valdez (eds.). *Puro Conjunto: An Album in Words and Pictures.* Austin, TX: CMAS, University of Texas and Austin and the Guadalupe Cultural Arts Center, 2001.
http://www.pbs.org/accordiondreams/all/index.html (PBS site accompanying the documentary *Accordion Dreams,* about Tejano music and culture).
http://www.lib.utexas.edu/benson/border/arhoolie2/raices.html (about Tejano and conjunto music).

THALÍA
Singer, Actor

Thalía is a successful singer and actress, and one of the most successful Mexican music and television stars in the United States and Latin America.

Ariadna Thalía Sodi Miranda was born on August 26, 1971, in Mexico City, Mexico. She was the youngest of five sisters of a privileged family and from the beginning was pushed to stardom. Her sister, Laura Zapata, has been a vital influence in her career. Zapata, a soap actress for Spanish-language broadcaster Televisa, served as Thalía's connection to Televisa's film, television, and music producers.

Singing beginnings

In 1981 Thalía started singing with the Din Din band and recorded four albums with them. In 1984 Thalía landed a part in the musical *Vaselina* (the Spanish equivalent of *Grease*). Two years later she received a call to form part of the famous Mexican children's band Timbiriche. Thalía stayed with the band for three years and recorded three albums. In 1990 she went to Los Angeles to prepare her first solo album, *Thalía.* The following year she completed a second album, *Mundo de Cristal.* This album was followed by *Love* (1992), which sold 200,000 copies and achieved platinum status. In 1994 Thalía signed a contract with EMI Music and recorded *En Extasis* (1995). Later she recorded her hits in English, Tagalog, and Spanglish on a special album for the Asian market: *Nandito Ako.*

Acting success

Thalía's acting career developed almost at the same time as her singing career, starting with a small part in the soap opera *La pobre señorita Limantour* (1983). Her first big part was in 1987, with *Quinceañera,* in which she landed a

▲ *A former child star, Thalía is a popular Latina singer who has had numerous hit albums.*

prime role and gained popularity among the public. Thalía next obtained starring roles in four soap operas: *María Mercedes* (1992), *Marimar* (1994), *María la del Barrio* (1995), and *Rosalinda* (1999). In 1998 Thalía acted in her first movie, *Mambo Café,* shot in the Bronx, New York.

Although Thalía was becoming a successful and popular actress, by the end of the 1990s she had decided to quit acting and pursue a full-time music career. In 2000 her album *Arrasando* earned her her first number one on the *Billboard* Latin Pop Album chart. She quickly followed from this success with six more albums: *Thalía con Banda* (2001), *Thalía* (2002), *Hits Remixed* (2003), *Thalía* (2003), *Thalia's Greatest Hits* (2004), and *El Sexto Sentido* (2005).

Thalía is married to Tommy Mottola, ex-husband of Mariah Carey and ex-CEO of Sony Music Entertainment. She is currently developing new musical material and collaborating with Mexican television.

See also: Carey, Mariah

Further reading: http://www.thalia.com (official Web site). http://www.emicatalogue.co.nz/Biography.aspx?artist=6430 (EMI Catalogue).

KEY DATES	
1971	Born in Mexico City, Mexico, on August 26.
1986	Sings with the Mexican band, Timbiriche.
1987	First big acting role in *Quinceañera.*
1990	Release of her first solo album, *Thalía.*
1998	Films her first movie, *Mambo Café.*
2000	Album *Arrasando* becomes her first number one on the *Billboard* Latin Pop Albums chart.

THOMAS, Piri
Author

Piri Thomas rose to stardom with the publication of his first novel, the autobiographical *Down These Mean Streets*. Having grown up in the impoverished barrio of Spanish Harlem, Thomas has remained committed to giving a voice to Latinos and other people of color who experience discrimination in the United States. He has used his writings to criticize a society where injustice and poverty prevail and where marginalized racial groups are relegated to a world of drugs and gangs.

As an acclaimed author in the Puerto Rican community, Thomas has traveled around the world giving lectures at universities and high schools to increase public awareness of the danger of abandoning the younger generation and to encourage politicians to develop programs that provide youth with an alternative to a life of crime.

Hard times
Born of Cuban and Puerto Rican parents in 1928 in New York City, Juan Pedro Tomás soon became familiar with the corrupting street environment of poverty, racism, and violence prevalent in his neighborhood of Spanish Harlem.

Although the Great Depression affected every stratum of society, it wrought havoc among working-class families in poor districts. The 1929 stock-market crash led to the closure of factories in Thomas's barrio. The few white-collar jobs available were filled by white workers. Meanwhile, skilled tradesmen of African descent—such as Thomas's dark-skinned father—were forced to take poorly paid unskilled work.

This racial discrimination convinced many migrants to change their names in order to hide their heritage. Perhaps it was with this idea in mind that Juan Pedro Tomás, emulating his father, obscured his Hispanic identity by taking the anglicized name John Peter Thomas.

Iconic name
The name Piri came from the spiritual influence of Thomas's mother. A Seventh-day Adventist, Dolores Montañez Tomás planned to raise her children according to her beliefs. Seventh-day Adventists believe that Christ's return is imminent. Dolores Tomás hoped her son Juan Pedro would become an Adventist priest. In adulthood Thomas was opposed to the hierarchical structure of the church, and this prevented him from accepting his mother's religion and plans for him. Nevertheless his

▲ *Piri Thomas battled through a life of crime and drug addiction to become one of the leading Nuyorican authors.*

mother's religious legacy remains in the name Thomas uses. Piri is a shortened form of *espíritu*, the Spanish word for "spirit."

Despite failing to instill her faith in her son, Thomas's mother's appreciation for Puerto Rican folklore helped awaken his passion for literature. As a teenager, Thomas usually spent hours in the public library on 110th Street, between Lexington and 3rd avenues, reading any book he got his hands on. Thomas's hunger to learn was never satisfied, and to continue his reading at home, he often sneaked three or four books out of the library under his jacket in addition to the two books he was permitted to borrow at a time. Thomas's dedication made him realize that there was a world of opportunity outside of Spanish Harlem and that he had to keep on working harder if he wanted to succeed in a racist society.

The dark years
Paradoxically Thomas's struggle for survival through education was interrupted at school, where he often got into trouble. In a district where children were used by gangs as robbers and drug dealers, Thomas's bad influences increasingly took him away from his studies and got him involved in street crime and drug abuse. In 1950 Thomas was wounded in a police raid. Having shot a

---

Although Thomas's father's conformism in an unjust society prevented him from becoming a strong role model for his son, his communist influences were crucial to the development of Thomas's ideology in adulthood.

Thomas frequently attended political meetings with his father, which brought him into contact with political figures, such as Vito Marcantonio (1902–1954), a member of the American Labor Party who served in the United States House of Representatives from 1935 until 1937.

Marcantonio spoke about social justice, human rights, and independence for Puerto Rico. Those ideas turned Thomas into a staunch defender of Puerto Rican culture. Since the publication of *Down These Mean Streets*, Piri Thomas has also talked to people about the terrible influence of racism. Thomas's message is based on the importance of building mutual understanding among members of all religions and races.

---

police officer in the encounter, he was arrested and sentenced to seven years in Bellevue and Comstock State prisons. In jail, Thomas thought a lot about the mistakes he had committed in the past and resolved to alter the direction of his life. Despite being incarcerated, he returned to education and completed his high-school studies. By the time of his release, Thomas had decided to become a teacher in the hope that he could help young people avoid becoming involved in crime and drugs.

Thomas settled in Puerto Rico. Although he was offered a fellowship to pursue a PhD in psychology at the University of Puerto Rico in San Juan, Thomas felt obliged to focus on the people who really needed his help. As a recovering drug addict, Thomas began by helping to develop a drug rehabilitation program at the Hospital of Psychiatry in Río Piedras, Puerto Rico.

A man of letters

Thomas's social work intensified in 1967 when he took to literature, financed by the Rabinowitz Foundation. His debut novel, *Down These Mean Streets*, was an electrifying and arresting autobiography that testified to the racism suffered by Hispanic and African Americans in the United States. Written in the tradition of Alex Haley's *The Autobiography of Malcolm X* (1965), and set in the 1940s and 1950s, *Down These Mean Streets* recounts Thomas's distressing psychological development into manhood as a Latino of African descent in New York City.

Being the only child in his family to inherit his father's skin color, Thomas's story is one of a tenacious adolescent who struggled to survive in a world of bigotry and social injustice. Given his ethnic background, Thomas's objective was to find his own identity in a society where, unlike his siblings, he could not distance himself from his African origins.

Trilogy

Not only did Thomas's anxiety fuel his internal rage and anger at the world, it also bestowed on him an uncommon creativity. Thomas's literary activity led to the completion of a trilogy of memoirs. The second book was published in 1972 under the title of *Savior, Savior, Hold My Hand*, which received widespread critical acclaim. Two years later came *Seven Long Times*, which is a description of his years in prison. In 1978 Thomas switched to fiction and published *Stories from El Barrio*, a collection of short stories he wrote to educate young people.

Nowadays, Thomas is a citizen of El Cerrito, California, where he retired to live with his wife, Daniela Calo. In 1999 he narrated a film called *The Double Life of Ernesto Gómez-Gómez*, the story of the son of Puerto Rican freedom fighters. Thomas's next projects consist of a sequel to *Down These Mean Streets* entitled *A Matter of Dignity*, and an educational film with the title of *Oye Familia Piri Thomas in a Dialogue with Society*.

KEY DATES	
1928	Born in New York City on September 10.
1950	Arrested and given a seven-year sentence.
1967	Publishes *Down These Mean Streets*.
1972	Finishes *Savior, Savior, Hold My Hand*.
1974	Completes his trilogy of memoirs with *Seven Long Times*.
1978	Publishes *Stories from El Barrio*.

Further reading: Thomas, Piri. *Down These Mean Streets*. New York, NY: Vintage Books, 1997.

http://www.cheverote.com/piri.html (Thomas's Web site).

TIANT, Luis
Baseball Player

Luis Tiant pitched four 20-win seasons, appeared in three All-Star games, and led the American League twice with his ERA (earned run average) statistics, but is best remembered for his cigar smoking, his protruding belly, and his "Fu Manchu" moustache. Tiant's joke-cracking personality, combined with his unorthodox delivery, made him one of Boston's most best-loved sports figures.

Early life

Luis Clemente Tiant Vega was born on November 23, 1940, in Marianao, Cuba. His father, Luis Tiant, Sr., was known as the best pitcher in Cuba, but he discouraged his son from playing. Luis Jr. ignored his father's advice and played baseball on the streets using cigarette cartons for gloves, sticks for bats, and corks with nails hammered into them for baseballs. Tiant showed promise, but his black skin prevented him from playing in Cuba's amateur leagues. Tiant finished high school and studied mechanics before a baseball scout discovered him and sent him to Mexico.

Pro career

Luis Tiant dominated the Mexican League, and in 1961 he was drafted to the Cleveland Indians; he made his major league debut in 1964. The way he twisted his upper body so that his back was to the plate during his pitching wind-up baffled batters. He released his pitches high, low, and everywhere in between to keep hitters guessing. Tiant finished his rookie year with a 10–4 record. In 1968 he compiled a 21–9 record with a league-best 1.60 earned run average (ERA). One year later, however, Tiant struggled, finishing with a 9–20 record. After his poor performance, the Indians traded him to the Minnesota Twins, where he injured his shoulder and was cut by the team.

▲ *A fine pitcher and a great personality, Luis Tiant was a popular baseball star.*

The Boston Red Sox gambled on the struggling pitcher when they signed Tiant on May 17, 1971. He lost seven games and won only one in his first season in Boston, but in 1972 Tiant pitched brilliantly, winning 15 games. He led the league with his ERA (1.91) and earned the "Comeback Player of the Year" award. He won 20 games in 1973, and 22 in 1974, but 1975 defined him. That year Tiant led the Red Sox to the World Series, where he shut out the powerful Cincinnati Reds in Game 1, and then pitched a complete Game 4: a 5-4 win for the Sox (the Reds went on to win the series). Tiant played for the Sox through the 1978 season, and then for the New York Yankees and Pittsburgh Pirates, before retiring with the California Angels in 1982.

Further reading: Aaseng, Nathan. *Baseball's Finest Pitchers.* Minneapolis, MN: Lerner Publications Co., 1980.
Tiant, Luis. *El Tiante: The Luis Tiant Story.* New York, NY: Doubleday, 1976.
http://www.baseballlibrary.com/baseballlibrary/ballplayers/T/Tiant_Luis_Jr.stm (career statistics).

KEY DATES

1940	Born in Marianao, Cuba, on November 23.
1964	Makes major league debut.
1971	Career appears over after the Minnesota Twins and Atlanta Braves release him from contract.
1972	Wins the "Comeback Player of the Year" award with the Boston Red Sox.
1975	Reunites with his parents for the first time since he left Cuba when he pitches in the World Series.

TIENDA, Marta
Sociologist

Marta Tienda is one of the United States's foremost sociologists and demographers (population scientists). Her pioneering research has focused on quantifying, tracking, and analyzing the inequalities faced by Hispanic Americans and other minority populations in key areas such as income, health, and education. Since 1998 Tienda has served as director of the Office of Population Research (OPR) at Princeton University, New Jersey—one of the country's leading demographic research centers.

A turning point

Tienda was born in south Texas in August 1950. Her father, Toribio, was a Mexican migrant worker who made his living picking fruit, while her mother, Azucena, was a Mexican American. Soon after Tienda's birth, her father took his family to live in Detroit, Michigan, where he found work in a steel mill. The Tiendas were often very poor, and sometimes the whole family had to work as agricultural laborers in order to supplement the household income.

Despite such disadvantages, Tienda did well at school, and in 1968 won a scholarship to study Spanish language and literature at Michigan State University. In her final year at Michigan State, Tienda did holiday work for the Michigan Cooperative Extension Service, where part of her

▼ *Marta Tienda is one of the United States's leading sociologists. Her work focuses on Hispanic groups.*

KEY DATES

1950   Born in south Texas in August.

1977   Awarded a doctorate degree in sociology.

1978   Begins a pioneering survey of "Hispanic-Origin Workers in the U.S. Labor Market."

1998   Appointed director of the Office of Population Research (OPR), Princeton University, New Jersey.

role was to certify migrant workers' eligibility for food stamps. The experience was a major turning point in Tienda's life, leading her to become interested in how economic inequalities can be shaped by race and ethnicity. After graduating with a bachelor's degree in 1972, Tienda took up postgraduate studies in sociology at the University of Texas at Austin, eventually specializing in Latin American demography. She received her master's degree in 1975 and her doctorate in 1977.

Teaching career

Tienda subsequently embarked on an impressive research and teaching career that began at the University of Wisconsin-Madison and led her to professorships at the University of Chicago and finally, in 1994, to Princeton University. Tienda began to forge a national reputation for her work as early as 1978, when the U.S. Department of Labor commissioned her to carry out a demographic analysis of "Hispanic-Origin Workers in the U.S. Labor Market." The result, published in 1981, was a pioneering survey that took Tienda to the top of her field and helped win her a string of prestigious research grants, including a fellowship (1993–1994) from the John Simon Guggenheim Memorial Foundation. In recent years Tienda has concentrated her research on access to higher education in minority populations, which has led her to become a passionate advocate of affirmative-action social and educational programs.

Further reading: Obermiller, Tim Andrew. "Necessary Dreams." *University of Chicago Magazine*, Vol. 87, No. 4 (April 1995) [available online at: http://www.magazine.uchicago.edu/9504/]. http://www.carnegie.org/reporter/08/interview/interview4.html (interview.)

TIJERINA, Felix
Civil Rights Activist

Felix Tijerina was the national president of the League of United Latin American Citizens (LULAC) from 1956 to 1960. During his leadership he oversaw educational programs to teach Hispanic American children the basics of English so they would not be disadvantaged when they enrolled in an English-language school.

American by right

Filberto Tijerina was born in Nuevo León, Mexico, in 1905. However, in 1956 a Houston judge determined that his legal birthplace was actually Sugar Land, Texas. The judge declared that Tijerina was a U.S. citizen.

The Tijerina family had come to the United States during the 1910 Mexican Revolution. Once in the United States, Filberto became known as Felix. The family worked as cotton pickers in southern Texas until Felix's father died in 1913. At the age of eight Felix had to work in the fields to help his family. When he turned 13, Tijerina convinced the family to relocate to Houston, Texas. There he began a long career in the restaurant business, first as a busboy. In 1928 he opened his own restaurant, the Mexican Inn.

During the Great Depression of the 1930s, Tijerina went broke. Nevertheless he opened Felix's Mexican Restaurant in 1937. He went on to build a chain of restaurants and became Houston's first Mexican American millionaire.

Educational reformer

Tijerina had struggled to learn English and did not succeed with the English-only curriculum in the Texas public schools. He never forgot the trauma of this failure.

As a young adult in Houston, he began promoting voter registration among Mexican Americans. He joined LULAC Council 60 in Houston and added education to his

▲ *Felix Tijerina was a successful businessman who became a civil rights leader and educational reformer.*

priorities. His leadership and philanthropy were widely recognized. He served as the council's vice president and president, and as its regional director. In 1956 Tijerina became the national president of LULAC, a position he held for four years.

In the summer of 1957 Tijerina personally funded a preschool program in Ganado, Texas. He hired a 17-year-old teacher to teach 400 basic words of English to Mexican American children. Every one of the children passed the first grade the subsequent year. The following year Tijerina expanded the program to nine other Texas cities. By 1960 he had managed to get the state to adopt his program and instruction began involving 614 schools and 15,805 Spanish-speaking children.

In Tijerina's honor LULAC established a scholarship fund in his name; some schools have also been named for him. Tijerina's papers are archived in Houston's Metropolitan Research Collection Public Library.

Further reading: Kreneck, Thomas H. *Mexican American Odyssey: Felix Tijerina, Entrepreneur & Civic Leader, 1905–1965.* College Station, TX: Texas A&M University Press, 2001. http://www.tsha.utexas.edu/handbook/online/articles/TT/fti8.html (biography).

KEY DATES

1905	Born in General Escobedo, Nuevo Leon, Mexico, on April 29.
1928	Opens first restaurant in Houston, Texas.
1956	Tijerina becomes national LULAC president.
1957	Founds the Little School of 400 program, the precursor to bilingual education in Texas.
1965	Dies in Houston on September 4.

TIJERINA, Pete
Civil Rights Attorney

Pedro (known as Pete) Tijerina helped set up the Mexican American Legal Defense and Educational Fund (MALDEF). This was the United States's first Hispanic legal advocacy group, and it tackled discrimination on a sustained basis throughout the Southwest. Today it provides opportunities and helps safeguard the rights of 40 million Latinos.

Taking a stand
Tijerina was born in 1923 in Laredo, Texas, the son of a Mexican truck driver. He left school at 16, and served in the United States Air Force as a mechanic during World War II (1939–1945). After returning home, Tijerina finally received his high school diploma.

It was while studying at the University of Texas in the 1940s that Tijerina started considering a legal career. He was outraged by the widespread discrimination against Chicanos, from signs in restaurants stating "No Mexicans" to many deliberately exclusive government policies.

Tijerina joined the League of United Latin American Citizens (LULAC) in 1946, and became their state civil rights chairman. The group had limited funds but employed a traveling squad to fight individual cases of discrimination. In 1951 Tijerina passed the bar, having studied at St. Mary's University in San Antonio, and practiced criminal trial law a year later. Hispanics were almost always tried by all-white juries, which often meant they did not receive a fair trial. In 1964 Tijerina represented a woman who had suffered an amputation following a car accident. He knew that the jury would award a lower level of compensation to a Mexican American, and he decided to take action.

Four years later, Tijerina set up the Mexican American Legal Defense and Education Fund (MALDEF), after receiving support from a similar group helping African Americans. His passion and energy were essential to MALDEF's success. He asked the Ford Foundation for financial assistance, and thanks to his persuasiveness, received $2.2 million, of which $250,000 was assigned to train Mexican American lawyers.

One of MALDEF's first successes was to argue before the Texas Court of Appeals that the exclusion of Latinos from juries was unconstitutional, thus ending decades of discrimination. It then fought for racial integration in schools, equal opportunity in employment, and bilingual education programs, with success. The not-for-profit group was soon established at the forefront of civil rights litigation.

Tijerina retired in 1992, having fought for the rights of Latinos for over 40 years. He died in 2003, at age 80.

See also: National Organizations

Further reading: www.maldef.org (MALDEF's Web site). http://historymatters.gmu.edu/d/6585/ (interview).

▼ *Pete Tijerina fought a lifelong and highly successful struggle for legal rights for Mexican Americans.*

KEY DATES	
1923	Born in Laredo, Texas, on August 4.
1941	Joins U.S. Air Force during World War II.
1943	Begins studies at the University of Texas.
1946	Joins League of United Latin American Citizens.
1951	First practices law.
1968	Sets up the Mexican American Legal Defense and Educational Fund.
2003	Dies in San Antonio, Texas, on May 14.

TIJERINA, Reies López
Activist

Reies López Tijerina was a major figure in the Chicano movement. He is best remembered for campaigning for the return of land that belonged to Hispanic American families that was taken away when territory was passed from Mexico to the United States in the mid-19th century.

Early life
Tijerina was born in 1926 in the fields outside Falls City, Texas. His was a large migrant-worker family. The poverty that shaped his childhood provided the foundation for his life-long mission to reclaim the Southwest's original land grants. These were made under the authority of the Spanish crown from the 16th century until 1848, when they were challenged after the United States took control of Mexico's northern territory.

Tijerina's mother, Herlinda, instilled in her son her own religious faith. She died when Tijerina was just six years old, and he began working alongside his father, Antonio, and his siblings on the harvest-worker route from Texas to Michigan. The Tijerinas moved often, and as a result Reies was educated at 20 different schools.

▼ *A leading figure in the early Chicano movement, Reies López Tijerina campaigned for the return of Mexican American property to its rightful owners.*

Tijerina abandoned the Catholic religion when he turned 18. However, his strong faith inspired him to become a preacher and he enrolled in a Pentecostal college at Ysleta, Texas, in 1944. Tijerina was a man of the people and not of institutions. He clashed with authorities on several occasions and left the college in 1946. He married a few months later and began circuit preaching for the Assembly of God Church. He continued to preach even after the church revoked his ministerial license in 1950.

The Valley of Peace
Tijerina stopped preaching in 1956 when he settled with his family in Arizona and founded a colony, the Valley of Peace. The Valley consisted of 17 families on 160 acres (64.5 hectares) of southern Arizona desert. It was to be a self-sufficient utopia that would put Tijerina's philosophy into practice. The good times were short-lived, however. Local state and federal authorities forced the commune to leave and Anglo citizens burned the schoolhouse. Tijerina was arrested on false accusations and served time in the Florence, Arizona, jail. On his release, he was again arrested for ostensibly helping his brother escape from jail. He jumped bail and became a fugitive in New Mexico for the next six years.

As a fugitive, Tijerina sought refuge in New Mexico for his wife, six children, and several followers from the Arizona commune. By 1960 Tijerina had settled in Albuquerque while intermittently traveling across New Mexico and Mexico investigating communal land grants.

Tijerina discovered many discrepancies in the Treaty of Guadalupe Hidalgo, the document that officially ended the Mexican War in 1848 and made the present-day Southwest a U.S. territory. Tijerina made the argument that the United States never lived up to its promises of property rights and full citizenship for Mexican Americans. Instead the authorities gave in to pressure from Anglo Americans bent on removing Mexican American landowners.

Tijerina believed that the reclamation of communal land would restore Mexican Americans to a rightful position of power in the U.S. establishment. New Mexico's Spanish American community—the Hispanos—would especially benefit.

On February 2, 1963, the anniversary of the signing of the Treaty of Guadalupe Hidalgo, Tijerina founded the Alianza Federal de Mercedes (Federal Land Grant Alliance),

INFLUENCES AND INSPIRATION

Throughout his activist years, Tijerina was in close contact with other Chicano leaders, such as César Chávez from California, Rodolfo "Corky" Gonzales from Colorado, and José Angel Gutiérrez from Texas. Despite their efforts, the Chicano movement remained fragmented across the Southwest. It was actually the African American civil rights leader Dr. Martin Luther King, Jr., who did the most to bring Tijerina to the national stage.

In 1967 King invited Tijerina to organize the Mexican American contingent of the Poor People's March on Washington, D.C. King was dead by the time the march took place in 1968. Tijerina brought protestors from New Mexico and was joined by a contingent from Colorado led by Gonzales.

When Tijerina was jailed the following year, he published *A Letter from Santa Fe Jail*. This is similar to King's own *A Letter*

from a Birmingham Jail of 1963. Both outline a vision of social justice. However, there were differences between the two leaders. King was jailed for nonviolent protest, while Tijerina served time for kidnapping.

After his release from prison Tijerina wrote a memoir about his life as an activist. His writings influenced a generation of Chicano scholars, who adopted his term "Indo-Hispano" to describe the people of New Mexico.

---

later changed to Alianza Federal de Pueblos Libres (Federal Alliance of Free Towns). The Alianza was an organization of the heirs of displaced Hispano landowners. The headquarters were in Albuquerque, New Mexico, but Tijerina organized and traveled throughout northern New Mexico, where most of the original heirs lived. Tijerina also broadcast on the radio and preached across the country promoting the plight of New Mexicans.

Activism and demise

Tijerina's combination of historical facts and religious parables spoke to the people of northern New Mexico, but it also alerted state and federal officials. The FBI began watching Tijerina in 1964 and reported on his activities throughout the decade. In 1966 the Alianza took over the

Echo Amphitheater Park, part of New Mexico's Carson National Forest, in the name of the San Joaquín del Río Chama land grant. As part of the Alianza's claim to the park, members arrested several public servants and subjected them to a court hearing. Tijerina chose this tactic because it temporarily usurped traditional authority. The police regarded it as kidnapping.

The demise of the Alianza occurred on June 10, 1967. On that day Tijerina and Alianza members entered the Tierra Amarilla Courthouse in northern New Mexico to make a citizen's arrest of the state's district attorney, Alfonso Sánchez. Their plans backfired, however, when the local Hispano deputies opened fire. In the resulting gunfight, two people were injured. Tijerina fled to the hills with two hostages, before 500 National Guardsmen moved in to take his followers and family into custody. Tijerina was arrested in Bernalillo, New Mexico, 10 days later. Tijerina was evntually sentenced to two years' imprisonment. While incarcerated, he spent a short time in a secure mental institution.

After two failed marriages, years on the run, and spells in jail and a mental hospital, Tijerina put his activist days behind him in 1971. He recently donated his archives to the University of New Mexico's Center for Southwest Research.

KEY DATES	
1926	Born near Falls City, Texas, on September 21.
1956	Founds the Valley of Peace colony in Arizona.
1963	Founds La Alianza Federal de Mercedes.
1966	Takes over Echo Amphitheater Park.
1967	Leads raid on the Tierra Amarilla Courthouse.
1968	Organizes the Mexican American contingent of the Poor People's March.
1971	Is released from federal prison.
1978	Memoirs are published in Mexico.
2005	Donates his archives to University of New Mexico.

See also: Chávez, César; Gonzales, Rodolfo; Gutierrez, José Angel

---

Further reading: Tijerina, Reies López. *They Called Me "King Tiger": My Struggle for the Land and Our Rights*. Houston, TX: Arte Público Press, 2000.

TIZOL, Juan
Musician

Juan Tizol was a well-respected jazz trombonist and composer. He is best known for his association with bandleader Duke Ellington.

Early life

Tizol was born in 1900 in San Juan, Puerto Rico, to a musical family. As a boy, Tizol took a serious interest in the slide and valve trombone. By age 20, Tizol had performed with various bands. In that year he was recruited by Ralph Escudero to go to the United States and play in the pit band of the Howard Theater in Washington, D.C. It was at this time that a young Duke Ellington was forming his first band in the D.C. area. The two musicians met at the Howard Theater, and, in 1929, Tizol joined Ellington's orchestra, where he remained for the next 15 years.

Tizol was quickly recognized as a standout musician who complemented Ellington's skills as a composer and arranger. However, Tizol is remembered more for his composing than his trombone playing. Compositions such as "Caravan," "Perdido," "Bakiff," "Pyramid," "Sphinx," and "Keb-Lah" were popular because of their excellent melodies and their emphasis on Latin rhythms, which were taking hold of jazz music at the time.

Tizol's two most popular and most recorded works were "Perdido" and "Caravan." Tizol composed and recorded "Caravan" with Ellington's orchestra in 1937, and sold the rights to Irving Mills for $25. It was Mills who later provided lyrics to the song. When the song became a worldwide hit, Mills gave the rights and royalties back to Tizol. Some argue that "Caravan" may have been the first real Latin jazz song, although others believe the song reflected Middle Eastern influences. Regardless of the debate, jazz orchestras were experimenting with Latin jazz rhythms as early as 1931. Ellington's orchestra also recorded Tizol's Latin jazz songs "Conga Bravo" and "Bakiff" during this time.

▲ *Juan Tizol was a talented trombonist who played and composed with bandleader Duke Ellington.*

Ellington's band recorded "Perdido" in 1942. Initially the piece was an instrumental, but two years later lyrics were written for the song by Ervin Drake and H. J. Lengsfelder. Jazz vocalists such as Sarah Vaughan and Dinah Washington recorded popular releases of the tune "Perdido."

Move to California

In 1944 Tizol left Ellington's band to join the Harry James Orchestra. While money may have been a factor, Tizol's wife was then living in California, where the Harry James Orchestra was based. By 1951 Tizol was back with Ellington and continued for another two years until retiring as a touring musician, preferring to live and work in Los Angeles, California. He continued working as a studio musician with Nelson Riddle's orchestra, recording albums for numerous singers, including Frank Sinatra. Tizol died in 1984.

Further reading: http://nfo.net/cal/tt2.html (composers and lyricists database).
http://musicofpuertorico.com/en/juan_tizol.html

KEY DATES	
1900	Born in San Juan, Puerto Rico, on January 20.
1937	Composes and records "Caravan."
1942	Composes and records "Perdido."
1984	Dies on April 23 in Inglewood, California.

TORAÑO, María Elena
Businesswoman, Activist

María Elena Toraño is a successful businesswoman and civil rights activist. She is the founder and former chief executive officer, president, and owner of META Inc. (Maria Elena Toraño Associates, Inc.). META Inc. is a consulting, contracting, and financial advisory firm based in Florida. Toraño has served on several government commissions and was a member of the U.S. Advisory Commission on Public Diplomacy.

The rise to prominence

Born in Havana, Cuba, Toraño studied at the University of Havana. In 1960 she moved to the United States with her family. Along with her husband, Leslie Pantín (1922–1989), the first Cuban to sit on the board of the Greater Miami Chamber of Commerce and the first Cuban on the Orange Bowl Committee, Toraño became a valuable member of the southern Florida Cuban community.

In the United States, Toraño continued her studies in business management, marketing, and communications. She had a unique understanding of different economic, political, and cultural systems, and it was that, together with her facility for languages—she is fluent in Spanish and English and reads Italian and French—that helped her rise to prominence in the business community.

As well as her business success, Toraño became known for her interest in politics and public affairs. In 1977 President Jimmy Carter appointed her as associate director for public affairs at the U.S. Community Services Administration. She held the post until 1979.

KEY DATES

1940s   Born in Havana, Cuba, at about this time.

1960   Moves from Cuba to the United States.

1977   Jimmy Carter appoints her as associate director for public affairs at the U.S. Community Services Administration.

1980   Sets up Maria Elena Taraño Associates (META).

1993   Chairs the first National Hispanic Women's Summit in Washington, D.C.

1994   Appointed to the U.S. Advisory Commission on Public Diplomacy.

2000   Sells META to her sons.

Company founder

In 1980 Toraño decided to set up her own company, the Miami-based META, a financial, contracting, and environmental advisory firm that had both U.S. and foreign clients. Toraño's business was very successful and within 20 years had grown to have revenues of more than $25 million a year.

Toraño was soon a wealthy woman and made several political donations, almost exclusively to the Democratic Party. In so doing she became a prominent figure in the Cuban anti-Castro politics of southern Florida.

Community member

Toraño has worked to improve the lives of other people both at home and abroad. For example, she helped USAID (United States Agency for International Development) develop a program that enabled 300 Guatemalan students to study at U.S. universities. In 1993 she organized and chaired the first National Hispanic Women's Summit in Washington, D.C., which brought together 46 carefully chosen leading Hispanic American women from different walks of life to discuss how best to increase the number of Latino women in positions of power.

In 1994, following her three-year appointment to the six-person U.S. Advisory Commission on Public Diplomacy, Toraño was sent on several international missions for the United States Information Agency, including to Europe, Latin America, and the Middle East, to look into such issues as the need for new diplomacy based on developments in communications and the growth of free markets and democracy.

Toraño has held several other important positions. She was president of the National Association of Spanish Broadcasters and director of Latin American affairs at the University of Miami. She is a trustee of St. Thomas University in Florida, a director of the Hispanic Television Network, and serves on the University of Miami Government Affairs and Public Policy Commission. Toraño retired from business in 2000 and sold META to her sons.

Further reading: http://www.count-me-in.org/about/maria.html (biography).
http://pdi.gwu.edu/aboutthecouncil/membership/torano (biography).

TORRES, Edwin
Attorney, Judge, Writer

Edwin Torres has led something of a double life. As a no-nonsense New York Supreme Court justice, he presides dispassionately over criminal cases, imposing severe punishment when necessary. Yet, as a crime novelist, he examines the back-street path of the criminal with insight and sensitivity.

Early life
Edwin Torres was born on January 7, 1931, in the Puerto Rican enclave of El Barrio, the then crime-ridden heart of Manhattan's Spanish Harlem. Raised by parents who were first generation Puerto Rican immigrants, Torres grew up in poverty but graduated from one of New York's best public schools, Stuyvesant High. He attended the City College of New York, followed by Brooklyn College School of Law and, in 1958, was admitted to the New York State Bar.

As a practicing lawyer, Torres earned a reputation for being especially tough on hardened criminals. In 1977 he was appointed to the New York State Criminal Court. Three years later he was elected to the State Supreme Court, where he currently serves as a justice representing the Twelfth Judicial District. In this latter capacity, Torres presided over a number of high-profile murder cases, including a highly publicized trial involving a Mafia-style

▼ *Edwin Torres uses his experiences as a criminal attorney and a judge to inspire his popular crime novels. All of his books have since become movies.*

KEY DATES	
1931	Born in Spanish Harlem, New York City, on January 7.
1958	Is admitted to the New York State Bar.
1975	Publishes his first novel, *Carlito's Way*.
1978	Writes *Q&A*, which becomes his first book to be made into a film.
1980	Elected to the New York State Supreme Court.

killing outside of a Manhattan nightclub and a 1991 case in which a tourist was slain on a New York subway platform. Affirming his belief that career criminals must be dealt with harshly, Torres unapologetically remarked, "A society that loses its sense of outrage is doomed to extinction."

After years of experience with criminals in the courtroom, Torres began to write about them, exploring criminality through character studies of gangsters, drug dealers, and crooked cops. In 1975 Torres debuted as a writer with *Carlito's Way*, a gritty novel that follows the rise and fall of Carlito Brigante, a Puerto Rican street hustler who ascends to the status of drug kingpin and is then arrested and sentenced to 30 years in prison. *After Hours,* the follow-up, chronicles Carlito's struggle to "go straight" after his release from prison. Although both novels were acclaimed for their readable prose and page-turning intensity, Torres's depiction of Spanish Harlem's urban jungle and Puerto Rican street culture was singled out for its authenticity.

In 1978 Torres wrote *Q&A*, which portrayed the investigation of a decorated New York police lieutenant suspected of corruption. It became the first of his novels to be translated into a Hollywood film. In 1992, *After Hours* was adapted into the hit film *Carlito's Way,* starring Al Pacino and Sean Penn. Thirteen years later, the first installment of Carlito's saga was released as the film *Carlito's Way: Rise to Power.*

Further reading: Torres, Edwin. *Carlito's Way* and *After Hours.* New York, NY: Saturday Review Press, 1975.
http://dvd.ign.com/articles/653/653491p1.html (an interview with Edwin Torres about his novels and their translation into films).

TORRES, Esteban E.
Politician

One of the United States's top Hispanic leaders, former Democratic congressman Esteban E. Torres served as a member of the U.S. House of Representatives from 1983 until his retirement in 1998. He represented the 34th Congressional District in southern California's San Gabriel Valley, which has a large Hispanic population.

While in office, Torres was a proponent of free trade, rights for illegal immigrants, disaster relief, and the cleanup of water resources. A former official with the United Auto Workers (UAW) union, Torres has also held positions with the International Monetary Fund, which fosters global financial cooperation, Fannie Mae (a home financing company), and the California Transportation Commission.

Political animal

Esteban Edward Torres was born in Miami, Arizona, in 1930. He served in the U.S. Army from 1949 until 1953, earning the rank of sergeant first class. After being discharged Torres worked as an assembly-line worker in the auto industry. He won his first elected position in 1954, when he was made chief shop steward at a Chrysler Corporation plant.

In 1955 Torres married Arcy Sánchez. The couple had a total of five children. Torres enrolled in East Los Angeles Community College in 1959, later transferring to Cal State, Los Angeles. He also studied at the University of Maryland in 1965, and in 1966 at American University, where he

▼ **Esteban E. Torres served eight terms as a representative in the U.S. Congress.**

KEY DATES	
1930	Born in Miami, Arizona, on January 27.
1955	Marries Arcy Sánchez.
1978	Is named U.S. ambassador to UNESCO by President Jimmy Carter.
1982	Elected to Congress as a representative of California's 34th District.
1998	Retires after 16 years in Congress.

studied international labor. By 1976 Torres had returned to Chrysler Corporation as assistant director for international affairs.

Federal posts

In 1978 Torres entered government service for the first time. President Jimmy Carter appointed Torres to the position of U.S. ambassador to the United Nations Educational, Scientific, and Cultural Organization (UNESCO) in Paris, France. Torres also served as an adviser on Hispanic affairs in the Carter administration.

Emboldened by his experiences under Carter, Torres stood as a Democrat for the congressional seat in California's 34th District in 1982. He was elected and went on to hold the seat for 16 years. While the population in California was beginning to turn against illegal immigration during his tenure in Congress, Torres held fast as a strong advocate for immigrants' rights. "Whenever there is a disaster in Mexico City, Bangladesh, or elsewhere, Americans are the first ones there and we never say we can't help these people," Torres told the *Los Angeles Times* in 1994. "You can't deny people here what we so generously give away from our borders."

Torres's district has one of the nation's largest potable water basins, and he was active in cleaning up hazardous waste in the region. Torres, who had served as a senior member of the House Banking Committee, is currently on the board of directors for Entravision Communications, a Spanish-language media company.

Further reading: http://www.forbes.com/finance/mktguideapps/personinfo/FromMktGuideIdPersonTearsheet.jhtml?passedMkt GuideId=165767 (biography).

TORRES, José
Boxer, Writer

José Torres was the first Latino world light heavyweight boxing champion. He won 43 out of 47 bouts as a professional, including 29 by knockout. Torres has remained closely involved with sports at the highest levels since retiring, and has also become involved in Puerto Rican issues, as well as becoming a successful writer.

Fighting machine

José Torres was born on May 3, 1936, in Ponce, Puerto Rico. His father had a trucking business and raised seven children in relative prosperity. At 18, Torres joined the U.S. Army. He had idolized boxer Sugar Ray Robinson since childhood, and took the first opportunity to learn to box. Within months Torres won the Caribbean Army Forces Championships, then, later, the All Army Championships.

In 1956 Torres qualified for the Olympics. He won three fights before meeting the previous gold medal winner, Hungarian Laszlo Papp, in the final bout. Torres lost, but won a silver medal as a junior middleweight.

On his professional debut in 1958, Torres knocked out George Hamilton in the first round. He also won his next 12 fights, with 10 wins by knockout, including impressive victories over Joe Shaw and Al Andrews. In 1963 Torres suffered a five-round loss to Florentino Fernández, his only defeat by knockout in his professional career. However, he made a determined return by beating Don Fullmer.

World champion

In 1964 Torres scored impressive victories over Carl Olson, Frankie Olivera, and José González. He finally gained the light heavyweight world title by defeating Willie Pastrano at

▲ *A former world-champion boxer, José Torres has lately turned his hand to writing.*

Madison Square Garden on March 30, 1965. Torres made three successful title defenses in 1966, but on December 16 he lost the title to Dick Tiger, in what was considered a shock result. The pair met again five months later, but Torres lost on a decision. Torres recovered from the loss to beat Bob Dunlop in Australia in 1967, then Charlie Green in 1969, by a second-round knockout, but after that he never fought again.

Torres later became a successful writer, producing biographies of Muhammad Ali and Mike Tyson. He has also been a spokesman for boxers and has represented New York's Puerto Rican community. In the 1980s Torres was appointed commissioner of the New York State Athletic Commission, while in the 1990s he served as president of the World Boxing Organization.

KEY DATES	
1936	Born in Ponce, Puerto Rico, on May 3.
1956	Wins silver medal at Olympic Games.
1958	Turns professional.
1965	Wins world heavyweight title from Willie Pastrano on March 30.
1969	Defeats Charlie Green and retires
1980	Becomes New York State Athletic Commissioner.
1990	Becomes president of the World Boxing Organization.

Further reading: Torres, José. *Sting Like a Bee: The Muhammad Ali Story*. New York, NY: McGraw Hill Companies; 2001.
Torres, José. *Fire and Fear: The Inside Story of Mike Tyson*. New York, NY: Warner Books Inc., 1989.
http://www.eastsideboxing.com/news.php?p=500&more=1

TORRES, Luis Lloréns
Writer

Luis Lloréns Torres is widely considered to be the national poet of Puerto Rico. He wrote most of his poetry in the early 20th century and used the Creole Spanish spoken by ordinary Puerto Ricans.

Torres used his work to express his deep love for his country and its people, language, and traditions. Throughout his life he was an ardent and outspoken supporter of Puerto Rican independence, first from Spain and then from the United States.

Early life
Torres was born on May 14, 1876, near the town of Juana Díaz, Puerto Rico. At this time Puerto Rico was a Spanish colony. The island, whose name means "rich port," had been discovered by Columbus in 1493 and claimed for the Spanish crown in 1508 by Juan Ponce de León. The island was then ruled by the Columbus family for many years.

The Torres family was wealthy and established. For generations the family had run coffee plantations in the Collores district of Juana Díaz. Torres grew up in privileged circumstances. Like many of the sons of the island's elite, he completed his education in Spain, where he studied first law at the University of Barcelona and later philosophy and literature at the University of Granada.

While in Spain Torres published his first books—a collection of essays on Puerto Rican history in 1898 and a volume of poetry, *Al Pie de la Alhambra* (At the Foot of the Alhambra), in 1899.

Returning home
Torres returned to Puerto Rico in 1901 and established a legal practice in the southern port city of Ponce, named for Spanish explorer Ponce de León. Only three years before, U.S. troops had occupied Puerto Rico. The island had been due to become independent from Spain but was instead ceded to the United State in 1898 by that year's Treaty of Paris. The treaty ended a war between the United States and Spain, and as part of the settlement Puerto Rico became U.S. territory, along with the Philippines and Guam. (The treaty also granted independence to Cuba.)

Like many other young Puerto Ricans, Torres became a passionate advocate for his country's independence, free from both Spanish and U.S. rule. He became active in the Partido Federal (Federal Party), which advocated democratic self-determination.

KEY DATES	
1876	Born in Juana Díaz, Puerto Rico, on May 14.
1888	Writes series of essays on the history of Puerto Rico while studying in Spain.
1899	Publishes first volume of poetry.
1901	Returns to Puerto Rico.
1916	Writes the patriotic play *El Grito de Lares* (The Cry of Lares).
1944	Dies in Santurce, Puerto Rico, on June 16.
1969	Complete works published in San Juan, Puerto Rico.

U.S. rule granted Puerto Ricans their own assembly—the Cámara de Delegados—but it had few powers. The U.S. president appointed a governor who could veto any law passed by the assembly. Torres was a member of the island's assembly between 1908 and 1910.

Love and patriotism
Meanwhile Torres was gaining a reputation as one of the island's foremost poets. Initially he published his works in literary journals but later he gathered them together in popular collections, such as the 1929 publication *La Canción de las Antillas y Otros Poemas* (The Song of the Antilles and Other Poems) and *Alturas de America* (The Heights of America) in 1940.

In 1913 Torres founded his own literary and political journal, *La Revista de las Antillas* (The Journal of the Antilles). Torres's work ranged from tender love poems to fiery political verse that expressed his patriotic pride.

In 1916 he also wrote a popular drama, *El Grito de Lares* (The Cry of Lares), which was set against the background of the Puerto Rican revolt against Spanish rule in 1868.

Torres died in Santurce, Puerto Rico, in 1944. A statue of the writer was later raised in his honor in a square in Juana Díaz, the place of his birth.

See also: Ponce de Leon, Juan

Further reading: http://www.elboricua.com/LuisLlorens Torres.html (biography and poems).

TREVIÑO, Jacinto
Folk Hero

Jacinto Treviño is a Texas folk hero. He is well known in South Texas as the subject of a ballad recounting his stand against acts of injustice along the border with Mexico. Little is known about his life—the place of his birth is unknown, for example—and what is known is at times contradictory. The ballad "El Corrido de Jacinto Treviño" has made the man a legend. Scholars such as Américo Paredes have used the song's lyrics and those of other "border ballads," or corridos, to shed light on the history and culture of Texas's Hispanic Americans.

Ordinary person

Treviño was born in the last half of the 19th century, but no one is sure when. He lived in a town named Los Indios, a few miles north of the border city of Brownsville, Texas. Like most men of his time and social standing, he was a hard-working farmer and was by all accounts considered a responsible law-abiding person.

Political turmoil

The Treviño story is set against the backdrop of the Mexican Revolution. This began in 1910, and had a powerful effect on the Tejanos (Mexican Texans) living along the border with Mexico. Tejanos were divided over the tumultuous events south of the border. Some supported the rebels. Others, along with many of their Anglo neighbors, resented the many families who were fleeing the violence and uncertainty in Mexico and seeking a new life in the United States. There were several violent clashes between the two camps along the border.

Only 60 years earlier the United States had defeated Mexico in war. Under the treaty that ended the conflict, half of Mexico's territory came under the control of the United States's government. This territory now forms the southwestern states. Under the arrangements for the transfer, Mexican citizens living in these areas were granted U.S. citizenship. Nevertheless, conflicts soon flared up between the Mexicans and the Anglos who now controlled the area. In many places Mexicans became second-class citizens.

Racist attack

In 1911, Treviño's half-brother was badly beaten by an Anglo-American named James Darwin at Ohio Station labor camp. It is said Treviño's brother was flirting with

KEY DATES

1910   Mexican Revolution breaks out, resulting in a mass migration from Mexico to the United States.

1911   Shoots the man who beat his brother to death and flees into Mexico; returns to Texas and foils a trap set for him by Texas Rangers.

Darwin's wife. Some reports say that Treviño's brother died from his injuries, others say that he survived but became deaf. Whatever the outcome, Treviño tracked down Darwin and shot and killed him. Treviño headed across the Rio Grande into Mexico to escape the Texas authorities. Rewards were offered for his capture, and he became known as a bandit.

Betrayal

As the story goes, Treviño's cousin Pablo rode into Mexico to find him. Pablo convinced Treviño that it was safe for him to return to Los Indios and that a feast had been arranged to celebrate his return. However, Pablo was lying. He had made a deal with the Texas Rangers.

In the legend, Treviño's horse became disturbed as they approached Los Indios. This concerned Treviño, who decided that he and Pablo should travel separately to their destination. When Treviño arrived, he found Texas Rangers lying in wait. He attacked the law officers and killed Pablo and a ranger. Treviño then slipped back into Mexico. Treviño's relatives in Los Indios were interrogated to give away his location, but nobody betrayed him.

The ballad that soon appeared turned Treviño into a celebrated outlaw—a peaceful man who was provoked into violence to defend his rights as a Mexican. There are no more facts about Treviño's life. He is reputed to have lived to an old age, and for years unexplained deaths of corrupt Anglos were attributed to the great Jacinto Treviño.

See also: Paredes, Américo

Further reading: Paredes, Américo. *Folklore and Culture on the Texas-Mexican Border.* Austin, TX: CMAS Books, 1993. http://www.sanbenito.k12.tx.us/Schools/BertaCabaza/READING%20DEPT/LopezPena/Jacinto_Trevino.html (biography).

TREVIÑO, Jesús
Filmmaker

Jesús Treviño is a Mexican American filmmaker and writer who has done more than any other Latino to put the history and culture of Hispanic Americans on screen. He is known for documentaries, television dramas, and feature films in both English and Spanish.

Early life

Jesús "Chuy" Treviño was born in El Paso, Texas, in 1946. His mother was a Mexican immigrant from Ciudad Juarez, Chihuahua. When he was three, Treviño's father left the family. His mother remarried Edward Shelton Farley. He took the the family, which also included Treviño's sisters Olinda and Rosalba, to live in Los Angeles, California. In Los Angeles Treviño discovered the Chicano movement while at Occidental College. The struggle for civil rights and social justice for Hispanic Americans would be an important influence in his early career.

Chicano events

Treviño realized that he had never been taught any Hispanic American history at school. His early films addressed the inherent prejudice of the school system and police against Chicanos. He got a job at KCET television station in Los Angeles and was a producer for the current-events show *Ahora!* Events in the Chicano movement gave him material for several award-winning documentaries, including *Yo Soy Chicano* (1972) and *Chicano! History of the Mexican American Civil Rights Movement* (1991).

▲ *Jesús Treviño has used his films to educate mainstream U.S. audiences about the history of Mexican Americans.*

On to Hollywood

Treviño has also had success writing, producing, and directing fictional films. His first was the 1976 feature film *Raices de Sangre* (*Roots of Blood*), which told the story of a Tejano labor union.

Treviño has directed many mainstream television dramas, including episodes of *ER, Prison Break, NYPD Blue, Crossing Jordan, Dawson's Creek, New York Undercover,* and *Star Trek.* He was also the director for the two-hour pilot of *Resurrection Boulevard* in 1999. The film, which starred Elizabeth Peña, told the story of three generations of the Santiago family. The pilot was a success, and *Resurrection Boulevard* ran for three seasons until 2002, with Treviño as a producer.

See also: Peña, Elizabeth

Further reading: Treviño, Jesús. *Eyewitness: A Filmmaker's Memoir of the Chicano Movement.* Houston, TX: Arte Público Press, 2001.
http://www.chuytrevino.com (Treviño's Web site).

KEY DATES	
1946	Born in El Paso, Texas, on March 26.
1968	Documents the student sit-in at the boardroom of the Los Angeles Unified School District.
1969	Is associate producer of *Ahora!*, the first Mexican American current affairs TV program.
1972	Writes and produces *Yo Soy Chicano* (I Am Chicano), the first documentary about Hispanic American history to be broadcast on a national television network.
1976	Writes and directs the Spanish-language feature film *Raices de Sangre* (Roots of Blood).
1999	Directs the pilot episode of *Resurrection Boulevard*, a successful TV drama about a Hispanic American family.

TREVINO, Lee
Golfer

Lee Trevino is the most successful Mexican American golfer of all time. He has won dozens of tournaments including three out of the four majors: the U.S. Open, the British Open, and the PGA Championship.

Early life

Lee Buck Trevino was born in Garland, a suburb of Dallas, Texas, in 1939. He never knew his father, and his mother gave him her father's surname. He and his two sisters were raised by his mother, uncle, and grandfather. In 1947 the family moved to an old four-room house with dirt floors and no plumbing or electricity. Their new home was next to a golf course on Walnut Hill Lane in Dallas, a few hundred yards from the seventh hole.

As a seven-year-old child, Trevino was fascinated by the men hitting balls with long sticks. Soon he was jumping the fence and venturing onto the course to find lost golf balls, which he sold to players. By the age of eight Trevino was a caddy earning $1.25 for 18 holes, or $1 for 5 balls, and he began to learn about the game. The Trevino family was extremely poor, and even young Lee's earnings were an important income for them.

Trevino quit school while in the eighth grade and took up working on the golf course full-time. This also gave him the opportunity to teach himself to play. The caddies practiced on their own time, using old clubs behind the clubhouse. Trevino also practiced on his own makeshift course near the house. He and other caddies played for money. It was here that he learned to handle pressure and developed the steady nerve that would serve him well in the professional game.

▲ *Lee Trevino lifts the trophy after winning the British Open, the world's oldest golf tournament, at Muirfield, Scotland, in 1972.*

KEY DATES	
1939	Born in Garland, Texas, on December 1.
1956	Joins the Marine Corps.
1961	Marries Linda, his first wife.
1964	Marries second wife, Claudia.
1966	Plays in first U.S. Open tournament in San Francisco, California, and finishes in 54th place.
1968	Wins the U.S. Open for the first time, scoring under 70 in all four rounds of the tournament.
1971	Named PGA Player of the Year; wins U.S. Open.
1975	Struck by lightning during the Western Open.
1981	Inducted into the World Golf Hall of Fame.
1990	Joins the Senior Tour.
1996	Career earnings top $10 million.
2005	Completes 34th season on the PGA tour.

INFLUENCES AND INSPIRATION

Golf is an individual sport, and all great players have worked hard to get where they are. Considering his childhood in poverty, perhaps Lee Trevino has come farther than most. For him, golf was a way out of poverty, first as a caddy and then as a player.

As a child, any money Trevino made from golf went toward supporting his family. His grandfather was a gravedigger, his mother cleaned houses, and his uncle worked as a manual laborer when he could. All contributed their meager earnings to the household income. The Trevinos also planted a garden to grow vegetables, and raised chickens, goats, pigs, and a cow on their small patch of land next to the golf course. Every year when the cow had a calf, they would fatten it and sell it as soon as possible.

Trevino's success as a professional golfer ended the hardship for his family. However, Trevino's grandfather died in 1969 as his grandson's career was still just beginning. Trevino's mother died from cancer in 1971.

Trevino's financial skills did not match his abilities on the golf course. In 1977, he was bankrupted by a series of poor investments.

The road out of poverty

At the age of 15, Trevino was hired to work building golf courses and driving ranges. He also played a lot of golf with anybody and everybody for money or for fun.

As a teenager he entered some amateur competitions, winning some and losing some. Despite his obvious skill, golf was not making him the money he needed to lift his family out of poverty. Instead he joined the U.S. Marine Corps at age 17. It took the Marines several months to make the strong-willed Trevino accept military discipline. However, he did profit from military life. By a lucky break he was assigned to a Special Services Unit. Trevino drove a bus for the football team and issued athletic equipment until his superiors found out about his golfing abilities. For the last 18 months of his tour, he played golf every afternoon with the officers.

The road to riches

After being discharged from the Marines, Trevino played in numerous local tournaments, and eventually qualified for membership of the Professional Golf Association (PGA) Tour. By 1965, he was winning minor tournaments across the United States and even in Mexico and other parts of Latin America. However, he was also spending as much money as he was winning.

With the birth of his daughter Lesley in 1966, Trevino moved his family to El Paso, Texas, so he could concentrate on qualifying for the PGA Tour. In his first outing in a major tournament, he finished 54th at the U.S. Open. Next Trevino came fifth in the United States Golf Association competition, just behind Jack Nicklaus. He picked up $6,000 in winnings.

Trevino then traveled to Cleveland, Ohio, for the next tournament. He did badly on purpose so he would not make the cut and be able to go home and celebrate his success.

By 1967 Trevino's successes prompted him to join the PGA Tour and drive across the country for competitions. He also played in the Canadian Open, finishing 4th and pocketing another $4,300. In 11 of 13 tournaments that year, Trevino won a total of $26,471, earning him the title 1967 Rookie of the Year.

Trevino won the U.S. Open in both 1968 and 1971; the Ryder Cup—between the United States and Europe—in 1969, 1971, 1973, 1975, 1979, and 1981; the Vardon Trophy in 1970, 1974, and 1980; the British Open in 1971 and 1972; and the PGA Championships in 1974 and 1984. Only the Masters' title eluded him.

Miracle man

In 1975, while playing in the Western Open at Butler National Golf Club in Chicago, Illinois, Trevino was struck by lightning. Miraculously he survived, but not without severe injuries to his arm, back, and internal organs. Trevino had to undergo several corrective surgeries to repair the damage to his lower vertebrae and arm. He continues to have back pain to this day.

In 1985, at age 46, Trevino retired from the professional tour, and joined the Senior Tour. He continued to win despite his injuries and the effects of years of drinking hard while on the road. Trevino's wins as a senior professional now outnumber his victories while on the regular tour.

Further reading: Trevino, Lee. *They Call Me Super Mex.* New York, NY: Random House, 1982.
Trevino, Lee. *The Snake in the Sandtrap (and Other Misadventures on the Golf Tour).* New York, NY: Holt, Rinehart, and Winston, 1985.
http://www.wgv.com/hof/member.php?member=1116 (World Golf Hall of Fame entry).

TRINIDAD, Felix
Boxer

Felix "Tito" Trinidad is one of the most successful boxers Puerto Rico has ever produced. As an amateur he was national champion in five weight divisions. As a professional he held world titles in three divisions.

Child fighter

Trinidad was born in Cupey Alto, Puerto Rico, in 1973. He has two brothers and three sisters. His father, Felix Sr., a boxer himself, began training him at age eight. Trinidad won his first amateur championship at the age of 12 in the 100-pound (45kg) division. As he gained weight with age, he moved up and captured championships in four more

▼ *Felix Trinidad celebrates knocking out Fernando Vargas in the 12th round of a fight in Las Vegas in 2000. Trinidad won the IBF junior middleweight title from Vargas to add to his WBA belt.*

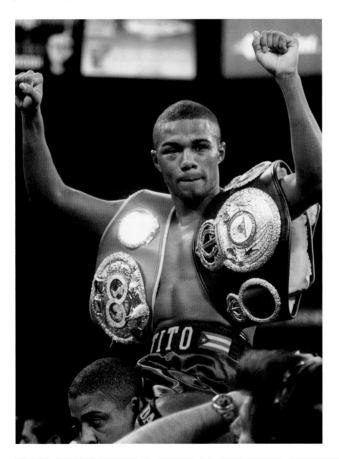

weight divisions. His amateur record was 51 wins to 6 losses, most by decision rather than knockouts.

Trinidad wanted to compete in the 1992 Olympic Games, but his father, who was also manager and trainer, advised him to turn professional instead. Felix Sr. argued that politics between the Puerto Rican and U.S Olympic teams would make selection uncertain. It would be better to cash in on his talent and earn some money. Trinidad turned professional on March 10, 1990.

Spectacular career

During his amateur years, Trinidad did not have a knockout punch. As he gained weight and height, however, his punching power increased. He amassed 29 knockouts in his first 33 fights, earning him the highest percentage of knockouts—90 percent—of any boxer in history.

Trinidad fought the biggest and the best, beating everyone in the welterweight and middleweight divisions, including Hector "Macho" Camacho, Oscar De La Hoya, and Fernando Vargas. All of his fights were spectacular displays of stamina, punching power, skill, and courage. He was knocked down in many fights, but never knocked out.

Perhaps Trinidad's most impressive victory was in 1999, when he beat the previously undefeated De La Hoya for the WBC (World Boxing Commission) welterweight title (147 pounds; 67 kg). The fight went the distance of 12 rounds with De La Hoya fading badly in the last three rounds, and having to run to avoid Trinidad. The judges awarded the fight to Trinidad in a split decision.

The fight set a pay-per-view record of 1.4 million paying viewers. On Trinidad's return to Puerto Rico, the celebration by the fans closed the capital city for a day.

Moving up a weight

After beating De La Hoya, Trinidad moved up to the 154-pound (70kg) junior middleweight division. He took on David Reid for the World Boxing Association (WBA) championship belt at Cesar's Palace, Las Vegas, Nevada, in 2000. He pounded out a unanimous victory. Later that year he went after the title of "Ferocious" Fernando Vargas, the undefeated and never-knocked-down IBF (International Boxing Federation) junior middleweight champion. Vargas floored Trinidad once, but the Puerto Rican sent Fernando to the canvas three times, twice in the first minute of the fight. The referee stopped the fight in favor of Trinidad in

INFLUENCES AND INSPIRATION

Felix Trinidad, Sr., was the guiding hand throughout his son's boxing career. Felix Sr. had been a successful boxer himself. In 1979 he held the Puerto Rican featherweight title. Featherweight fighters weigh between 122 and 126 pounds (54 –57kg). Felix Sr. even went five rounds with the legendary Mexican fighter Salvador Sánchez (1959–1982) at a bout in San Antonio, Texas.

Encouraged by his father, Felix Jr. grew up always wanting to be a boxer. His father had him in the training ring at the age of eight. As the boy grew, Felix Sr. moved him up the amateur weight divisions. By the time he turned professional at the age of 17, Trinidad had won 51 fights and lost only six.

Trinidad's professional career was managed very closely by his father. The decision for Trinidad to turn professional caused many Puerto Ricans to criticize Felix, Sr. Many boxing fans had expected Trinidad to compete at the 1992 Olympic Games in Barcelona, Spain, where he could follow in the footsteps of the island's most celebrated Olympian and fellow boxer, Juan Venegas.

For all the work and effort over the long years as manager and trainer, Felix Trinidad, Sr., was voted the Boxing Writers' Association of America (BWAA) Trainer of the Year in 1995. In 2000 he was both Trainer and Manager of the Year. It was the first time in the history of the BWAA that anyone had won both awards in the same year. Felix Sr. now trains a stable of younger Puerto Rican contenders.

the last round. Boxing pundits and sports writers declared the contest the fight of the year.

Tasting defeat

In 2001 boxing promoter Don King proposed a middleweight world championship between Trinidad and three other champions to determine who was the undisputed middleweight champion. Eager to earn the title last held by the great Sugar Ray Leonard after defeating the legendary Marvin Hagler in 1987, Trinidad signed up and began putting on weight. He beat William Joppy, a true middleweight, in just five rounds. Bernard Hopkins disposed of Keith Holmes to set up an elimination match between Trinidad and Hopkins at New York City's Madison Square Garden on September 15, 2001.

The fight was postponed for two weeks in the aftermath of the terrorist attacks of September 11. Trinidad tasted defeat in the professional ring for the first time. He was shattered by the experience, and Hopkins refused a rematch to settle the score.

Taking the knocks

Boxing takes its toll on fighters. Trinidad suffered hand injuries in 1991, plus countless punishing blows to his body and head over the years. In 2002, after a final victory, Trinidad decided to retire rather than risk injury in nonchampionship fights.

In 2004 Trinidad was lured out of retirement, however. He beat Ricardo Mayorga in New York that year, but lost to Ronald Wright at the MGM Grand, Las Vegas, in May 2005. Trinidad retired once more to enjoy family life in Puerto Rico.

KEY DATES	
1973	Born in Cupey Alto, Puerto Rico, on January 10.
1985	Begins to compete as a boxer.
1990	Turns professional.
1993	Wins IBF world welterweight title in San Diego, California.
1999	Beats WBO welterweight champion Oscar De La Hoya to become undisputed champion of the world.
2000	Becomes undisputed world junior middleweight champion by defeating David Reid and Fernando Vargas.
2001	Claims WBA middleweight title after beating William Joppy; loses for the first time against Bernard Hopkins as he attempts to unify the middleweight titles.
2002	Retires from boxing.
2004	Makes a comeback but retires the following year after losing his second fight.

See also: Camacho, Héctor; De La Hoya, Oscar; Vargas, Fernando; Venegas, Juan E.

Further reading: http://www.boxrec.com/boxer_display.php?boxer_id=003254 (biography).

TRUAN, Carlos
Politician

Carlos Truan has been a politician all his life. He won his first election—for class president—in the sixth grade. He never looked back, and overcame poverty and prejudice to become one of the longest-serving Texas politicians of modern times. He has also held state and national positions in the League of United Latin American Citizens (LULAC).

Early life
Truan was born in Kingsville, Texas, in 1935. This was during the Great Depression and life was hard for the young Truan. His father left when he was young and he lived with his mother in a two-bedroom shack in the barrio. As a child, Truan worked shining shoes, sweeping floors, washing windows, and cooking hamburgers.

▼ *Carlos Truan served in the Texas state legislature for more than 30 years.*

KEY DATES	
1935	Born in Kingsville, Texas, on June 9.
1968	Elected state representative for Nueces and Kleberg counties.
1976	Elected state senator for District 20.
1995	Named dean of the Texas Senate in 1995.
2002	Retires from public office.

Truan suffered at school because of the English-only curriculum and prejudice of the Anglo pupils and staff. He managed to graduate from high school at age 20. During college he worked at a gas station on weekends and as a clerk after classes. After college Truan began a long career selling insurance with American Life and later the New York Life Insurance Company.

Civil rights and politics
Truan joined LULAC in 1960 and became involved with the farmworker strike against La Casita Farms in Starr County, Texas. He participated in the early Raza Unida Conferences and served on various civil rights commissions and boards. He also helped found the Mexican American Legal Defense and Educational Fund (MALDEF) and sought election to the Texas House of Representatives. After eight years as a state representative, Truan ran for and won a state Senate seat where he remained until his retirement in 2002.

Legislation
As a policymaker, Truan championed several causes and passed important legislation in Texas. He is known for authoring the Public Housing Authority and Bilingual Education Act (1969), Adult Education Act (1973), Interstate Placement of Children and Child Care Licensing Act (1975), and the Birth Defects Registry (1993). He pushed for creation of a Regional Academic Health Center and School of Pharmacy in South Texas. For his contributions, several buildings in South Texas are named in his honor and Kingsville has a boulevard named for him.

Further reading: http://libraries.uta.edu/tejanovoices/interview.asp?CMASNo=084 (interview with Truan).

TRUJILLO, Severino
Journalist, Educator

Severino Trujillo was an important figure in the Mexican community of northern New Mexico in the late 19th century. Through his newspaper, *La Estrella de Mora* (The Star of Mora), Trujillo set out to speak for the territory's Latino population—the Nuevo Mexicanos—whose communities and traditional way of life were increasingly under threat from the dominant Anglo culture of the United States. Trujillo believed that by improving standards of education and knowledge among Nuevo Mexicanos, they would be able to regain economic and political power in their homeland.

A church education

Severino Trujillo was born into a poor family in the mountain village of Guadalupita, in the Mora Valley of northern New Mexico. Today the region is included in Mora County.

Trujillo's childhood was shaped and overshadowed by New Mexico's recent history. Formerly a Spanish colony and then a frontier province of independent Mexico, New Mexico had become a territory of the United States only in 1848. The people of the Mora Valley had put up stout resistance to U.S. occupation of their land, but had subsequently found their livelihoods and rights whittled away as Anglo settlers and entrepreneurs came to dominate the local economy.

Trujillo was educated at the Christian Brothers School, a Roman Catholic school founded in Mora in 1865. There he became the protégé of Mora's French parish priest, John B. Guerín, and later worked as his assistant. In return, Trujillo received a bed, food, and extra classes.

Guerín encouraged Trujillo to become a priest, and in 1872 the young Nuevo Mexicano traveled to Paris to enroll at the Seminary of Saint Suplice. He completed his studies in 1876.

Educating the people

In 1877 Trujillo returned to Mora but by now had decided against becoming a priest. While he remained a devout Catholic throughout his life, he now believed that he could best serve his fellow Nuevo Mexicanos by campaigning for better education in the territory.

In 1879 Trujillo founded a local newspaper, *La Estrella de Mora*, as a platform for his ideas and as a voice for his community. The newspaper was one of a number of

KEY DATES	
1850s	Born in Guadalupita, New Mexico, about this time.
1865	Begins education at the Christian Brothers School, in Mora County, New Mexico.
1872	Travels to Paris, France, to train as a priest.
1876	Is ordained as a priest.
1877	Returns to New Mexico.
1879	Founds the newspaper *La Estrella de Mora*.
1884	Relocates to Trinidad, Colorado.
1889	Represents Mora County at a convention on the future of New Mexico.
1897	Founds school in Wagon Mound, New Mexico.
1911	Dies in New Mexico about this time.

Spanish-language publications set up in New Mexico at this time as part of a wider drive for Nuevo Mexicano self-empowerment.

In 1884 Trujillo moved for a short while to Trinidad, Colorado, where he set up a Mexican American mutual-aid society known as the Asociación de Mutuo Adelantamiento. By this time Trujillo was also becoming actively involved in politics. He was part of the campaign for New Mexico, still a territory, to be admitted to the Union as a full state.

In 1889 Trujillo was chosen to represent Mora County at a convention held in the territorial capital, Santa Fe, to decide on the constitution of the future state of New Mexico. Trujillo retired from politics in the 1890s, and in 1897 founded a private school at the ranching village of Wagon Mound, Mora County. The exact date of his death is unknown but was some time after 1911.

Further reading: Meléndez, A. Gabriel. *Spanish-Language Newspapers in New Mexico, 1834–1958.* Tucson, AZ: University of Arizona Press, 2005.
Meléndez, A. Gabriel. *So All Is Not Lost: The Poetics of Print in Nuevo Mexicano Communities, 1834–1958.* Albuquerque, NM: University of New Mexico Press, 1997.

TURLINGTON, Christy
Model

Christy Turlington is a celebrated model, known as the face of Maybelline cosmetics and Calvin Klein's Eternity perfume. On the catwalk, Turlington has modeled clothes by the world's top designers, including Armani, Versace, Chanel, and Lacroix. Turlington was one of the first "supermodels," an elite group of models who could command million-dollar fees for their assignments. With a career spanning three decades, Turlington is also one of a select few models to have appeared on over 300 magazine covers.

KEY DATES	
1969	Born in Walnut Creek, California, on January 2.
1982	Discovered by photographer Dennis Cody.
1987	Becomes a full-time model.
1989	Wins multimillion-dollar modeling contract with Maybelline Cosmetics.
1994	Appears in fashion-world movie *Pret-A-Porter.*

Early life
Christy Nicole Turlington was born on January 2, 1969, in Walnut Creek near Oakland, California. Her father was of European-American heritage and her mother came from El Salvador. Turlington was discovered at the age of 13, while horse riding, by photographer Dennis Cody. She was subsequently signed by a San Francisco modeling agency and her first assignment was for store chain Emporium Capwell. Turlington was soon signed by the prestigious

▼ *Christy Turlington is a famous supermodel, but she also devotes time to campaigning and charity work.*

Ford agency and appeared in American *Vogue* while a student at the Monte Vista High School in Danville, California. Ford tried unsuccessfully to establish Turlington's career in Paris, and she fared better when introduced to New York City's fashion world, becoming highly sought after. On completing her education at the age of 18, Turlington took up modeling full-time.

Becoming a supermodel
Making the cover of Italian *Vogue* launched Turlington's career, and international fame as a "supermodel" soon followed. She was frequently grouped with the modeling elite, including Linda Evangelista and Naomi Campbell. Challenging popular assumptions about supermodels, Turlington gained a reputation for being well-mannered and professional. Her contract with Maybelline Cosmetics rewards Turlington with $3 million for just 12 days' work a year. In 1989 Turlington won the exclusive contract as the face of Calvin Klein's Eternity fragrance.

Turlington appeared in the fashion world feature film *Pret-A-Porter* (1994) and the documentary *Unzipped* about fashion designer Isaac Mizrahi (1995). She was also the subject of the documentary biography *Catwalk* in 1996.

Since retiring from the catwalk Turlington has continued to model for magazines, and has established herself as a successful businesswoman. She is active in publicizing campaigns against smoking and wearing animal fur, and supports educational charity work in El Salvador. Turlington married actor Ed Burns in 2003.

Further reading: Halperin, Ian. *Bad and Beautiful: Inside the Dazzling and Deadly World of Supermodels.* New York, NY: Citadel Press, 2001.
http://christy.turlington.com (official Web site).

UNANUE, Joseph
Businessman, Philanthropist

Former chairman and chief executive officer (CEO) of Goya Foods, Inc., Joseph A. Unanue built his family's small Manhattan-based food distribution company into the largest Latino-owned food company in the United States. A well-known philanthropist, Unanue dedicates his time to helping the Hispanic community.

Early life
Unanue was born in Brooklyn, New York, on either March 13 or 14, 1925. He was the second of four sons of Spanish immigrant Prudencio Unanue and his wife, Puerto Rican-born Carolina Casal. His father worked as a broker for Spanish companies with economic ties to the United States and became aware of a growing demand for traditional Hispanic food products. In 1936, he established a small import and distribution company in lower Manhattan called Goya Foods. Unanue's father insisted that his children learn about the business. As a child, Unanue bottled olives after school.

In 1943, at the height of World War II (1939–1945), Unanue's studies at a college in Tacoma, Washington,

▼ *Joseph Unanue and his family support initiatives to improve Hispanic cultural understanding, education, and programs to help Hispanic immigrants.*

KEY DATES	
1925	Born in Brooklyn, New York.
1936	Father, Prudencio, establishes Goya Foods.
1943	Drafted into U.S. Army; wins Bronze Star.
1976	Becomes president of Goya Foods, Inc.
2004	Steps down as chairman and CEO of Goya Foods, Inc., in favor of his two nephews, Robert and Francisco.

were interrupted when he was drafted into the U.S. Army. Sent to Europe in 1944, Unanue and his company joined General George S. Patton's 3rd Army in France at the Battle of the Bulge. Only 19 years old at the time, Unanue was made platoon leader after his sergeant died in action. A natural leader, Unanue took his men to safety and was awarded a Bronze Star Medal for his courageous service.

A successful businessman
After returning home in 1946, Unanue enroled in the Catholic University of America in Washington, D.C., where he earned a degree in mechanical engineering. Dissatisfied with the second-rate employment offers that he received, Unanue decided to dedicate his skills to building up the family business.

Unanue, helped by his brothers, turned the company into a multimillion dollar venture. After becoming president of Goya in 1976, Unanue capitalized on the growing number of Latino immigrants in the United States, supplying supermarkets with Hispanic foodstuffs. Goya became the largest Latino-owned food distributor in the country, employing more than 2,000 people and making more than $800 million in annual revenues.

In 1995 Unanue's son, Joseph, became vice president of operations. After his death in 1998, his younger brother, Andy, replaced him. In early 2004 Joseph Unanue stepped down as CEO and chairman of Goya and retired to live in New Jersey. He was succeeded by his two nephews, Robert and Francisco.

Further reading: http://utopia.utexas.edu/explore/latino/narratives/06Unanue_joseph.html (discussion of Unanue's background and leadership qualities).

URREA, Luis Alberto
Writer

Luis Alberto Urrea is an award-winning and best-selling Chicano writer who has published books in a wide variety of genres—from journalistic nonfiction and an autobiography, to poetry, short stories, and novels. In much of his work, Urrea writes movingly about the experience of impoverished Mexicans living and working along the Mexican–U.S. border, as well as about the predicament of immigrants trying to forge a new life in *El Norte* (the United States). Since 1999, Urrea has served as an associate professor of English and creative writing at the University of Chicago in Illinois.

On the border
Luis Alberto Urrea was born in 1955 in the Mexican border city of Tijuana. He is the son of a Mexican father and an American mother. At the age of three, Urrea's family moved to San Diego, California, where he was educated at a Roman Catholic elementary school and at Claremont High School. He became the first person in his family to gain a bachelor's degree, graduating from the University of California at San Diego in 1977. For the next five years, he worked as a bilingual teaching assistant and tutor at Mesa College in San Diego before going on to teach writing at Harvard.

Urrea had begun writing while still at high school, and published his first short story in 1980. However, it was only in the early 1990s, after he had turned to writing full time, that he published his first major work, *Across the Wire: Life and Hard Times on the Mexican Border* (1993), a collection of powerful essays rooted in his own experience as a relief worker in Mexico.

The book was followed by volumes of poetry, including *The Fever of Being*, in 1994, novels, and a memoir—*Nobody's Son: Notes on an American Life* (1998). In 1997, Urrea also gained a master's degree in creative writing from the University of Colorado at Boulder.

▲ *Luis Alberto Urrea is an award-winning Chicano novelist. He was born in Mexico but has U.S. citizenship because his mother was from New York.*

National acclaim
In 2004 Urrea became famous across the United States for *The Devil's Highway*, an account of 26 Mexican immigrants who, in 2001, were smuggled across the border only to find themselves lost without water or food in the Arizona desert. The book won several awards, and highlighted the suffering of thousands of illegal Mexican immigrants. Urrea followed this success with *The Hummingbird's Daughter* (2005). The acclaimed novel tells the story of Teresa Urrea, a distant relative of the author, who, in the late 19th century, won renown as a healer in Sinaloa, Mexico.

See also: Urrea, Teresa

Further reading: Urrea, Luis Alberto. *The Devil's Highway*. New York, NY: Little Brown and Company, 2005.
www.luisurrea.com (Urrea's Web site).

KEY DATES	
1955	Born in Tijuana, Mexico, on August 20.
1993	Publishes *Across the Wire: Life and Hard Times on the Mexican Border*, a collection of essays.
2004	Publishes *The Devil's Highway*.
2005	Publishes the novel *The Hummingbird's Daughter*.

URREA, Teresa
Healer

Teresa Urrea was born in Sinaloa, Mexico, to Cayetana Chavez, a Yaqui Indian, and Tomas Urrea, a boss at the ranch where Chavez lived. Urrea was a healer, and many said she had mystic powers. Her popularity was so great that she treated numerous people on both sides of the U.S.–Mexico border.

Early life
As an adolescent, Urrea was left in a trance or coma for several days. During this coma she was said to have heard voices telling her to serve the ill. She believed this was her purpose in life and devoted the remainder of her life to healing others, especially the poor. Before this incident, Teresita, as she was known, had already learned aspects of healing from an indigenous healer, including rituals and remedies.

Revolutionary healer
Later, Teresita's family moved to a ranch in Cabora, Sonora, Mexico. Here she acquired her following, mostly among Yaqui Indians. She became known as La Santa de Cabora (The Saint of Cabora). During this time, the government became suspicious of her activities with the Yaqui Indians. Teresita was thought to be associated with revolutionary movements, and this caused great controversy. Although the charges were never proven, they followed Teresita throughout her life. President Porfirio Diaz eventually had Teresita and her father arrested, and then had them exiled to the state of Arizona. The family later moved to El Paso, Texas, then back to Clifton, Arizona.

In 1896, while Teresita and her father lived in Nogales, Arizona, a group of Yaqui and Tomochi followers, calling themselves Teresitas, attacked a Mexican customhouse. The president blamed Teresita for the incident, accusing her of inciting revolution. It was an accusation that was never proven, but would become part of her mystique.

▲ *A Christian healer, Teresa Urrea also used the teachings of local Mexican Indians to help the sick.*

Teresita never stopped healing. She often treated 200 people a day while living in El Paso. Her method of healing was through prayer and herbal medicines, and she never charged for her services. Teresita met rich and poor, Mexican and Anglo, and became something of a celebrity.

At one point in her life, Teresita joined a medicinal company that toured the United States offering advice and other services. In spite of her busy schedule, Teresita married twice and had two children by her second husband, whom she married in 1900. Disillusioned with the sharp practices of the medicinal company, she returned to Arizona where she lived in a house which also served as a medical facility.

Teresita died of tuberculosis in 1906, at the age of 32. Her legend is still powerful today in Sonora, Mexico, and the southwestern United States. The town of Santa Teresa, just outside El Paso, is named after her.

See also: Urrea, Luis Alberto

Further reading: Castro, Rafaela G. *Chicano Folklore.* New York, NY: Oxford University Press, 2001.

KEY DATES	
1873	Born in Sinaloa, Mexico, on October 15.
1896	Indian uprising blamed on Urrea's influence.
1906	Dies in Clifton, Arizona.

VALDES-RODRIGUEZ, Alisa
Writer

Alisa Valdes-Rodriguez is a best-selling novelist. Sometimes compared to the African American novelist Terry McMillan, Valdes-Rodriguez writes mainly about strong, often professional Latinas. Valdes-Rodriguez has said that, although she is very proud of her Hispanic heritage, she does not want to be perceived by ethnicity alone. In 2005, *Time* magazine named Valdes-Rodriguez as one of the 25 most influential Hispanics.

Early life

Born in 1969 in Albuquerque, New Mexico, Valdes-Rodriguez is the daughter of a Cuban father and an Anglo-American mother with Irish and Native Indian ancestry. Her parents divorced when she was 11, and Valdes-Rodriguez was brought up by her liberal father, who taught her that she could achieve anything she wanted in life.

Valdes-Rodriguez knew that she wanted to be a writer from about the age of 13. Despite that, she went to the Berklee College of Music to study the saxophone, but she decided to concentrate on a career in journalism because she found the music world too sexist.

Journalism

Valdes went on to earn a master's degree in journalism from Columbia University, New York. In 1994, she became one of the *Boston Globe*'s youngest-ever staff writers. She received a Pulitzer prize nomination for her stylish work.

In 1999, Valdes-Rodriguez moved to the *Los Angeles Times,* where she wrote about music. She also married magazine editor Patrick Jason Rodriguez. In 2000, she resigned after she became pregnant. She was very unwell during her pregnancy with hyperemesis, a condition that

▲ *Valdes-Rodriguez's books often deal with such controversial subjects as religion and homosexuality.*

causes excessive vomiting, dehydration, and malnutrition. She required hospitalization, and suffered further complications after the birth of her son, Alexander.

Fiction

In 2003, Valdes-Rodriguez published her first novel, *The Dirty Girls Social Club*. Focusing on the reunion of six Latinas from Boston University 10 years after graduation, the book received an advance of $475,000 and sold more than 350,000 copies following its publication.

Valdes-Rodriguez went to work as a features editor at the *Albuquerque Tribune*, and continued to write fiction. In 2005 she published *Playing with Boys*, which examined the entertainment world's portrayal of ethnic minorities. Her third novel, *Make Him Look Good*, was published in 2006. She also wrote *Haters*, a novel for young people.

Valdes-Rodriguez's Web log, "Queen Sucia," in which she examines sometimes controversial subjects, has a substantial following. She also set up Dirty Girls Productions, Inc., which is dedicated to improving Latinos' exposure to the media. Valdes-Rodriguez is producing a TV version of *The Dirty Girls Social Club*.

KEY DATES	
1969	Born in Albuquerque, New Mexico.
1994	Goes to work for the *Boston Globe*.
1999	Joins the *LA Times*.
2003	Publishes *The Dirty Girls Social Club*.
2005	Publishes *Playing with Boys*; also founds Dirty Girls Productions Inc, a media company.
2006	Publishes *Make Him Look Good* and *Haters*.

Further reading: Valdes-Rodriguez, Alisa. *The Dirty Girls Social Club.* New York, NY: St. Martin's Press, 2003. www.alisavaldesrodriguez.com (official Web site).

VALDEZ, José Antonio
Priest

José Antonio Valdez served as a Roman Catholic priest in Texas during the turbulent period that led up to the state's annexation by the United States in 1845. Valdez's story illustrates the difficulties faced by Catholic officials as they struggled to maintain the church's influence in beleaguered Hispanic settlements across the Southwest, and to counter the strong anti-Catholic prejudices of many Anglo-American settlers.

Chaplain at the Alamo

Valdez was born in about 1787, and grew up in San Antonio, the provincial capital of Texas. At the time, Texas was part of the northernmost territory of the vast Spanish viceroyalty (colony) of New Spain. The colony encompassed modern-day Mexico, and included for much of its history (1535–1821) the present southwestern United States, Florida, Central America, the Antilles, part of northern South America, and the Philippines.

Valdez lived in San Antonio until 1803. His relative, Gavino Valdez, was the town's priest. Valdez then moved to an unknown location, probably in Mexico, to study. By the time he returned to San Antonio in February 1811, he had been ordained as a Catholic priest. He was appointed chaplain of the Alamo Company, whose headquarters were at the Alamo in San Antonio. The Alamo had formerly been a Franciscan mission, but from the late 18th century it had been reinforced by Spanish troops as a deterrent against a possible U.S. invasion. The building is best known as the site of a famous battle in 1836 when a band of Texas rebels was besieged in the fortress for 13 days by several thousand Mexican soldiers.

Trouble in Texas

The first threat of war in Texas came not directly from U.S. settlers, but from Tejano (Texas Mexican) revolutionaries who wanted to create a republic that was independent of both Mexico and Spain. In 1813, there was a widespread uprising in the state, and the Mexican troops, including the Alamo Company, were forced temporarily to leave the province. Valdez, left behind in San Antonio, found himself in rebel hands. He soon managed to escape, however, and rejoined Mexican government troops just as they were returning to take on the rebels. In August 1813, Mexican troops won a significant victory over Texas rebels at the Battle of Medina.

KEY DATES	
1787	Born in Mexico about this time, and raised in San Antonio, Texas, then the capital of a colony of New Spain.
1811	Appointed chaplain to the Spanish Army unit stationed at the Alamo fort in San Antonio.
1813	Captured by rebel Tejano forces but soon escapes.
1816	Appointed chaplain in La Bahía, Texas (later the city of Goliad).
1835	Imprisoned by Tejano rebels during the Texas Revolution.
1846	Dies in Saltillo, Coahuila, in November.

In 1816, Valdez was appointed as both military chaplain and parish priest of La Bahía, a southern Texas settlement that was later renamed Goliad. There, Valdez settled down with his widowed mother, and established a cattle ranch close by. Despite recurring bouts of ill health and several crises of faith, Valdez proved a popular parish priest, especially among the town's poorer inhabitants. In 1821, Mexico finally won its independence from Spain, although Spanish troops remained garrisoned in the town until 1828. Valdez continued to serve as their chaplain throughout the final days of empire.

In 1835, the Texas Revolution broke out as U.S. settlers and their Tejano allies broke away from Mexico and formed their own government. Goliad was captured in February 1836. The Mexican garrison fled, and its civilian inhabitants were forced into hiding. Valdez, however, remained, and fell into enemy hands. He was accused of being a Mexican spy, and imprisoned. The Mexican army recaptured Goliad a few weeks later, and Valdez was freed.

By the end of April 1836, Texas won its independence. Valdez returned to San Antonio, where he was denounced by the new U.S.-dominated Catholic church. No longer able to serve as a priest in Texas, Valdez moved to Saltillo, Coahuila, Mexico, where he died in 1846.

Further reading: Campbell, Randolph B. *Gone to Texas: A History of the Lone Star State*. New York, NY: Oxford University Press, 2003.
http://www.tsha.utexas.edu/handbook/online/articles/VV/fva1.html (biography).

VALDEZ, Luis M.
Playwright

Luis M. Valdez is often referred to as the founding father of Chicano theater. He founded the influential El Teatro Campesino in 1965, and built a successful career as a playwright and Hollywood movie writer and director.

Life in the fields

Luis Valdez was born in Delano, California, in 1940 into a family of Mexican farmworkers. Delano lay at the heart of migrant-worker country. Later, César Chávez chose Delano as the place to launch his campaign to organize farmworkers to strike for better working conditions.

Valdez's parents had owned their own farm. They lost it during the Great Depression (1929–1939), and were forced into migrant work. Valdez was six years old when he started work in the fields. His early schooling was patchy, but he graduated from Lick High school in San Jose. He then won a scholarship to San Jose State University.

Valdez started to write plays while at college. His first one-act play, *The Theft* (1961), won an award, and his play *The Shrunken Head of Pancho Villa* was staged by the college drama department.

Following his graduation with a BA in English in 1964, Valdez went to join the San Francisco Mime Troupe. The troupe comprised a group of highly political actors who were opposed to the Vietnam War. Valdez learned about the techniques of popular theater. The next year, he returned to Delano to help the activist Chávez in his support of striking grape pickers. Valdez set up a theater group to help the strike—El Teatro Campesino (The Farmworkers' Theater).

The group had no props or trained actors, but Valdez used his experience of mime to educate migrant workers about their legal rights and the need to join together. Valdez did this through a series of short sketches he called "*actos*." They were one-act plays that explained the significance of the Delano strike through actions and the use of masks and signs. The success of the venture encouraged Valdez to perform more works that examined the position of Chicanos in mainstream society.

Message plays

El Teatro Campesino performed Valdez's plays through the 1960s and into the 1970s. He tackled different subjects, such as the school system forcing cultural assimilation on minorities in *No Saco Nada de la Escuela* (I Don't Learn Nothing in School; 1969), and the large numbers of

▼ *Luis Valdez (right) and César Chávez outside the Winter Garden Theatre on New York's Broadway, where Valdez's* **Zoot Suit** *was playing in 1979.*

INFLUENCES AND INSPIRATION

Valdez belonged to a large family. He was the second of 10 children. His family played an important part in his life, instilling in him the importance of shared values and the strength and unity to be drawn from a family. Valdez involved his family in El Teatro Campesino, with at least one of his brothers and one of his sisters working for the theater group. Valdez's own sons have also followed him into the art world, and he is proud of the contribution they have made as actors, writers, directors, and filmmakers. Valdez says of his family's involvement in his work: "We've anchored it in family because it is through family that you get a sense of community." Valdez believes in the continuity of the family. He believes that he carries his parents and grandparents with him, and his children will carry him with them one day.

Chicanos serving in the Vietnam War. However, after the failure in 1974 of a production of his controversial drama *La Gran Carpa de la Familia Rascuachi* (The Great Tent of the Rascuachi Family; 1971), Valdez decided to move away from protest plays.

Commercial success

By the middle of the 1970s, El Teatro Campesino was becoming more commercial. It found a wider audience with its biggest hit, *Zoot Suit* (1978). Valdez based *Zoot Suit* on the 1942 Sleepy Lagoon case, in which a group of young Chicanos in East Los Angeles were convicted of murder on flimsy circumstantial evidence and sentenced to life imprisonment. The play was a big hit among Mexican Americans in California. It was the first play to draw many Mexican Americans to see a mainstream American theater production. Following a sell-out run in Los Angeles, it transferred to Broadway in New York City. However, the production there flopped. Valdez lashed out at critics who gave negative reviews, branding them as racists.

Despite the failure on Broadway, Valdez continued to write plays, and also started to work in Hollywood. In 1982, he wrote and directed the movie version of *Zoot Suit*, but it was also not a success. Valdez returned to work with El Teatro Campesino, and in the 1980s had a largely favorable reception for *I Don't Have to Show You No Stinking Badges*. The play was an examination of a middle-class Chicano family and its attempt to assimilate into Anglo-American culture. With the success of the play, Valdez returned to Hollywood, where he enjoyed a smash-hit with the movie *La Bamba* in 1987.

Written and directed by Valdez, *La Bamba* tells the story of Ritchie Valens. Valens was a Chicano singer who enjoyed great success before he was killed, aged just 17, in the 1959 plane crash that also killed singer Buddy Holly. Since the success of *La Bamba*, Valdez has continued to work sporadically in Hollywood, including on the 1994 television film *The Cisco Kid*, starring Jimmy Smits.

Recent work

During the late 1990s little was heard from Valdez. He did not produce a new play until 2000, when *The Mummified Deer* appeared. The play examines the Yaqui Indian influence on Mexican American culture and marks a return to Valdez's interest in the roots of his culture. Valdez's absence was due to his concentration on academia. He is a faculty member of the Teledramatic Arts and Technology Department of California State University at Monterey Bay.

Over the decades, Luis Valdez's impact on Chicano arts has been immense. He can be credited with creating Chicano theater where nothing existed before. El Teatro Campesino has won many awards, and Valdez himself has been awarded many honorary degrees and awards.

See also: Chávez, César; Smits, Jimmy; Valens, Ritchie

Further reading: Valdez, Luis. *Zoot Suit and Other Plays.* Houston, TX: Arte Público, 1992. http://www.galegroup.com/free_resources/chh/bio/valdez_l.htm (biography).

KEY DATES

1940	Born in Delano, California, on June 26.
1961	His first one-act play, *The Theft*, wins a prize.
1965	Founds El Teatro Campesino.
1978	His play *Zoot Suit* enjoys great success in Los Angeles, California.
1987	Writes and directs hit movie *La Bamba*.
2000	First play for 14 years, *The Mummified Deer,* is staged.

VALENS, Ritchie
Musician

Ritchie Valens was a rock-and-roll star for only eight months in 1958–1959, but during that brief period he recorded some of the most influential and lasting pop songs of the era.

Early life

The son of migrant Mexican farmworkers, Richard Steven Valenzuela was born in 1941 and raised in his native town of Pacoima, California. He began playing guitar at age nine, encouraged by his uncle, John Lozano, who gave him his first lessons on the instrument, and sowed the seeds of his lasting interest in traditional Mexican music.

Valenzuela first appeared on stage at Pacoima Junior High School in 1953, at age 12. His performance attracted great attention locally, and he was soon in demand for private parties. Then, at San Fernando High School, he was first exposed to rhythm and blues and rock and roll music. In 1957, he began playing with a local garage band, The Silhouettes, as a vocalist and guitarist.

In 1958, Doug Macchia, a graduate of San Fernando High, taped a Silhouettes' performance and played it to Bob Keane, the owner of Del-Fi Records, a respected independent label. Keane was impressed, and went to see the band live in concert. Although he enjoyed The Silhouettes, he most admired the singing and playing of Valenzuela. Keane invited the young man to his Gold Star Studios in Hollywood to make some demonstration recordings (demos).

Recording success

The demo sessions confirmed Keane's belief that Valenzuela had star quality. The problem was that, at the time, very few Mexican Americans had ever had a national hit record. The few successful Chicano artists who were in the charts around then included Little Julian Herrera, with "Lonely, Lonely Nights" (1957), and Freddy Fender, with "Before the Next Teardrop Falls" (1959).

In order to distract attention from Valenzuela's ethnicity, and also to give him a name that could be more easily pronounced by non-Spanish-speaking Anglo-American record buyers, Keane persuaded his protégé to adopt the name Ritchie Valens.

Valens signed his first recording contract on May 27, 1958. From then on, his rise was meteoric. His debut single, "Come On, Let's Go," released in September 1958,

▲ *Ritchie Valens became an instant national hit when he released his first records in 1958. On the verge of celebrity, he was killed in an airplane crash the following year.*

reached number 42 in the U.S. pop chart, and sold 750,000 copies. On the strength of that success, Valens almost immediately embarked on an 11-city national tour. At the end of it, in October 1958, Valens returned to the studio and recorded "Donna" and "La Bamba." Both songs were also hits, "Donna" reaching number 2 on the charts, and "La Bamba" number 22. The events transformed Valens's life: In less than a year, he had gone from small-town guitarist to national pop idol. Valens gave performances all over the United States, and appeared several times on national television, most notably on the popular show *American Bandstand*.

INFLUENCES AND INSPIRATION

Richard Valenzuela's earliest inspiration was the traditional Mexican *mariachi* music that he heard as a child. When he first performed on stage at school, his act was plainly indebted to Little Richard, and it was his similarity to the African American star that first attracted the attention of Bob Keane, the record producer who invented the name "Ritchie Valens" and guided the performer's subsequent career.

Despite his brief life and small output, Valens has exerted a strong posthumous influence on a range of pop musicians. Chris Montez publicly acknowledged Valens as the inspiration for his 1962 hit "Let's Dance." Echoes of Valens may also be heard in the music of Joan Baez and Carlos Santana. "Twist and Shout"— written by Phil Medley and Bert Russell, and famously covered by The Beatles—is similarly indebted.

The best-known pop reference to Valens occurs in "American Pie," the 1971 hit single by Don McLean. The famous lyric describes the plane crash that killed Valens, Buddy Holly, and the Big Bopper on February 3, 1959, as "the day the music died."

In 1987, Los Lobos, a Chicano group from East Los Angeles, recorded the soundtrack to the movie *La Bamba*, a fictionalized biography of Valens.

Greatest hits

"Donna" and "La Bamba" are Valens's greatest records, the works on which his lasting reputation is based. The former was his own composition, inspired by his girlfriend, Donna Ludwig. The latter was an updated version of a traditional Mexican folk song that had been popular since at least 1775. Valens was originally reluctant to record "La Bamba." Some historians claim that his unwillingness was based on the fear that his Spanish was not good enough to do justice to the material, but, according to Keane, Valens was concerned that it would demean his culture. The producer eventually persuaded him, however. Released in December 1958, "La Bamba" stayed on the charts until April 1959. By that time, Ritchie Valens was dead.

Tragic death

During the months following the release of "La Bamba," Valens played at many concerts to promote his recordings. The popularity of his music led to an invitation to join the Winter Dance Party Tour. Among the other featured artists in the traveling show were Buddy Holly and the Crickets, Dion and the Belmonts, and the Big Bopper (J. P. Richardson), a Texas disc jocky who had recorded a couple of hit songs. On February 3, 1959, the group had finished a show in Clear Lake, Iowa. The next scheduled stop on the tour was Fargo, North Dakota. The tour bus had developed problems with its heating system, and so Buddy Holly chartered a plane in order to avoid the cold of the Midwest and to make some extra rest time before the next gig. The aircraft had only three passenger seats, and Holly invited the Big Bopper and Valens to accompany him on the flight.

The plane hit a snowstorm shortly after takeoff, and crashed within a few miles of Clear Lake airport. The pilot and all three passengers were killed. The youngest was Ritchie Valens, who was only 18, and had been a professional musician for just over eight months.

Legacy

Ritchie Valens was buried in San Fernando Mission Cemetery in Mission Hills, California. His tomb has since become a place of pilgrimage for subsequent generations of rock fans. He has a star on the Walk of Fame in Hollywood. A successful bio-pic, *La Bamba*, written and directed by Luis M. Valdez, was released in 1987. The role of Valens was played by Lou Diamond Phillips. In 2001, Valens was inducted into the Rock and Roll Hall of Fame.

See also: Fender, Freddy; Los Lobos; Valdez, Luis M.

Further reading: Mendheim, Beverly. *Ritchie Valens: The First Latino Rocker.* Tempe, AZ: Bilingual Press, 1987.
http://www.history-of-rock.com/ritchie_valens.htm (biography).

KEY DATES

1941   Born in Pacoima, California, on May 13.

1958   First single, "Come On. Let's Go," reaches no. 42 on the U.S. pop chart; the follow-up, "Donna," later reaches no. 2; "La Bamba" released in December.

1959   Dies in a plane crash near Clear Lake, Iowa, on February 3; also killed are Buddy Holly and the Big Bopper.

1987   Premiere of *La Bamba,* a bio-pic of Ritchie Valens.

2001   Inducted into the Rock and Roll Hall of Fame.

VALENTÍN, Bobby
Musician

Puerto Rican-born musician Bobby Valentín is a leading salsa bandleader and arranger. Valentín plays several instruments, including trombone and trumpet, but he is best known as a bassist. He is sometimes known as "El Rey del Bajo" (The King of Bass).

Early life
Born in Orocovis, Puerto Rico, on June 9, 1941, Roberto Fred Valentín showed a love of music from an early age. He was taught to play the guitar by his father from age four. Later, at the suggestion of a teacher who had noticed his musical talent, Valentín went to study at the José Quinton Academy of Music. There he learned to play the alto saxophone but decided to concentrate on the trumpet. In 1956, Valentín moved to New York City, where he went to George Washington High School and studied the trumpet privately. In New York, Valentín met musicians Joe Quijano and Chu Hernandez. The three men formed a band named Los Satelites.

Professional career
In 1958, Valentín began playing professionally with Quijano, then moved on to play with and arrange music for Willie Rosario's orchestra. During this time, Valentín learned to play the bass, switching between that and the trumpet. He played bass with Charlie Palmieri, and arranged songs for Johnny Pacheco in the early 1960s. From 1963, Valentín played with Tito Rodriguez for about 18 months. He traveled with Rodriguez's band to Puerto Rico, later touring there with his own orchestra, which he formed in 1965. Valentín and his orchestra recorded their first album, *El Mensajero,* for Fonseca Records the same year. Their second recording, *Young Man with a Horn* (also 1965), was made for Fania Records, Johnny Pacheco's new label.

▲ **Bobby Valentín is a multitalented instrumentalist and musical arranger of Latin salsa.**

Valentín had a long relationship with Fania, which lasted even after he moved back to Puerto Rico in 1968. While recording *Algo Nuevo* (1970), Valentín switched to become a bass player. Although Valentín stopped recording with Fania in 1975, when he formed his own label, Bronco Records, he continued to collaborate with Pacheco as an arranger and toured with the Fania All-Stars until the 1990s.

In 1978, Valentín began recording for his own label, releasing *La Boda de Ella* to critical acclaim. In addition to touring and recording, Valentín also arranges songs for other artists, and is considered by many music commentators to be the best salsa arranger of his generation. Valentín has also performed with many leading Latin stars, including Cheo Feliciano and Celia Cruz.

See also: Cruz, Celia; Fania All-Stars; Feliciano, Cheo; Pacheco, Johnny; Palmieri, Charlie

Further reading: http://www.allmusic.com/cg/amg.dll?p=amg& uid=MIW060604031911&sql=11:n7yvadokv8w4~T0 (biography and discography).

KEY DATES	
1941	Born in Orocovis, Puerto Rico, on June 9.
1952	Studies at Jose Quinton Academy of Music in Coamo.
1965	Forms orchestra; records first album; signs with Fania Records.
1968	Moves back to Puerto Rico.
1978	Begins recording with own label, Bronco Records.

VALENZUELA, Fernando
Baseball Player

The youngest of 12 children, Fernando Valenzuela was born on November 1, 1960. He grew up in a small adobe house in the farming village of Etchohuaquila in southern Sonora, Mexico. Early in life, Valenzuela developed an interest in baseball. His six brothers all played baseball on the home-town team, and he learned the game from them. His older brothers liked to pitch, and used Valenzuela as a catcher. It was while observing from behind the plate that Valenzuela learned the art of pitching.

A catapulted path to fame

By age 13, it was obvious that Valenzuela was a cut above his peers in baseball prowess. He became part of the town team and, two years later, at age 15, he signed up with a Mexican professional baseball team. For the next five years, Valenzuela played on several minor league teams throughout Mexico, gaining confidence and experience.

On March 17, 1978, Los Angeles Dodgers' scout Mike Brito witnessed Valenzuela's pitching skill and sent an encouraging report to the Dodgers' manager. On July 6, 1979, Valenzuela became the property of the Los Angeles Dodgers for $120,000. After a short stint in the Dodgers' minor league system at the end of the 1979 season,

▼ **One of the legends of baseball, Valenzuela amassed an impressive pitching record and many enthusiastic fans during 10 years with the Los Angeles Dodgers.**

Valenzuela was sent to Double-A team San Antonio for the 1980 season. After an impressive record at San Antonio, Valenzuela was called up by the Los Angeles Dodgers, where he pitched his first major league baseball game on September 15, 1980.

Fernandomania

Fernando's performance as a relief pitcher at the end of the 1980 season was outstanding, but it was nothing compared to the 1981 season, when he became a starter for the team. Fernando pitched the first game of the season, and went on to accumulate a 17–7 record with a 2.48 earned run average (ERA). Fernando was instrumental in the Dodgers clinching the National League pennant with a 2–1 win against the Seattle Expos. He also won the second game of the World Series against the New York Yankees, and helped the Dodgers take the World Series that year.

For the next 10 years with the Dodgers, Fernando became not only a celebrity but a baseball phenomenon. As he amassed an impressive pitching record, Latinos and many other fans began attending games in large numbers just to watch him pitch.

Fernando was traded to the California Angels in 1991. He also played for the Baltimore Orioles, the San Diego Padres, and the St. Louis Cardinals. He retired at the end of the 1997 season after a successful and glorious career.

Further reading: Gloeckner, Carolyn. *Fernando Valenzuela.* Mankato, MN: Crestwood House, 1985.
www.baseball-reference.com/v/valenfe01.shtml (career statistics).

VALENZUELA, José Luis
Theater and Film Director

A leading Latino theater and film director, José Luis Valenzuela is the founder and artistic director of the Los Angeles, California-based Latino Theater Company (LTC). Much of his work for stage and screen has explored contemporary Hispanic American life, and he remains best known for his direction of the hit Latino film *Luminarias* (2000), written by and starring his wife, the Hollywood actress and screenwriter Evelina Fernández, and Chicano actor Cheech Marin.

A Latino in Norway

A native of East Los Angeles, Valenzuela did much of his early work as a director in Norway, where he was mentored by the leading Norwegian director Stein Winge. Among Valenzuela's notable productions were Henrik Ibsen's epic play *Peer Gynt* at the Norland Theater and a stage version of Manuel Puig's novel *Kiss of the Spider Woman* at the National Theater of Norway in Oslo.

Back in the United States, Valenzuela developed the LTC (initially know as the Latino Theater Lab) during the late 1980s. The LTC later made its permanent home in the historic Los Angeles Theater Center.

Collaborations

Valenzuela's work first came to the fore in the mid-1990s, when he directed his wife's script *Luminarias* for the stage. The play—the story of four middle-aged, middle-class Latinas in Los Angeles—was a huge success with Hispanic American audiences. With the help of funding from members of the Latino community, Valenzuela was able to go on to produce and direct a new version of the drama for the big screen.

Latino critics have often criticized Hollywood cinema for its stereotypical portrayal of Hispanic Americans, often with good reason. They almost unanimously praised *Luminarias* for its pioneering, naturalistic portrayal of everyday Latino life.

▲ *As well as being a director, José Luis Valenzuela is a professor of drama at the University of California, Los Angeles (UCLA).*

Bright future

The Latino Theater Company has gone from strength to strength. In 2002, Valenzuela went on to direct another of his wife's plays, *Dementia*, for the company. Once again, the story—about a young gay Latino who is dying of AIDS, and who struggles to overcome intolerance from his own community and family—showed the director's willingness to confront stereotypes. The play won the 2003 Gay and Lesbian Alliance Against Defamation (GLAAD) Award.

In 2006, with a $4-million grant, the LTC, headed by Valenzuela, bought the lease to its longtime home, the prestigious but dilapidated Los Angeles Theater Center. Valenzuela hopes that the revitalized center will become a showcase for multicultural theater in Los Angeles. In 2003, Valenzuela won the Hispanic Heritage Month Local Hero of the Year Award for his services to the Latino community.

See also: Fernández, Evelina; Marin, Cheech

Further reading: www.latinotheater.com (Web site of the LTC.)

KEY DATES	
2000	Releases the motion picture *Luminarias*.
2002	Directs the award-winning play *Dementia* for the Latino Theater Company (LTC).
2006	LTC buys the lease of the Los Angeles Theater Center.

VALLEJO, Mariano Guadalupe
Politician

Mariano Guadalupe Vallejo was a politician and military commander who was a pivotal figure in California's history. He followed in the footsteps of his family, who had distinguished themselves in war and peace from the time of Christopher Columbus. Vallejo's father, Ignacio, was born in Mexico and moved to Alta California (Upper California) as a soldier in the Spanish army.

Vallejo was born in 1808, in Monterey, the capital of Alta California. During his lifetime, California was ruled successively by Spain, Mexico, and the United States.

Meteoric career

Vallejo began attending school in 1815 and excelled in his studies. In 1823 he became a cadet in the Monterey militia. Mexico had won its independence from Spain in 1821, and Vallejo worked as secretary to California's Mexican governor in 1825.

Vallejo then joined the army where he rose quickly through the ranks. He was made a first ensign in 1827 and a lieutenant in 1835. At this time Vallejo was involved in battles against Native Americans. In 1835 he was given

▼ *Mariano Guadalupe Vallejo was an important figure in California's transition from Mexican province to U.S. state. The city of Vallejo, California, is named for him.*

KEY DATES	
1808	Born on in Monterey, California, on July 7.
1835	Founds the town of Sonoma, California.
1836	Made comandante general of California.
1890	Dies in Sonoma on January 18.

orders to build a town at the San Francisco de Solano mission. He named the settlement Sonoma. Sonoma is now at the heart of California's wine-making industry. Vallejo was responsible for distributing land to settlers, and for curtailing Russian expansion in the area.

Vallejo also had great success in the civil arena. Under Mexican rule, at the age of just 19, Vallejo was selected as a delegate to the Provincial Legislature meeting in Monterey in 1829.

U.S. rule

In 1836 Upper California rebeled against Mexico and declared itself an independent state. Vallejo was not directly involved in the rebellion, but was later made commandante general of the country. Soon, the Mexican government accepted the rebels as leaders of Upper California in exchange for the territory's return to Mexico.

Throughout the 1840s, conflicts arose between Californios—Hispanic Californians—and Anglo settlers from the United States. In 1846 Mexico and the United States were at war, and Vallejo, now a colonel, was briefly captured by Anglo rebels. As eventual victors in 1848, the United States took control of California along with the rest of the Southwest.

Vallejo sided with the new U.S. authorities, becoming a state senator in 1850. He offered to build and pay for a new state capitol on his land. The location was named Vallejo in his honor. However, the building was poorly constructed and was only used for one year before the capitol was moved to Sacramento, where it remains today.

Further reading: Rosenus, Alan. *General Vallejo and the Advent of the Americans: A Biography.* Berkeley, CA: Heyday Books/Urion Press, 1999.
http://www.pbs.org/weta/thewest/people/s_z/vallejo.htm (biography).

VARGAS, Elizabeth
Journalist

Elizabeth Vargas is one of the most popular Hispanic American broadcasters working in U.S. television. A respected journalist, Vargas is known for her dedication to work and her ability to tackle a wide range of subjects, from *The Da Vinci Code* to in-depth investigative reports on weighty subjects such as the former East German government's drugging of athletes.

Early life
Born in Paterson, New Jersey, on September 6, 1962, Vargas is of mixed Puerto Rican and Irish American descent. Her father was a colonel in the U.S. Army, and Vargas spent much of her youth living in Europe and Japan.

After graduating from the University of Missouri at Columbia with a degree in journalism, Vargas debuted as a reporter with the University of Missouri-owned KOMU-TV, an affiliate of NBC. From 1986 to 1989, Vargas worked as lead reporter for KTVK-TV, the ABC affiliate in Phoenix, Arizona, after which she spent four years working for WBBM-TV, the CBS affiliate in Chicago, Illinois.

A formidable career
In 1993, Vargas moved to the NBC network, where she gained valuable journalistic experience on *Dateline NBC*, covering several topical issues such as breast cancer research and drunk-driving. She also filled in as a substitute anchor on the NBC *Nightly News* and *Today* shows.

In 1997, Vargas went to work for ABC, where she was involved in the station's Children First Safety Special and its March Against Drugs. Vargas was a news anchor on

▲ *A talented journalist, Elizabeth Vargas is known as a host of ABC television's* **World News Tonight.**

ABC's *Good Morning America* show (1996–1997) and an investigative correspondent on the *20/20* news program (1997–2004). Vargas presented *20/20 Downtown* (1999–2002), and replaced Barbara Walters as coanchor of *20/20* following the latter's retirement from the show in 2004. In 2005, Vargas was asked to fill in for veteran anchor Peter Jennings on *World News Tonight* after the latter's announcement that he had terminal cancer. In January 2006, Vargas became Bob Woodruff's coanchor on the show and the first female journalist since Connie Chung to host an evening news broadcast. Woodruff was then seriously injured while on assignment in Iraq. Vargas anchored the show alone until May, when she stepped down owing to a difficult pregnancy. She was replaced by Charlie Gibson.

Vargas won an Emmy in 1999 for her coverage of the case of the Cuban refugee Elian Gonzalez.

KEY DATES	
1962	Born in Paterson, New Jersey, on September 6.
1993	Joins NBC Television.
1996	Moves to ABC Television.
1999	Wins an Emmy award for her coverage of the story of Elian Gonzalez, the Cuban child castaway.
2001	Marries Grammy-winning songwriter Marc Cohn.
2004	Replaces Barbara Walters as coanchor of *20/20*.
2006	Becomes coanchor with Bob Woodruff of ABC's *World News Tonight*; steps down as anchor.

Further reading: http://usliberals.about.com/od/thepressand journalist1/p/EVargas.htm (biography).

VARGAS, Fernando
Boxer

Mexican American Fernando "Ferocious" Vargas is one of the United States's best-known boxers, revered for his powerful punch and reckless courage in the ring. As an amateur he won 100 of his 105 fights, and as a professional he has twice been world junior middleweight champion. However, Vargas's aggressive "bad-boy" persona has often attracted criticism, as has his much publicized antipathy to fellow boxer and East Los Angelean Oscar De La Hoya.

El Feroz

Fernando Vargas was born in the Mexican state of Michoacán on December 7, 1977. Soon after his birth, his mother took him to the United States, where she raised him in the Hispanic La Colonia district of Oxnard, California. Vargas was often in trouble at school, and was frequently suspended for fighting with other students. At the age of 10, he began attending a local boxing club, where his talent and determination soon impressed his trainers. Over the following years, Vargas established himself as one of the country's most formidable amateur boxers, winning a series of tournaments, including the National Championships in 1994.

In 1995, Vargas was selected to compete for the United States at the 1996 Atlanta Olympics, but lost in the second round of competition after what was widely considered to be a controversial scoring decision. In 1997, the undaunted Vargas turned professional, and launched his career by defeating his first opponent, Jorge Morales, with a knockout in just 56 seconds. Then, in 1998, Vargas won national fame when he captured the International Boxing Federation (IBF) junior middleweight title. Over the following two years, Vargas fiercely defended his title, and was toppled only in December 2000, when he met the more experienced Felix Trinidad.

▲ *Boxer Fernando Vargas is nicknamed* **El Feroz** *(The Ferocious) for his fierce determination.*

Double world champion

In September 2001, Vargas retook the IBF title and won the World Boxing Association (WBA) junior middleweight crown by crushing José "Shibata" Flores. A year later, Vargas was challenged for the titles by Oscar De La Hoya, in what was billed as a classic meeting of rivals. In the fight, De La Hoya's speed and experience eventually paid off, and Vargas was forced to concede victory in the 11th round. The defeat left Vargas bruised both physically and mentally, and it was a low point that later deepened when he was found guilty of taking steroids in the run-up to the match.

Since the loss to De La Hoya, Vargas has led a checkered career, with long periods out of the boxing ring interspersed with "comeback" victories that have left some critics unimpressed.

See also: De La Hoya, Oscar; Trinidad, Felix

Further reading: www.fernandovargas.com (Vargas's Web site). boxing.about.com/od/records/a/vargas.htm (boxing record).

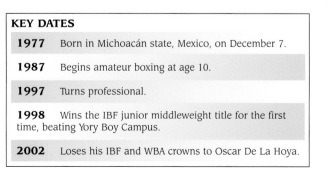

KEY DATES	
1977	Born in Michoacán state, Mexico, on December 7.
1987	Begins amateur boxing at age 10.
1997	Turns professional.
1998	Wins the IBF junior middleweight title for the first time, beating Yory Boy Campus.
2002	Loses his IBF and WBA crowns to Oscar De La Hoya.

VARGAS, Jay R.
Medal of Honor Recipient

Jay R. Vargas is one of 37 Latinos who have received the Congressional Medal of Honor, the United States's highest military decoration. He won the award while serving as a Marine major in a three-day battle near the Vietnamese village of Dai Do in 1968. Now retired, Vargas continues to be active in veteran affairs.

A hero of the Marines

The son of a Mexican American father and an Italian mother, Vargas was born in Winslow, Arizona, on July 19, 1940. At high school, he excelled both as a student and as an athlete, and won a scholarship to Arizona State University. He graduated in 1962 with a bachelor's degree in education, and soon after enrolled in the U.S. Marine Corps. Vargas completed his basic training in Quantico, Virginia, the following year, and was initially assigned to the 1st Battalion, 5th Marines of the 1st Marine Division. Vargas saw his first active duty in the Vietnam War (1965–1975).

In 1968, Vargas—by now promoted to captain—was serving as a company commander in the 4th Marine

▼ *Jay R. Vargas was an officer in the U.S. Marine Corps during the Vietnam War. His bravery earned him the Congressional Medal of Honor.*

KEY DATES	
1940	Born in Winslow, Arizona, on July 19.
1968	Serves as a company commander in the 4th Marine Division during the Vietnam War; leads significant assaults on Dai Do and Dinh To.
1970	Presented with the Medal of Honor for his actions at Dai Do, Vietnam, between April 20 and May 2, 1968.
1991	Retires from service as a colonel.

Division. On April 30, he and his men took part in an assault on an enemy stronghold based in the village of Dai Do near the demilitarized zone (DMZ) between North and South Vietnam. On the following day, under intense enemy fire, Vargas led his own men and two other companies across the surrounding rice paddies, where they seized enemy gun emplacements and gained a secure foothold in the village before nightfall.

The next day, the battle continued relentlessly. Vargas led his men on a second advance on the neighboring village of Dinh To, but they were driven back by intense enemy counterattacks. Despite having been repeatedly wounded during the previous days' fighting, Vargas risked his life to rescue a fellow officer who had fallen injured on open ground. He dragged the wounded man to safety in a protected position.

Thirty years of service

Soon after the battles at Dai Do and Dinh To, Vargas was promoted to the rank of major. In 1970, President Richard M. Nixon presented him with the Congressional Medal of Honor for his courage in rescuing the wounded soldier at Dai Do. Because Vargas's mother had only recently died, he asked for her name, Sando Vargas, to be inscribed on the medal in place of his own. Vargas went on to pursue a successful military career in operational roles across the United States, and eventually rose to the rank of colonel. He retired from the U.S. Army in 1991, after more than 30 years of service, and lives in San Diego, California.

Further reading: http://www.medalofhonor.com/JayVargas.htm (Medal of Honor citation.)
www.amgrunt.com/VargusBio.html (biography).

VARGAS, Kathy
Artist

Kathy Vargas is an internationally renowned painter and photographer. Inspired by both Mexican painting and German photography, Vargas was particularly influenced by the surrealist Hans Bellmer, who used hand-painting in his work, a technique that Vargas herself employs. Vargas also incorporates text in her work, such as in the series "Miracle Lives," in which subjects were asked to recite the miracles that had occurred during their lives.

Vargas often draws on her own past to create her art: Following her mother's death in 1996, Vargas dedicated *Broken Column: Mother* to her. She also used old family photographs in the Este Recuerdo series (2001–2005), stating, "I wanted to create a memory of … [my family], so that their names would not be forgotten."

▲ *Kathy Vargas's work hangs in the Smithsonian American Art Museum, the Museum of Fine Arts in Houston, and the Southwestern Bell Collection.*

Early life
Born in San Antonio, Texas, on June 23, 1950, Vargas was brought up in a politically active household. Her father was involved in the Democratic Party and her mother was involved in local grassroots church groups. Vargas's Spanish-speaking grandmother lived with the family and Vargas grew up speaking Spanish and learning about her Mexican heritage. Vargas's mother gave her a Diane camera when she was five. Her uncle, Antonio Valdez, a photojournalist based in Mexico, taught her how to hand-color photographs during his visits to the Vargas family home. Vargas attended the Our Lady of Perpetual Help and St. Gerard High School, where she was encouraged by her art teacher to become an artist.

An artistic environment
While still at school Vargas began working for Martín Ibarra at his galley in San Antonio. Ibarra paid Vargas in drawing lessons. Following her graduation from school, Vargas went to study at the San Antonio Art Institute but she thought it too "Anglo." She continued her lessons with Ibarra, spending most of her time working at his gallery. In the late 1960s she met Bill and Jerry Hayes, who offered Vargas a paid job as a receptionist in their gallery. Vargas also worked as a translator on a film they were making about the Mexican surrealist Salvador Valdez-Galindo.

When the Hayes decided to close their gallery and open an animation studio instead, Vargas went to work in their art department, learning to ink and paint. She also took painting lessons from Alberto Mijangos at the Mexican Cultural Institute, and in the early 1970s began taking photographs of rock and roll stars.

Focusing on photography
In the mid-1970s Vargas studied photography at San Antonio College. In 1974 the artist Melesio Casas invited her to join Con Safo (1972–1975), a Chicano group of artists. However, she left the group because she thought that its definition of Chicano art was too restrictive.

In 1977 Vargas studied at the University of Texas at San Antonio (UTSA). In 1984 she received an MFA from UTSA. She became director of the visual arts program at Guadalupe Cultural Arts Center in San Antonio in 1985. Since 2000 Vargas has been chair of the art and music department at the University of the Incarnate Word.

KEY DATES	
1950	Born in San Antonio, Texas, on June 23.
1974	Joins Con Safo.
1984	Graduates with an MFA from UTSA.
2000	Becomes chair of the art and music department at the University of the Incarnate Word in San Antonio, Texas.

Further reading: http://www.uiw.edu/thewordonline/fall05/campusnews.html (news article).

VASQUEZ, Richard
Writer

A writer and journalist, Richard Vasquez is best known for his 1970 novel *Chicano*, a best seller about the Sandoval family and the attempts of its members to establish themselves in the United States. Vasquez's work examines how mestizos, or people of mixed heritage, come to terms with their identity. The book was unusual for a work by a 1970s' Latino author because it was published by a major publishing house.

Early life
Vasquez was born into a Mexican American family in Southgate, a neighborhood close to downtown Los Angeles, California, in 1928. One of 10 children, he was raised in the San Gabriel Valley outside Los Angeles.

In 1945, Vasquez started a construction company. When that folded, he became a cab driver until 1959, when he started work as a journalist. Vasquez joined the *Santa Monica Independent* before going to work as a reporter for the *San Gabriel Valley Daily Tribune* between 1960 and 1965. Another change of career beckoned in 1965, and Vasquez spent the next five years working first as a historian for a book publisher and then for the Wilshire Boulevard Public Relations company.

Vasquez quit public relations in 1970 to work as a feature writer on the *Los Angeles Times*. His appointment followed the police killing of the newspaper's Chicano reporter Rubén Salazar, who was protesting against the Vietnam War. The same year, Vasquez published *Chicano*, which became a best seller.

Fact and fiction
Chicano was loosely based on Vasquez's own family. The novel spans four generations of the Sandoval family as they establish themselves in the United States. The family leaves Mexico in 1910 following the Mexican Revolution, and the story traces their move to Los Angeles. The fast rate of change within the Sandoval family is mirrored by the growth of the city. The older generation of the family enjoy the modern conveniences they had not had in Mexico, such as electricity and plumbing. The younger family members clash with their elders as traditional Mexican ways conflict with U.S. values.

The central theme of *Chicano* is Vasquez's belief that skin color is at the heart of how a mestizo is treated. The paler the skin, the less discrimination they experience. The

KEY DATES	
1928	Born in Southgate, California, on June 11.
1945	Starts construction company.
1959	Works as a reporter for California newspapers.
1965	Begins to work in publishing and public relations industries.
1970	Publishes his first novel, *Chicano*.
1977	Publishes *The Giant Killer*.
1980	Publishes *Another Land*, his final work.
1990	Dies in Los Angeles, California.

problems caused by a mixed heritage raised in *Chicano* inspired many later Hispanic American novels, such as Sandra Cisneros's *House on Mango Street* (1983).

Other work
Vasquez followed *Chicano* with *The Giant Killer* in 1977. That novel's protagonist, Ray García, is a Mexican American reporter who thinks it is important to assimilate into the dominant Anglo-American culture. Over the course of the novel, García's attitude is tested. Vasquez's final novel, *Another Land* (1980), is set in Los Angeles and deals with the issues of borders and immigration.

While Vasquez questioned the position of Mexican Americans in the United States in his fiction, his newspaper journalism dealt with barrio life and aspects of Chicano life that would interest a mainstream audience. He also wrote several short poems.

Vasquez's work made an important contribution to the understanding of the growth of the city of Los Angeles and the development of the border crossing between Tijuana, Baja, and San Diego, California. His work also serves as a reminder of the cultural diversity of the United States. Richard Vasquez died in 1990 in Los Angeles. Since his death, *Chicano* has been republished several times.

See also: Cisneros, Sandra; Salazar, Rubén

Further reading: Vasquez, Richard. *Chicano*. New York, NY: HarperCollins, 2005.

VASQUEZ, Tiburcio
Bandit

Tiburcio Vasquez was one of California's most famous Mexican American outlaws. He has come to symbolize the turbulent years of interracial strife that occurred after the United States acquired the state from Mexico.

Murderer

Vasquez was born José López to a law-abiding family in Monterey, California, in 1835, 10 years before California became U.S. territory. He grew up during the lawlessness and unrest of California's Gold Rush, and was attracted to a life on the wrong side of the law. As a teenager, Vasquez became a friend of the robber Anastacio Garcia. In 1854, the pair killed a police officer in a barroom brawl. Vasquez fled, and adopted his new name to evade capture. By 1856, he had his own gang, which committed a series of robberies, hold-ups, and horse thefts.

Prison and escape

Vasquez was arrested in Los Angeles in 1857 for horse theft, and sentenced to five years in San Quentin Penitentiary. He escaped once, but was recaptured a year later. After his release in 1863, Vasquez first made a living from gambling, but soon returned to his old life. He was jailed again for robbing a store in Mendocino. On his release in 1867, Vasquez returned to Monterey. However, he was forced to flee yet again after suffering serious injuries in a fight over another man's wife.

In 1873, having carried out a string of robberies in San Benito County, Vasquez decided to hide out in the mountains of southern California. He was pursued there by the Los Angeles County sheriff, William Rowland. Vasquez hid in the canyonlands around Tejon Pass, now known as Vasquez Rocks. However, he was betrayed by one of his own men, Abdon Leiva, with whose wife he had had an affair. When the authorities came for Vasquez, he survived a shoot-out and escaped.

▲ *Tiburcio Vasquez was a California bandit. Although he was a murderer and robber, he was admired as a worthy adversary of the Anglo authorities.*

Dead or alive

With a hefty price on his head—$8,000 alive or $6,000 dead—Vasquez parted from his gang. He took refuge with family members in Los Angeles. Again, his eye for women proved to be his downfall. While in hiding, he made his own niece pregnant. In revenge, the girl's parents informed Sheriff Rowland where he could find Vasquez.

Early on the morning of May 6, 1874, Vasquez was awaked by six intruders. One shot him, but he reminded them that, "You get two thousand dollars for being kind." Vasquez's reputation was unharmed by his capture. While in jail, he signed countless autographs for female visitors. On being sentenced to death for the murders, Vasquez stated: "I had many fights in defense of what I believed to be my rights and those of my countrymen. I believed we were unjustly deprived of the rights that belonged to us." He was hanged on May 19, 1875.

Further reading: Boessenecker, John. *Gold Dust and Gunsmoke: Tales of Gold Rush Outlaws, Gunfighters, Lawmen, and Vigilantes.* New York, NY: John Wiley, 1999. www.digitalhistory.uh.edu/mexican_voices/voices_display.cfm?id=80 (statement by Vasquez from an 1874 newspaper).

KEY DATES	
1835	Born in Monterey, California, on August 11.
1854	Murders a police officer during a brawl.
1857	Enters California's San Quentin Penitentiary for the first time.
1875	Hanged in San Jose, California, on May 19.

VASQUEZ VILLALPANDO, Catalina
Businesswoman, U.S. Treasurer

Catalina Vasquez Villalpando's Mexican father stressed the value of hard work and passed on his business acumen to his daughter. He was a hardware store clerk doing sales, inventory, stocking, and public relations—anything and everything to service clients. Cathi (as she was nicknamed) followed determinedly in her father's footsteps, becoming not only a very successful businesswoman, but also a powerful political figure and, for a time, Treasurer of the United States.

Early years
Vasquez Villalpando was born in San Marcos, Texas, on April 1, 1940, to immigrant parents from Mexico. After graduating from high school, Vasquez Villalpando enrolled in the Austin College of Business, Texas, in a two-year program. She was interested only in business and making money, rather than academic learning, and the desire for money continually interrupted her higher education. Vasquez Villalpando attended several colleges, including Southwest Texas State College in her hometown, but became a clerk-typist rather than continue as a student. Vasquez Villalpando also attended Southern Methodist University in Dallas, but never managed to finish a degree. She worked instead, as a jewelry store clerk and then as an accounting clerk for Mid-South, a Dallas oil company.

Vasquez Villalpando's skills and personality caught the attention of her superiors and she was promoted often, eventually becoming vice president of Mid-South. Vasquez Villalpando then accepted a job as senior vice president of Communications International, located in Atlanta, in 1969.

While changing careers, Vasquez Villalpando also switched her political affiliation, from Democrat to Republican. A tireless political mover as well as a successful businesswoman, Vasquez Villalpando was elected vice president of the Republican National Hispanic Assembly of Texas, and later its national president. She had now become a player in national Republican circles and her timing would prove to be excellent.

Moving up
Becoming a Republican was not merely a change in voting behavior. Vasquez Villalpando also engaged actively in party work: volunteering, canvassing, running get-out-the-vote campaigns, electioneering, and donating time and money with regularity. Her volunteer work soon paid off.

▲ *Catalina Vasquez Villalpando (pictured here with President George H. W. Bush) is a former U.S. Treasurer who was infamously sentenced to prison for tax evasion in 1994.*

Her visibility in Hispanic Republican circles got her a government job; she became assistant to the regional director of the Community Services Administration (CSA). Vasquez Villalpando served in the post for a decade, long enough to make extensive political contacts in government circles and nationwide. She formed her own company, V. P. Promotions, when she left CSA. V. P. Promotions was set up to help minority vendors with assistance in business contacts and contracts, including work for the federal government.

When George H. W. Bush contested with Ronald Reagan for the Republican presidential nomination of 1980, Vasquez Villalpando volunteered for Bush and then for the Reagan-Bush ticket. After Reagan won the nomination and then, in 1981, the presidential election, Vasquez Villalpando immediately joined Reagan's transition team, putting together the personnel for the new administration. She also assisted in planning and coordinating events during the inauguration ceremonies. The "Reaganites" were so impressed with Vasquez

Catalina Vasquez Villalpando displayed no emotion on February 17, 1994, as she pleaded guilty in a U.S. District Court in Washington, D.C., to evading federal income taxes, obstructing an independent counsel's corruption investigation, and conspiring to conceal financial links with her former company.

Vasquez Villalpando assured Judge Thomas F. Hogan that she understood the gravity of the offenses and the terms of the plea agreements. In a written statement made outside the courtroom she said: "While devoting all my attention and energies to the demands of my public office, I neglected to attend to some personal matters with the care and immediacy they required." Describing her court appearance as "a most painful and sad day for me," Vasquez Villalpando said she accepted "full responsibility for my mistakes" and that her admission "marks the first step in what I understand will be a long journey back."

Villalpando that she was named special assistant to the president for Hispanic affairs. She also was appointed to the U.S. Commission on Civil Rights.

From pinnacle to prison

When Vice President Bush became president in 1989, he asked Vasquez Villalpando to become the 39th Treasurer of the United States, succeeding Katherine Ortega. All the time, effort, and money that Vasquez Villalpando had invested in her career had paid off. She was sworn into office in 1989, and served until 1993. Her official signature appeared on millions of U.S. bills issued during that period.

That such bills are now collector's items is a result of what happened next. Vasquez Villalpando fell dramatically from power when she became the first U.S. Treasurer in history to be convicted of a federal crime and sentenced to a prison term.

Vasquez Villalpando's legal problems stemmed from her long association with Communications International, Inc. (CII), from which she resigned when she became U.S. Treasurer. As part of her severance terms, she received considerable payments from CII while she was U.S. Treasurer. Federal law prohibits government employees from receiving material benefits and services from private companies or individuals. Prospective federal employees are expected to reveal all sources of income, benefits, services, assets, and gifts. Vasquez Villalpando did not make full disclosure. She chose not to reveal substantial income received from CII in 1989 and 1990, and she failed to report those amounts (approximately $214,914) as income when she filed her income tax returns in 1990 and 1991.

Discredit

Vasquez Villalpando pleaded guilty to obstruction of justice, and received a four-month prison term plus a fine and community service. In order to avoid a sentence of 15 years and a $750,000 fine, Vasquez Villalpando cooperated with Department of Justice officials and the Office of Independent Counsel investigating corruption related to her case. There was a related matter involving the Department of Housing and Urban Development and her testimony before a federal grand jury in the District of Columbia. The plea bargain settled all those matters apart from the nonpayment of income taxes, for which Vasquez Villalpando is still under investigation.

See also: Ortega, Katherine

Further reading: http://www.usdoj.gov/opa/pr/Pre_96/ September94/521.txt.html (account of verdict and sentence).

KEY DATES

1940   Born in San Marcos, Texas, on April 1.

1969   Appointed assistant to the regional director, Community Services Administration.

1980   Becomes staff assistant in the White House Office of Personnel.

1983   Is appointed special assistant to the president of the United States.

1987   Takes up presidency of Republican National Hispanic Assembly.

1989   Becomes U.S. treasurer on November 20.

1993   Resigns from office.

1994   Sentenced by U.S. District Judge Thomas F. Hogan for crimes committed before and during her period of office as U.S. Treasurer.

VÉA, Alfredo, Jr.
Writer, Lawyer

Alfredo Véa, Jr., is a critically acclaimed Mexican American novelist. His work has been favorably compared with that of the Colombian Gabriel Garcia Márquez and the U.S. authors John Steinbeck and Raymond Chandler. The _Los Angeles Times_ named Véa's third novel, _Gods Go Begging_, one of the best books of 1999.

Early life
Many commentators regard Véa's life as the American Dream come true: He rose from extreme poverty to become a respected lawyer and writer. Born in 1952 in an immigrant transit camp in Arizona, Véa is of mixed Spanish and Yaqui ancestry. From an early age, he worked as a migrant farmworker near Phoenix, Arizona. In the 1960s he was drafted to fight in the Vietnam War. His experiences there had a lasting impact on his life, and he later wrote about them extensively.

Professional training
After the war, Véa took advantage of the GI Bill to go to law school, working a range of menial jobs to support himself during his studies. After graduating, he moved to San Francisco, California, where he represented young people from the Potrero Hill housing project who had been accused of drug and weapons offenses. He began to draw parallels between the poor young men from ethnic minorities who served in the infantry in Vietnam and the teenage gang members—also known as "soldiers"—whom he saw caught up in the drug and turf wars of the 1980s and 1990s.

From law to literature
After practicing as a criminal defense attorney, Véa, who suffered from post-traumatic stress syndrome, decided to write down his thoughts and anxieties. In 1993, he published his first novel, _La Maravilla_. The _Washington Post_ called it "brilliant, rich, and extravagant." The book, which follows the life of a nine-year-old boy living in an impoverished Phoenix suburb in the late 1950s, is viewed by many commentators as a classic, and became a featured text in several Chicano studies programs.

Véa's second novel, _The Silver Cloud Café_ (1996), was also well received by critics. Drawing again on his own experiences, Véa created the character of Zeferino Del Campo, a San Francisco lawyer who defends a hunchback accused of murder. As the story unfolds, Del Campo is forced to face his own memories of a murder that took place when he was a child in a migrant labor camp in the late 1950s.

Breakthrough work
Véa's next work, _Gods Go Begging_, drew directly on his experiences during the Vietnam war. The protagonist carries dog tags around with him to remind himself of a friend, a black soldier named Amos, who was killed in combat. Véa recalled that they used to pass the time in Vietnam by playing a fantasy game called "Supposings." Amos's favorite dream was that he was back in the United States opening a restaurant with his wife, Persephone. The novel opens with the killing of Persephone and her partner, Mai, just days before they open the café. The man accused of the slayings is defended by Jesse Pasadoble, a former infantry soldier.

War memories
In interviews, Véa is often asked about his experiences in Vietnam. While he prefers not to discuss the most harrowing details, he has said that the moment that epitomized the conflict for him occurred on April 4, 1968. He and his comrades in arms had to learn about the death of Martin Luther King, Jr., from North Vietnamese Hanoi radio. In Véa's view, "The American military was afraid that troops of color would sit down, and refuse to fight if they heard about the assassination in Memphis."

Further reading: Véa, Alfredo, Jr. _Gods Go Begging_. New York, NY: Dutton Books, 1999.
http://us.penguingroup.com/static/rguides/us/gods_go_begging.html (brief biography and summary of literary works).

KEY DATES	
1952	Born in Arizona.
1960s	Serves in Vietnam; qualifies as lawyer.
1993	Publishes _La Maravilla_.
1996	Publishes _The Silver Cloud Café_.
1999	Publishes _Gods Go Begging_.

VEGA, Bernardo
Activist

Bernardo Vega was a labor activist who worked in New York City's fledgling Puerto Rican community in the early 20th century. Throughout the 1920s and 1930s, Puerto Ricans poured into the city, settling in East Harlem, Soon the region became known as Spanish Harlem. Today Spanish Harlem is more often referred to by Latino and Latina residents as el barrio. The neighborhood extends from East 96th Street to East 125th Street, and is bound by the Upper East Side, East River, Harlem, and Central Park. Thanks in part to the activism of Vega, New York's Puerto Ricans have forged one the city's most vibrant communities, the self-styled Nuyoricans (New York Puerto Ricans).

In 1940 Vega wrote his autobiography, which was eventually published posthumously in 1977 as *Memorias de Bernardo Vega* (an English translation followed in 1984—*Memoirs of Bernado Vega*). The work, quite apart from its merit as literature, is an invaluable source of information about the experience of early Puerto Rican migrant workers in New York City.

Jíbaro from the mountains
Vega was born in the agricultural town of Cayey, in southeastern Puerto Rico, in 1885. He was a *jíbaro*, a white person from the Puerto Rican countryside. After a basic education, Vega worked as a *tabaquero*, or cigar maker. As a young adult, he became involved in the radical, socialist politics that swept through the island at the turn of the century. The surge of political activity was the result of Puerto Rico being denied independence as it was passed from the control of one colonial power, Spain, to another, the United States, in 1898.

One benefit of U.S. rule, however, was a right of abode on the mainland. In 1916 Vega set sail for New York City, joining the increasing numbers of young Puerto Ricans who were settling there in the hope of making a better life.

Life in New York
The city's Puerto Rican community was still small at the time—fewer than 8,000—and most lived in the crowded apartment blocks of East Harlem. Vega initially worked in a munitions factory but later returned to his profession as a *tabaquero*. As they were back home in Puerto Rico, cigar factories were hotbeds of political radicalism. Soon Vega was deeply involved in attempts to organize workers—both male and female—across the city's Puerto Rican community, in a struggle to win better employment rights and combat widespread discrimination.

Forging a community
As the Nuyorican community grew throughout the 1920s and 1930s, Vega and his close friend Jesús Colón were at the forefront of radical politics in the community. In 1924, both he and Colón helped form the Alliance of Puerto Rican Workers and the Puerto Rican and Hispanic League in 1926. Vega also worked as a journalist, and was one of the founders and editors of the influential Spanish-language journal *Gráfico*, which was published between 1926 and 1931. Its principal goal was to preserve the culture and language of New York's Puerto Ricans.

Such activities did not prevent Vega from being a committed U.S. patriot. He supported the United States's military efforts during World War I (1914–1918), and he served as an official censor. However, in the McCarthy era of the early 1950s, both he and Colón came under suspicion from the Un-American Activities Committee in Washington, D.C. Vega escaped prosecution, however, and in the late 1950s he returned to live in his native Puerto Rico, where he devoted his remaining years to the island's independence movement.

KEY DATES	
1885	Born Cayey, Puerto Rico.
1898	Puerto Rico is ceded from Spain to United States.
1916	Sails for New York City.
1924	Helps form the Alianza Obrera Puertorriqueña (Alliance of Puerto Rican Workers).
1926	Sets up the Spanish-language magazine *Gráfico*.
1965	Dies in Puerto Rico.

See also: Colón, Jesús

Further reading: Vega, Bernardo. *Memoirs of Bernardo Vega: A Contribution to the History of the Puerto Rican Community in New York: Memorias de Bernardo Vega.* New York, NY: Monthly Review Press, 1984.

VEGA, "Little" Louie
Disc Jockey, Musician, Record Producer

A record producer, musician, and disc jockey, "Little" Louie Vega is best known for his influential remix work with Masters At Work partner Kenny "Dope" Gonzalez. Their style is a fusion of house music, hip-hop, Latin, jazz, and soul, and their trademark sound is a combination of live instruments with sampled beats, typified by their releases under the name NuYorican Soul. Rather than simply adding dance beats to create a remix, Masters At Work introduced the notion of transforming a song. Consequently they produced some of the most innovative dance remixes of the 1990s and new millennium and earned Grammy-award nominations.

KEY DATES	
1965	Born in the Bronx, New York City, on June 12.
1990	Begins working with Kenny "Dope" Gonzalez.
1997	*NuYorican Soul* album nominated for a Grammy.
2004	Masters At Work nominated for Grammy for Best Remixed Recording.

Musical upbringing

Luis Fernando Vega was born into a musical family in the Bronx, New York City, on June 12, 1965. His Puerto Rican father was acclaimed saxophonist Louie Vega, Sr., and his uncle was Hector Lavoe, a salsa vocalist with the world-famous musical collective the Fania All-Stars. As a teenager, Vega Jr. began playing records at high school parties and hip-hop events in the Bronx, soon progressing to become a disc jockey at New York City's Devil's Nest nightclub. As his reputation grew, Vega was able to command crowds of 4,000 at the legendary nightclub Studio 54.

Vega's first remix was Information Society's "Running," and in 1989 he released *Keep Pumpin' It Up* under the name Freestyle Orchestra. However, Vega's creative partnership with younger disc jockey Kenny "Dope" Gonzalez established his wider reputation. Initially introduced by DJ Todd Terry, Vega and Gonzalez quickly realized their potential as a partnership and began remixing as Masters At Work.

▼ *New York DJ "Little" Louie Vega is one half of the popular remixing duo, Masters At Work.*

From underground to mainstream

Masters At Work's first remix, Debbie Gibson's "One Step Ahead," became an underground hit along with "The Ha Dance," which unusually combined house beats with samples. Many pioneering remixes followed, including Tito Puente's "Ran Kan Kan," combining house music and mambo, and the duo's distinctive acclaimed remix of Saint Etienne's "Only Love Can Break Your Heart." As their sound became common in nightclubs, so Masters At Work became in demand by prestigious labels and artists. In 1997, Masters At Work recorded their Grammy-nominated album *NuYorican Soul*, which is frequently credited with changing the direction of dance music. Vega continues to remix and disc jockey worldwide. He produced Grammy-nominated band Los Amigos Invisibles, and released his solo album *Elements of Life* in 2004.

See also: Fania All-Stars; Gonzalez, Kenny "Dope"; Lavoe, Hector; Puente, Tito

Further reading: Fikentscher, Kai. *You Better Work! Underground Dance Music In New York City.* Lebanon, NH: University Press of New England, 2000.

VEGA YUNQUÉ, Edgardo
Writer

The Puerto Rican-born writer Edgardo Vega Yunqué, also known as Ed Vega, has published a number of novels that examine the Irish–Puerto Rican community in New York City. His work has led him to be called a "Celtorican" novelist. Vega Yunqué, who lives in Brooklyn, New York, is the stepfather of the singer Suzanne Vega.

Early life
Born in Ponce, Puerto Rico, in May 1936, Vega Yunqué was the son of Alberto Vega Lebron and Abigail Yunqué Martinez. He grew up in the town of Cidra in the mountains. In 1949 Vega Yunqué joined his parents in the United States, where his Baptist minister father had been appointed head of a Spanish-speaking congregation in the South Bronx, New York.

A love of literature
In 1954, Vega Yunqué joined the U.S. Air Force, serving until 1958. During that time he developed a love of literature. In 1955, while on leave, he helped his sister clear out a house, and found hundreds of books by major U.S. writers. After reading them, Vega Yunqué fell in love with the work of William Faulkner and John Steinbeck. The title of Vega Yunqué's 1977 short story "Wild Horses" is a reference to Faulkner.

After leaving the Air Force, Vega Yunqué studied at Santa Monica College in California and then at New York University, earning a BA in 1963. He worked in a number of jobs before embarking on an academic career. Vega Yunqué joined Hunter College of the City University of New York (CUNY) in 1969; he also taught at other universities.

▲ **Edgardo Vega Yunqué has published more than 17 books, including 14 novels.**

In 1982 Vega Yunqué embarked on a freelance writing career. Vega Yunqué wrote for a number of publications including *Nuestro, Revista Chicano-Riquena, Maize, Americas Review,* and *Portable Lower East Side.* His early work was published under the name Ed Vega. He published his first novel, *The Comeback*, in 1985 and followed it with a collection of short stories, *Mendoza's Dreams*, two years later. *Casualty Report* was published in 1991; this was followed by a long period during which Vega Yunqué did not publish any new novels.

The author now publishes under his full name of Edgardo Vega Yunqué. His recent work includes: *No Matter How Much You Promise to Cook or Pay the Rent You Blew It Cauze Bill Bailey Ain't Never Coming Home Again: A Symphonic Novel* and *The Lamentable Journey of Omaha Bigelow into the Impenetrable Loisaida Jungle* (both 2004).

Further reading: Vega Yunqué, Edgardo. *The Lamentable Journey of Omaha Bigelow into the Impenetrable Loisaida Jungle.* New York, NY: The Overlook Press, 2004. www.members.authorsguide.net.edgar (comprehensive biography of the author).

KEY DATES	
1936	Born in Ponce, Puerto Rico, in May.
1949	Comes to the United States to join his parents.
1954	Joins U.S. Air Force.
1963	Graduates with a BA from New York University.
1977	Publishes first short story, "Wild Horses."
1985	Publishes first novel, *The Comeback.*
2004	Publishes *The Lamentable Journey of Omaha Bigelow into the Impenetrable Loisaida Jungle.*

VELASQUEZ, Baldemar
Labor Leader

Baldemar Velasquez was inspired to make a difference to the lives of impoverished farmworkers by personal experience. As the founder of the Farm Labor Organizing Committee (FLOC), he now represents more than 6,000 migrant workers. His efforts helped farmworkers win the right to join unions, and have secured substantial wage increases and improved working conditions.

Early life
Velasquez was born in Pharr, Texas, in 1947. His parents were migrant farmworkers of Mexican descent, and the family usually lived in barns or converted chicken coops. Velasquez started picking berries and tomatoes at age six. The family was once stranded in Ohio after the harvest, too poor to return to Texas, and was forced to work unpaid to pay off its debts, eventually returning seven years later.

Farm Labor Organizing Committee
Velasquez founded the FLOC in 1967, while studying for a bachelor of arts in sociology. He received help from his close friend, labor organizer César Chávez. At first, the FLOC targeted the growers who employed the farmworkers, but, by 1971, Velasquez's focus instead became the powerful food corporations, a policy vital to his success. Velasquez's tactics included letter-writing, prayer vigils, and protest marches that frequently led to his arrest. As a last resort, he called for national boycotts of corporations' products.

In a breakthrough in 1993, the FLOC negotiated employee status for 7,000 workers in the pickle industry. In the same year, Velasquez founded the Farm Worker Network

▲ **Baldemar Velasquez has worked tirelessly for the rights of exploited U.S. farmworkers.**

for Economic and Environmental Justice, to increase collaboration by farmworker organizations and make it more difficult for corporations to refuse union requests.

By 1995, the FLOC had signed agreements with Heinz, Vlasic, and Dean Foods. Many Ohio and Michigan pickle and tomato workers received wage increases. The same year, Velasquez discovered that cucumber pickers for the Mount Olive Pickle Corporation were earning as little as 55 cents for each 33-pound (15 kg) bucket, and were living in the corporation's dilapidated housing. He called for a national boycott of the corporation's products. In 2004, an agreement was finally reached, leading to an increase in wages and improved housing and health care.

Velasquez also broke new ground by setting up an independent commission to function as a labor relations board. Widely accepted by the agricultural industry, the board held discussions with growers and corporations.

See also: Chávez, César

Further reading: Sowash, R. *Heroes of Ohio: 23 True Tales of Courage and Character*. Bowling Green, OH: Gabriel's Horn Publishing Company, 1998.
www.floc.com (FLOC's official Web site).

KEY DATES

1947 Born in Pharr, Texas, on February 15.

1967 Founds Farm Labor Organizing Committee (FLOC).

1989 Wins Macarthur Fellowship, the so-called "genius award."

1991 Ordained as a chaplain; wins the Hispanic Leadership Award of the National Council of La Raza.

1993 Negotiates employee status for 7,000 pickle workers. Also founds the Farm Worker Network for Economic and Environmental Justice.

1995 Negotiates deals with Heinz, Vlasic, and Dean Foods; signs a pact with the Mount Olive Pickle Corporation.

VELÁSQUEZ, Willie
Activist

Willie Velásquez was the founder of the Southwest Voter Registration Education Project (SVREP). The organization encourages members of the Hispanic American community to register as voters, and promotes the importance of taking part in elections.

Early life

William C. Velásquez was born in Orlando, Florida, in 1944 while his father William, Sr., was stationed there during his military service in World War II (1939–1945). The family returned to San Antonio, Texas, after the war, and that is where Velásquez spent the rest of his life.

Velásquez's father, a butcher by trade, was a strict disciplinarian. He sent his children to private schools, where they received a conservative Catholic education. William, Sr., was a labor activist and a staunch Democrat. His son was like his father in many respects, plain-speaking and tough. The pair often clashed.

After graduating from St. Mary's University, a Catholic school in San Antonio, Velásquez enrolled in the master's program. He soon quit to dedicate himself to the Chicano movement, the Latino campaign for civil rights. He became a prominent figure at the first conferences held by the political grouping La Raza Unida in south Texas cities during the late 1960s. (La Raza Unida was formed into a political party by José Angel Gutiérrez in 1970.)

Velásquez headed the San Antonio boycott committee for Texas farmworkers on strike in the Rio Grande Valley. With other students from St. Mary's University, he formed the Mexican American Youth Organization (MAYO), which pushed for educational reform in curriculum, personnel, and financing of education in Texas. The group of Chicano

▲ **Willie Velásquez (left) founded the Southwest Voter Registration Education Project.**

activists promoted and organized hundreds of protests, marches, school walkouts, demonstrations, and boycotts across the state.

Money and votes

In 1967, MAYO's leaders formed a tax-exempt organization, the Mexican American Unity Council, which still pursues social justice in San Antonio. Velásquez became its first executive director, and then moved on to help build the Southwest Council of La Raza in Phoenix, Arizona.

Velásquez became focused on getting Chicanos registered to vote. He set out his proposals for a voter registration and education project to labor unions and corporations and received funding in 1972. By 1974, he had established SVREP. From then until his early death at age 44, Velásquez worked tirelessly to register voters across the five southwestern states: Texas, Arizona, New Mexico, Colorado, and California. His organization has registered millions of voters, mostly Chicanos. Six months before he died of cancer, Velásquez founded the Southwest Voter Institute, a research and training arm of SVREP.

See also: Gutiérrez, José Angel

Further reading: Sepúlveda, Juan. *The Life and Times of Willie Velásquez.* Houston, TX: Arte Público Press, 2003.
http://www.svrep.org/aboutsvrep/willie_bio.html (biography).

KEY DATES	
1944	Born in Orlando, Florida, on June 15.
1966	Graduates with a degree in economics from St. Mary's University, San Antonio, Texas.
1967	Helps found Mexican American Unity Council in San Antonio.
1974	Founds Southwest Voter Registration Education Project.
1988	Dies in San Antonio, Texas, on June 16.

VELAZQUEZ, Loreta Janeta
Writer

Hailed by some historians as a "lost heroine of the Confederacy," and denigrated by others as an opportunist and hoaxer, Loreta Janeta Velazquez is the author of one of the most bizarre war memoirs ever written. The title says it all: *The Woman in Battle: A Narrative of the Exploits, Adventures, and Travels of Madame Loreta Janeta Velazquez, Otherwise Known as Lieutenant Harry T. Buford, Confederate States Army.*

KEY DATES

1842	Born in Cuba.
1861	Joins the Confederate Army disguised as a man.
1876	Publishes her memoir, *The Woman in Battle*.
1897	Dies about this time.

Fact or fantasy?
Velazquez was born in Cuba in 1842 into a distinguished family. The daughter of a French American mother and an aristocratic Spanish father, Velazquez fantasized about being Joan of Arc as a child. At the age of eight, she was sent to live with her aunt in New Orleans, Lousiana. At 14, she eloped with her first husband, William. She later gave birth to three children, but they all died in infancy.

When the Civil War broke out in 1861, William resigned his post with the U.S. Army and joined the Confederates. Velazquez decided to follow him. She cut her hair, donned a fake moustache, and a padded uniform fitted with a wire

▼ *Loreta Janeta Velasquez is remembered for her account of many unlikely Civil War adventures.*

frame to conceal her female form, and transformed herself into Lieutenant Harry T. Buford. Recruiting more than 200 men in just four days and equipping them from her own funds, she led the group to Florida, where her husband was stationed. Although William was shocked when she revealed her identity, he nonetheless took command of the soldiers. He was killed shortly afterward during a training exercise.

Grief-stricken, Velazquez left her unit and headed north to forge her own destiny. As Lieutenant Buford, she supposedly engaged in a number of key battles, and had a string of outrageous adventures that included spying for the Confederate side, meeting President Abraham Lincoln and his secretary of war, and claiming to have crossed much of the nation at a time when transportation was difficult. Her identity as a woman was discovered twice, but both times she somehow eluded punishment for her charade. Once, in the North, officials unwittingly hired her to search for a spy passing as a Southern woman— Velazquez herself. She married three more times, only to have all three husbands die. She traveled to Europe and then Venezuela, returning to the United States in the 1870s pregnant and penniless.

Unreliable evidence
Velazquez's 600-page memoir was published in 1876. It was written in the bombastic style of an era in which novelty and romanticism held sway. *The Woman in Battle* contains numerous exaggerations and inaccuracies that prompted the hoaxing accusations. Still controversial after all these years, Loreta Janeta Velazquez's historical significance may lie as much in the telling of her tall tale as in the handful of truths that inspired it.

Further reading http://docsouth.unc.edu/velazquez/velazquez.html (digital copy of Velazquez's memoir).

VELÁZQUEZ, Nydia M.
Politician

Congresswoman Nydia M. Velázquez made history in 1992, when she became the first Puerto Rican woman to be elected to the U.S. House of Representatives.

In education
Velázquez was born in 1953 in Yabucoa, a small town in southeast Puerto Rico. One of nine children in a modest household, Velázquez was a precocious student, excelling in her studies from an early age. As a child, she was surrounded by politics. Her father was a labor activist. She would listen to his political conversations at the dinner table and accompany him to rallies fighting for the rights of sugar cane workers. Velázquez developed an interest in advocating social rights and equality among citizens.

At age 16, Velázquez began her college career at the University of Puerto Rico in the town of Río Piedras. She

▼ *Nydia Velazquez celebrates in 1992 on becoming the first Puerto Rican woman to win election to the U.S. Congress.*

graduated magna cum laude in 1974, earning a bachelor's degree in political science. She was the first member in her family to obtain a college degree.

Velázquez subsequently earned her master's degree from New York University. In 1974, she began work as a professor at the University of Puerto Rico, staying in the job for the next five years. She then joined the faculty at the Center University of New York's Hunter College in 1981, teaching Puerto Rican studies.

Political career
Velázquez was still interested in politics. In 1983 she worked as an assistant to Democratic congressman Edolphus Towns, who represented Brooklyn, New York. In 1984, Velázquez became the first Latina to serve on the New York City Council. By 1986 she was director of the Department of Puerto Rican Community Affairs in the United States.

As a committed leader, Velázquez set about launching one of the most ambitious Latino development programs in the United States. She organized a successful voter

LEGACY

As a Latina politician, Nydia Velázquez has produced an impressive legacy. In honor of her leadership in the political and business arenas, and for her work to increase opportunities for minority groups in commerce, she was named "Woman of the Year" by *Hispanic Business Magazine* in April 2003.

In 2005, Velázquez passed an amendment to the Border Protection, Antiterrorism, and Illegal Immigration Control Act. The amendment enables the Department of Homeland Security to ease the enormous backlog in applications from migrants—many of them Hispanic—that has stalled the immigration process in the United States.

Velázquez is one of the most active members of Congress. She serves on a number of caucuses and task forces, including the Asian Pacific American Caucus, the Congressional Caucus on the Census, the Congressional Children's Caucus, the Empowerment Zone, the Enterprise Community Caucus, Hispanic Caucus, Human Rights Caucus, and the Women's Issues Task Force, among several others.

Velázquez is also a supporter of the nation's entrepreneurs. She has a seat on the Small Business Committee and the House Financial Services Committee.

registration drive, called Atrévete (Dare to Go for It!), a program that registered more than 150,000 new voters in the Puerto Rican communities.

In 1992, Velázquez was elected to the U.S. House of Representatives to represent New York's 12th District. The district is a very diverse neighborhood, with a large Latino community as well as Polish and Chinese residents. It includes sections of Brooklyn, Queens, and the Lower East Side of Manhattan. It is the only triborough district in the New York City congressional delegation.

In Congress, Velázquez fought for the equal rights of all under-represented populations, and has proposed a wide range of economic, housing, education, health, and environmental reforms for the poor and for working-class families in her district and across New York City.

Leading figure
In February 1998, Velázquez became the ranking Democratic member of the House of Representatives' Small Business Committee. She became the first Latina to serve as a chair or ranking member of a committee in the history of the House of Representatives. As part of the committee, Velázquez has managed federal programs and contracts totaling $200 billion annually. She has also developed programs that would benefit small business owners and entrepreneurs, establishing various legislative projects on tax regulations, contracting, and trading opportunities, as well as technology, health care, and retirement reforms.

Current work
In the 21st century, Velázquez remained a member of the Small Business Committee and the House Financial Services Committee. In those roles, she endeavors to facilitate the work of entrepreneurs and the growth of small companies. She also advocates for the rights of the historically underserved communities of her district. For her dedication to the empowerment of minority groups, and for her commitment to social equality, Nydia Velázquez is widely admired in both the United States and her native Puerto Rico.

KEY DATES	
1953	Born in Yabucoa, Puerto Rico, on March 28.
1969	Begins college education at the age of 16.
1981	Joins the faculty of Hunter College, New York.
1983	Appointed as special assistant to New York congressman.
1984	Becomes first Latina elected to serve as a member of New York City Council.
1992	Is elected to the House of Representatives for New York's 12th District.
1998	Becomes ranking Democratic member of the House Small Business Committee.
2003	Is named "Woman of the Year" by *Hispanic Business Magazine*.
2005	Composes an amendment to the Border Protection, Antiterrorism, and Illegal Immigration Control Act.

Further reading: http://www.loc.gov/rr/hispanic/congress/velazquez.html (biography).
http://www.house.gov/velazquez/biography.htm (biography).

VÉLEZ, Lauren
Actress

Lauren Vélez is an actress of Puerto Rican heritage who has had many lead roles in feature films, on stage, and in popular television series. Vélez is best known for her portrayals of Lisette Linares in the film *I Like It Like That* and Detective Nina Moreno in the TV series *New York Undercover.* Her other lead roles include Carol in the movie *I Think I Do,* Dr. Gloria Nathan in the HBO prison drama *Oz,* and Mayme in the off-Broadway show *Intimate Apparel.*

Early life
Lauren Vélez and her twin sister, Loraine, were born on November 2, 1964, in Brooklyn, New York City, to Puerto Rican parents José and Coco Vélez. They had six other siblings, and with their father's police officer salary the large family was able to relocate to the borough of Queens. The twin sisters enjoyed performing at school and one of Vélez's early roles was as a groundhog in a second grade

▼ *Lauren Vélez has starred on stage, on film, and on TV. Her best-known roles are on TV, and include Detective Nina Moreno in* **New York Undercover.**

KEY DATES

1964	Born in Brooklyn, New York, on November 2.
1970s	First television role, in *Ryan's Hope*; first major stage role, in Broadway musical *Dreamgirls.*
1994	First lead film role in *I Like It Like That.*
1995	First regular TV role, as Detective Nina Moreno in *New York Undercover.*

school play. On graduating from Kingsborough Community College, both Vélez sisters were awarded scholarships to the Alvin Ailey Dance School. However, a knee injury caused Vélez to change her career course and she began studying at the Acting Studio. Her first small television role came in the 1970s' ABC program *Ryan's Hope,* and her first stage role was in the Broadway musical *Dreamgirls.* Vélez later became understudy for Phylicia Rashad in the Broadway show *Into the Woods.*

From stage to screen
Vélez's film debut and first lead role came in 1994, as Lisette Linares in the comedy drama *I Like It Like That*. In 1995, Vélez attained her first regular television role, as Detective Nina Moreno in the popular police series *New York Undercover.* Vélez received nominations for the Independent Spirit Award and the Desi Award for the role. The following year, Vélez starred in the thriller film *City Hall,* and in 1997 she had lead roles in the comedy film *I Think I Do,* and the HBO prison-drama series *Oz.* Vélez appeared in the Spanish-language film *Buscando un Sueño* (*In Search of a Dream*) in 1997, and *The LaMastas* in 1998.

Vélez also had television roles in *Thicker Than Blood* (1998), *St. Michael's Crossing* (1999), and *Love and Treason* (2001). In 2000, Vélez starred in the feature *Prince of Central Park* and the following year, *Prison Song.* Following guest appearances on several television shows, in 2005 Vélez starred in the feature film *Serial,* and the short film *Barely Buzzed.* She starred as Mayme in the Broadway play *Intimate Apparel* in 2004.

Further reading: Borgenicht, David. *A Biographical Handbook of Hispanics and United States Film.* Tempe, AZ: Bilingual Review Press, 1997.

http://www.angelfire.com/ny5/LVelezBLS (tribute Web site).

VELEZ, Lupe
Actress

Lupe Velez was a popular actress in both Mexico and the United States, acting in Spanish and English. In Hollywood in the 1930s and 1940s Velez played stereotyped Mexican characters. Much like Carmen Miranda and her "tutti-frutti" hat, Velez is best remembered for her "hot tamale" image, versus the more serious reputations enjoyed by contemporaries Rita Hayworth and Dolores del Rio.

Early life

Born Maria Guadalupe Velez de Villalobos, in 1908 in San Luis Potosi, Mexico, Velez was sent to convent school in San Antonio, Texas, by her army officer father and opera singer mother. Velez returned to Mexico briefly after the death of her father to help support the family. While in Texas, she made her theatrical debut at the Teatro Principal in 1924, in the musical review *Ra-Ta-Plan.*

Velez moved to Hollywood later that year, and was discovered by producer Hal Roach. Her first movie was *The Gaucho* in 1927, starring Douglas Fairbanks. In 1928, Velez became a Western Association of Motion Picture Advertisers (WAMPAS) Baby Star, one of 13 young women chosen annually who WAMPAS believed to be Hollywood star material.

Velez starred in a series of eight "Mexican Spitfire" movies, playing the eponymous lead role of Carmelita. The character was funny, intelligent, and often out-witted Anglo-American characters in the films. It was a recognizable, continuing role, stereotypical but not totally flat, and helped increase Velez's profile.

In *Palooka* (1934), a variation on the "great brown hope" genre, Velez played a gold digger who lures a boxer into the fast life, which eventually leads to his ruin. Her character, unable to exercise self-restraint, again emphasized the stereotypical representation of Latinas

▲ *Famous for her role as Carmelita, the "Mexican Spitfire," Lupe Velez was a movie star of the 1930s and 1940s. She committed suicide in 1944.*

as weak and out of control in comparison to their stronger, more rational Anglo-American counterparts.

As with many Latinas, Velez was called on to play other types of ethnic characters. Despite these limited roles, Velez was a Hollywood role model for young Mexican American women. She was one of the few Hollywood actresses to make the transition from silent movies to "talkies," because, according to Velez, "Art has neither nationalities nor borders." Velez was honored with a star on the Hollywood Walk of Fame.

Velez married actor Johnny Weissmuller of *Tarzan* fame in 1933, and divorced five years later. She also had a brief relationship with Gary Cooper, another Hollywood actor. Velez committed suicide on December 13, 1944, with an overdose. She was pregnant at the time, but estranged from the father of the child, Harold Raymond.

KEY DATES	
1908	Born in San Luis Potosi, Mexico, on July 18.
1927	First credited film role in *The Gaucho.*
1940	Beginning of "Mexican Spitfire" series of movies.
1944	Stars in her last movie, *Nana.*
1944	Dies in Beverly Hills, California, on December 13.

See also: Del Rio, Dolores; Hayworth, Rita; Miranda, Carmen

Further reading: Rodriguez, Clara E. (Ed.). *Latin Looks: Images of Latinas and Latinos in the U.S. Media.* Boulder, CO: Westview Press, 1997.

VENEGAS, Juan E.
Boxer

Juan Venegas was the first Puerto Rican boxer to win a medal in an Olympic Games. Venegas was a bantamweight boxer, which means that he and his opponents had fighting weights of between 112 and 118 pounds (51–53.5kg).

The pinnacle of Venegas's career came early. He was just 20 years old when he represented Puerto Rico at the 1948 Olympic Games in London, England. Despite being a U.S. territory, Puerto Rico fields its own team at the Olympic Games. The London games was the first Olympics in which a Puerto Rican team was entered. Before that Puerto Rican athletes had to fight for a place on the U.S. team. Today, Puerto Ricans who are good enough to make the grade can choose to compete on either the U.S. or Puerto Rican teams.

The Olympic Hero

Juan Venegas was born in a working-class district of Puerto Rico's capital, San Juan, in 1928. Like many other poor Puerto Ricans of African origin, Venegas saw boxing as a way out of a life of poverty and discrimination. He started training and competing at an early age. He grew up idolizing Sixto Escobar, the Puerto Rican boxer who had become the bantamweight world champion and a much-loved national hero in 1936.

In 1948 Venegas was chosen to represent Puerto Rico at the London Olympics. The event was the first Olympics since the 1936 games in Berlin, Germany. London's games were a symbol of the world's peoples coming together in peace after the destruction of World War II (1939–1945).

KEY DATES	
1928	Born in San Juan, Puerto Rico.
1948	Wins the bronze medal in the bantamweight boxing competition at the Summer Olympic Games in London, England.
1949	Becomes a professional boxer, but loses his first two fights.
1950	Wins first professional fight against Jerry Kortright in Puerto Rico.
1958	Retires from the ring after his 14th professional bout.
1980s	Dies about this time.

Puerto Rico's national squad was tiny. Venegas was one of just three athletes. Nevertheless, the team became the focus for an upsurge in national pride. Venegas was a southpaw, a lefthander. With their guards up, southpaws lead with their right hands, but their left hands deliver the stronger punch. Such fighters are notorious for being difficult opponents, and Venegas was no exception. He was the most successful Puerto Rican at the games that year, coming away with a bronze medal. He was beaten only by Tibor Csik of Hungary and Giovanni Battista Zuddas of Italy, who won the gold and silver medals respectively.

The professional boxer

Soon after a triumphant return to his home country, Venegas became a professional featherweight boxer. Featherweight is a heavier class than bantamweight. Fighters are between 118 and 126 pounds (53.5–57kg). His first fight took place in 1949 against fellow Puerto Rican Art Llanos in Long Island City, New York. Venegas lost on points. His next fight was another defeat. Mexican American Eddie Chavez knocked him out in one of New York City's most prestigious boxing venues, the St. Nicholas Arena.

This unpromising beginning was followed by some hard-fought wins against the likes of Cuban Black Pico in 1955 and fellow Puerto Rican Iggy Maldonado in 1957. However, Venegas's professional career was a disappointment. In 1958, he lost two fights in a row and opted to retire from the ring. Of his 14 fights, Venegas won eight, lost five, and drew one. Venegas lived the remainder of his life in near obscurity and died in San Juan sometime in the 1980s. The exact date of his death is unknown.

Venegas's achievement not only helped to consolidate boxing's reputation as one of Puerto Rico's major national sports, but also served to raise the island's international profile at a time when it was just beginning to assert its identity after a half-century of direct rule from Washington, D.C. One of Puerto Rico's most important boxing fixtures, the Juan Evangelista Venegas Tournament, is named in the Olympian's honor.

See also: Escobar, Sixto

Further reading: www.boxrec.com/boxer_display.php?boxer_id=075854 (Venegas's boxing records)

VIGIL, Donaciano
Politician

Donaciano Vigil was a Mexican politician who became the governor of New Mexico when the territory was occupied by the United States during the U.S.–Mexico War (1846–1848). Vigil was a *rico* (rich man), a member of the New Mexican elite. Along with others, such as the Luna and Otero families, he attempted to benefit from the Anglo-American conquest of the territory.

From rebel to leader
Vigil was born into a family of landowners in New Mexico in 1802. At that time, the territory was still the northern frontier of the Spanish colony of New Spain. In 1821, New Mexico become a province of an independent Mexico.

By 1837, Vigil and other *ricos* had become resentful of the Mexican government's attempts to rule from Mexico City. They wanted more local decision-making. The poor also resented the Mexican government for taxing corn too highly. Vigil helped lead a rebellion against Albino Pérez, the unpopular governor of New Mexico. Pérez was killed in the revolt, and José Angel Gonzales declared himself governor. However, he was soon unseated by Manuel

▼ *Donaciano Vigil was the governor of New Mexico after it became U.S. territory.*

KEY DATES	
1802	Born in Nuevo México, a northern province of the Spanish colony of New Spain, now known as New Mexico.
1834	Serves as an officer in a rebel New Mexican force.
1847	Becomes governor of New Mexico after the U.S. occupation.
1877	Dies in New Mexico.

Armijo (1793–1853), who was backed by Mexico City to retake the province. Vigil soon deserted the rebels and allied himself with the government's new representative.

Vigil went on to become a celebrated leader during Mexico's battles with Texas. Texas had become independent from Mexico in 1836. In 1842 and 1843, Texas attempted to invade New Mexican territory with U.S. backing. Although the New Mexico *ricos* had trading links with Texas and the United States, they fought back. In the process, Vigil was promoted to captain in the Mexican Army.

The coming of the U.S. Army
In 1845, the U.S. Army under Colonel Stephen Kearny marched into New Mexico. The *ricos* offered little resistance, and again Vigil changed sides. He was named as interim territorial secretary. In 1847, New Mexicans revolted against the occupation. Charles Bent, the U.S. governor of New Mexico, was killed, and Vigil was appointed in his place by the U.S. military. The move helped restore order to the region.

Vigil used his political position to boost trade with Anglo-Americans. This benefited him personally, as well as other *ricos*. Vigil became wealthy buying and selling land. Some thought that he was self-serving, but others regarded him as a masterful statesman, who was able to bridge cultures and political systems. Vigil would be the last Mexican governor in New Mexico for many years. He was replaced by U.S. military figures in 1848.

See also: Otero Family

Further reading: http://www.digitalhistory.uh.edu/mexican_voices/voices_display.cfm?id=57 (transcript of a 1847 speech by Vigil).

VILLA, Beto
Musician

Saxophonist Beto Villa is known as the father of *Orquesta Tejana*, which literally means "Texas Mexican orchestra," but is now used to denote a general musical style. He recorded with some of the leading musicians of his time.

Early life

Alberto "Beto" Villa was born in Falfurrias, Texas, on October 26, 1915. During the Mexican Revolution that began in 1910, his family had fled Monterrey, Nuevo Leon, Mexico, and settled in Texas.

Villa's father, Alberto, was a musician and tailor, who had his own *orquesta típica*. He insisted that his son play an instrument and gave Villa a saxophone when he was 10. Villa played with the local school band before forming his own group, Sonny Boys, which played at local fiestas. The group was contracted as the house band at the Barn in Freer, Texas, playing six nights a week. However, Villa did not earn enough to support his family and worked in a meat market to supplement his income.

▼ *Beto Villa made several recordings for Ideal Records with the renowned accordionist and conjunto star Narciso Martínez.*

KEY DATES

1915	Born in Falfurrias, Texas, on October 26.
1947	Records first hit singles "Las Delicias" and "Porque Te Ries" with Ideal label.
1954	Signs to RCA.
1986	Dies in Corpus Christi on October 26.
2000	Inducted into the Chicano Music Hall of Fame, Alice, Texas.

Road to fame

During World War II (1939–1945) Villa served in the U.S. Navy. Upon his discharge, he returned to South Texas, where he continued to play. In 1946 he approached Armando Marroquín and Paco Betancourt at the Texas-based Ideal Records and persuaded them to let him record a few songs in a new musical style. Villa combined the big-band sound popular in the United States with conjunto music, mixing his sets with polkas, *danzones*, and *rancheras* to create a unique sound.

In 1947 the Beto Villa Orquesta recorded "Las Delicias" and "Porque Te Ries," which were released to great success. In the following year he recorded with the legendary accordionist Narciso Martínez, backed by brass and drums. Villa's music appealed to working-class Mexicans on both sides of the border, and his style influenced other saxophonists.

In the 1950s Villa and his band dominated the *orquesta* scene in Texas, and they began to incorporate the more popular samba and mambo music into their sets. In 1954 Villa and his orchestra signed with RCA, becoming the first Tejano *orquesta* to do so. In 1960 health problems made Villa stop touring with the band; his son-in-law, Wally Armendariz, took over as saxophonist. Villa died in 1986. He was inducted into the Chicano Music Hall of Fame in Texas in 2000.

See also: Martínez, Narciso

Further reading: Pena, Manuel. *The Mexican American Orquesta.* Austin, TX: University of Texas Press, 1999. http://userwww.sfsu.edu/~josecuel/sax.htm (article on saxophonists and music).

VILLANUEVA, Alma Luz
Writer

Alma Luz Villanueva's autobiographical poetry has found a wide audience. Her turbulent early life is documented in her poems, as are her meditations on being a woman. Her poetry also explores many other themes, including violence, poverty, sexual abuse, racism, and war.

Early life

Villanueva was born in Lompoc, California, in 1944. Her father was a German national, but Villanueva had no contact with him. Until she was 11, her Mexican maternal grandmother raised her in the Mission District of San Francisco, California. When her grandmother died, Villanueva moved back to live with her mother.

Villanueva's early life was tough. When she was only 14 she discovered she was pregnant and dropped out of 10th grade. (She did not finish her education until much later, finally earning a master's from Vermont College in 1984.)

Becoming a poet

Until she was 30 years old, Villanueva concentrated on bringing up her children, living on welfare in a poor neighborhood of San Francisco. She started work on the poetry that would form two of her major works as she approached her 30th birthday. In 1977, just three years after she had started to write regularly, her first collection of poetry appeared. *Bloodroot* was a collection of 47 poems that Villanueva saw as an affirmation of being a woman. This work won her the Third Chicano Literary Prize. *Mother, May I?,* published the following year, is a long autobiographical poem that traces her emotional childhood. In the poem Villanueva looked at the women who had influenced her, including her mother and grandmother, as well as the events that had shaped her own life. Villanueva describes each period of her life

▲ *Poet and novelist Alma Villanueva achieved success without a formal education, having dropped out of school in the 10th grade to have a child.*

through a particular event associated with that time. For example, her childhood with her grandmother is told through her memories of making tortillas.

Villanueva's next collection, *Life Span*, appeared in 1985. It celebrates nature and her happiness at living in a remote part of California.

Novelist

Villanueva has also written three novels to date. The first, *The Ultraviolet Sky* (1988), won the American Book Award of the Before Columbus Foundation. Her second novel, *Naked Ladies* (1994), won the PEN Oakland Josephine Miles Award. Her most recent novel, *Luna's California Poppies*, written in the form of a diary, appeared in 2001.

Villanueva has published three further collections of poetry. *Planet* (1993) won the Latin American Writers Institute Award in Poetry. It concentrated on racism, sexual abuse, and poverty. Her next two collections, *Desire* (1998) and *Vida* (2002), celebrated life in a more joyful mood. Villanueva lives in Santa Fe, New Mexico.

Further reading: http://voices.cla.umn.edu/vg/Bios/entries/
villanueva_alma_luz.html (biography).

KEY DATES	
1944	Born in Lompoc, California, on October 4.
1977	Publishes her first book of poetry, *Bloodroot.*
1978	Publishes a second poetry collection, *Mother, May I?*
1988	Publishes the novel *The Ultraviolet Sky*, which wins the American Book Award.
2002	Publishes poems in *Vida*.

VILLANUEVA, Tino
Poet

Tino Villanueva is a highly regarded poet who writes in both English and Spanish. Villanueva's work reflects what he calls *bisensibilidad* or double sensibility. He believes that Hispanic Americans see the world from two perspectives, that of their Hispanic heritage and that of the U.S. culture they live among.

Early influences
Villanueva was born in San Marcos, Texas, in 1941 to Mexican migrants. He spent his summers as a child helping his parents in the fields. He could not return to school until he had helped with the October harvest.

After high school, Villanueva worked in a furniture store for four years before being drafted into the Army in 1963. He was stationed at the Panama Canal and while there he started to read the poetry of the Nicaraguan poet Rubén Darío and the Cuban revolutionary Jose Martí.

When he left the Army, Villanueva enrolled at Southwest Texas University and started writing his own poetry. After graduating with his bachelor's degree in 1969, Villanueva moved to the Northeast to study for a master's degree at Buffalo, New York.

In 1972 Villanueva published his first collection of poetry, *Hay Otra Voz: Poems*, which was written in Spanish. The poetry concentrated on the injustices he had experienced as a Chicano. Although the book received little critical attention at the time, it has come to be seen as a work of great importance in the Chicano literary canon.

After completing his master's degree, Villanueva moved to Boston University, where he completed his PhD in 1981. Since then, he has taught Spanish at the university.

▲ **Tino Villanueva has been publishing poetry for more than 30 years. He has also established an influential journal for Hispanic American poets.**

Poet of distinction
In 1984 Villanueva began to publish *Imagine: International Chicano Poetry Journal*. He wanted the magazine to publish poetry in any language, accompanied by English translations, although the emphasis was on Chicano work.

Villanueva has continued to publish poetry. In 1984 *Shaking Off the Dark* appeared, followed by *Autobiographical Disclosures* in 1988. In the 1990s he published three further collections. The 1993 *Scene from the Movie Giant* won the 1994 American Book Award. It was based on the 1956 movie *Giant*, which contained a scene in a Texas roadside diner when an Anglo customer is beaten up as he tries to prevent the owner from throwing out a Hispanic man. *Chronicle of My Worst Years* (1994) was a translation of an earlier Spanish volume from 1987. Villanueva published his most recent work, *Primera Causa/First Cause*, in 1999. He continues to live and teach in Boston.

See also: Martí, José

Further reading: Villanueva, Tino. *Chronicle of My Worst Years.* Evanston, IL: TriQuarterly Books, 1994.
www.library.txstate.edu/swwc/archives/writers/villanueva.html (biography).

KEY DATES

1941   Born in San Marcos, Texas, on December 11.

1969   Graduates from Southwest Texas State University in San Marcos.

1972   Publishes his first poetry collection.

1981   Earns PhD in Spanish from Boston University.

1984   Founds Imagine Publishing and starts publishing *Imagine: International Chicano Poetry Journal.*

1999   Publishes collection of poetry, *Primera Causa/First Cause.*

VILLARAIGOSA, Antonio
Politician

Elected mayor of Los Angeles in 2005, Antonio Villaraigosa became the first Hispanic mayor of the city since 1872. His life began in poverty and violence in East Los Angeles, progressed to the campus of the University of California, Los Angeles (UCLA), and then into the halls of political power. The charismatic and energetic mayor became an effective leader, learning to rally support from widely diverse constituencies.

Tough early years
Antonio Villar (he would later change his name) was born on January 23, 1953, in the Boyle Heights section of East Los Angeles to Antonio Villar and Natalia Delgado, both

▼ *Antonio Villaraigosa was elected mayor of Los Angeles, California, in 2005, thanks in part to his ability to attract non-Latino support.*

Mexican Americans. Villar was the oldest of four children. During Villar's youth, Boyle Heights was a generally harmonious mixture of Hispanics, Jews, African Americans, and Japanese Americans. The model influenced his thinking for his later political development.

As a boy, Villar witnessed his father, usually drunk, beating his mother, and was helpless to stop him. His father eventually left the family, and visited infrequently. It was Villar's mother who kept the family together. The teenage Villar got into many fights, often returning home bleeding. He was kicked out of Cathedral High, and was soon chased out of Wilson High by gangs. He never finished high school, but after motivation and inspiration from his mother, he shook off his gang-member lifestyle, enrolled in night classes, and earned an honorary degree from Theodore Roosevelt High.

Getting it together
Villar continued his studies at East Los Angeles College and was then accepted to UCLA, where he received a degree in history in 1977. During his time at UCLA, Villar led campus protests over the Vietnam War, Chicano rights, and farmworker protection. He also became involved with the radical civil rights organization Movimiento Estudiantil Chicano de Aztlán (MEChA; the Chicano Student Movement of Aztlán). The organization had recently been formed to promote awareness of Chicano history among Chicano youth through education and political action. MEChA's motto was "La Unión Hace La Fuerza," or "Unity Creates Strength."

After graduating from UCLA, Villar went on to study law at the unaccredited People's College of Law, but failed his bar exam four times. Instead of pursuing law any further, Villar decided to focus on labor. Villar already had experience in the area. From the age of 15 years, he had been volunteering with the farmworkers' movement. Now Villar became a field organizer for the United Teachers of Los Angeles (UTLA). There Villar became close to individuals who would later help him move into a political career. These figures included James M. Wood and Miguel Contreras, both executive treasurers of the Los Angeles County Federation of Labor, AFL-CIO.

During this period Villar was also president of the Los Angeles chapter of the American Civil Liberties Union and the American Federation of Government Employees.

INFLUENCES AND INSPIRATION

It is difficult to overstate the positive influence that Villaraigosa's mother, Natalia, had on her son's life. After enduring beatings from her husband, and then abandonment, Natalia insisted on raising her four children as normally as possible. She supported them by working as a secretary for the California Department of Transportation. She stocked the family's small duplex with classic books, read to her children often, and encouraged them to visit a nearby library after school until she arrived home from work. They couldn't visit the park, because it was ruled by gangs. She insisted on sending her children to Catholic school for a strict moral education. When her unsteady teenage son seemed in danger of wasting his life after being expelled from school, she handed him a letter that said, "You may have lost faith in yourself, but I will never lose faith in you." The rebellious Antonio was deeply touched. He studied at night classes, and against great odds finished college and became a major political leader—something of which Natalia, who died in 1991, would most certainly have been proud.

A new name and a new career

In 1987 Villar married Corina Raigosa, a Los Angeles schoolteacher, and combined their names to Villaraigosa. By this time Villaraigosa had begun to pursue his political aspirations and, in 1991, was given his first political post, on the Los Angeles Metropolitan Transportation Authority board. He was a rare voice on that panel, speaking on behalf of bus riders' rights.

In 1994 Villaraigosa was elected as a Democrat to the California State assembly from Los Angeles. Just four years later his fellow assemblymen voted him speaker of the Assembly, making him the first speaker from Los Angeles in 25 years. Villaraigosa became well known as a charismatic and effective political leader, as he successfully championed such landmark legislation as modernizing public schools, delivering health care to disadvantaged children, and banning assault weapons. He was unafraid to ruffle political feathers and proved a brilliant deal-maker, but with little concern for the details of policymaking.

Villaraigosa next returned to Los Angeles, his political home base. In 2001 he lost the citywide election for mayor by 8 percent in a run-off against fellow Democrat James Hahn. Embittered, he stayed out of politics for two years. Both his alma mater, UCLA, and the University of Southern California (USC) appointed him a distinguished fellow. In that role, he co-authored "After Sprawl," a study laying the groundwork for his future term as mayor.

In 2003 Villaraigosa defeated 14th District incumbent Nick Pacheco to become a member of the Los Angeles City Council. He was able to show constituents and the press his energy and hands-on leadership in solving urban problems. He repaired a flaw of his first mayoral campaign by adding more African Americans to his existing coalition of Hispanics, labor unions, and progressive whites. The strategy worked.

On May 17, 2005, Villaraigosa finally won the race for mayor, over the previous incumbent, James Hahn (58.7 percent to 41.3 percent), in a run-off election. Villaraigosa was sworn in as the 41st mayor of Los Angeles on July 1 of that year. As mayor of the nation's second-largest city, and the first Hispanic to hold that post in well over a century, Villaraigosa was instantly catapulted into the national spotlight. The mayor's ambitious agenda included a takeover of the city's public schools, an expanded police department, and completing a subway to the Pacific Ocean. His campaign slogan was "Si, se puede," which means "Yes, we can." The same mantra was used for decades by labor organizer César Chávez.

See also: Chávez, César

Further reading: "Mayor Shares Vision for L.A.," *Los Angeles Times*, Dec. 9, 2005, California section, Metro desk, part B, p.1 (overview of agenda).
http://www.lacity.org/mayor/bio1.htm (official Web site for Mayor's Office).

KEY DATES

1953	Born in Boyle Heights, Los Angeles, on January 23.
1977	Graduates from UCLA.
1994	Is elected as Democrat to California State Assembly.
1998	Takes up post of speaker of California State Assembly, the first speaker from Los Angeles in 25 years.
2005	Is elected as mayor of Los Angeles on May 17; he becomes the first Latino to hold the office since 1872.

VILLARREAL, José Antonio
Writer

The Mexican American author José Antonio Villarreal occupies an important place in the canon of Chicano literature, and is often called its founding father. In 1959 he published his coming-of-age novel, *Pocho*, which was to launch a whole new genre of novels.

Life in the fields

Villarreal was born in Los Angeles, California, in 1924 to itinerant Mexican farmworkers. His parents had arrived in the United States in 1921 in the wake of the Mexican Revolution. They traveled through California following the seasonal harvest and worked as casual farm laborers. Villarreal was one of 17 children, 12 of whom survived to adulthood. When he was young, he lived with his parents in tents pitched in the fields around the state. The family spoke only Spanish at home as their father forbade the speaking of English.

The Villarreal family did not settle until José was six. They moved to Santa Clara, California, where Villarreal attended elementary school. His first-grade teacher could not speak Spanish, so Villarreal had to learn English to communicate with her. By third grade, he was reading English so well that he was promoted to fourth grade and began writing stories and poems in English.

In 1942 Villarreal graduated from high school and entered the U.S. Navy. He saw action during World War II (1939–1945) in the Pacific theater. Villarreal left the Navy in 1945 and attended college on the GI Bill. Five years later, he graduated from the University of California at Berkeley with a bachelor's degree in English.

▲ *José Antonio Villarreal was one of the first Mexican American writers to achieve critical acclaim.*

During the 1950s Villarreal concentrated on family life. He had married Barbara Gentles in 1953, and their three children were born between 1954 and 1958. To provide for the family he worked a number of jobs, including as a technical editor and writer, a career that continued into the 1970s. The family moved between Mexico and the United States, and it was while in Mexico in 1956 that Villarreal

INFLUENCES AND INSPIRATION

From an early age, Villarreal knew he wanted to be a writer. Although he writes novels, Villarreal has always considered himself to be an oral storyteller. He credited his love of storytelling to his early upbringing in the fields of California.

During those early years, Villarreal was completely isolated from mainstream North American culture, living entirely among Mexicans. In the evenings, the workers would tell stories of their lives back home. Villarreal met new people continually, since every job only lasted a few weeks. Each night there was a steady supply of new stories.

In his own words, Villarreal said: "Long into the night I listened until I dropped off to sleep and my father would pick me up onto his lap as he continued to talk of the Revolution. Then off we would go to the next harvest, where new people would gather and there would be new tales to be told and heard. I knew when I was six years old that the one thing I most wanted from life was to be a storyteller."

KEY DATES

1924	Born in Los Angeles, California, on July 30.
1959	Publishes his first novel, *Pocho*.
1974	Publishes second novel, *The Fifth Horseman*.
1984	Publishes third novel, *Clemente Chacón*.
1994	Spanish translation of *Pocho* is published.

finished the novel *Pocho*, on which he had been working for some time. Villarreal did not find a publisher for the book until 1959.

Migrant's story

The novel tells the story of Richard Rubio and is largely autobiographical. Villarreal's experiences as the child of Mexican immigrants is reflected through the main character. Richard is caught between two cultures. His loyalty to his Mexican roots and culture is severely tested by his interest in and attraction to the country of his birth. The novel begins in Mexico as the revolution is drawing to a close, and follows Richard's father, Juan Rubio, as he moves to the United States. Juan Rubio is a typical product of a macho rural Mexican culture. Richard and his siblings represent a generation that is in transition and belongs in neither world. At the end of the novel, the family falls apart and Richard leaves to serve in World War II unsure if he will return.

Pocho is more than a story of a culture clash. It has been compared with Irishman James Joyce's *A Portrait of the Artist as a Young Man* (1916), which tells of the struggle of an artist to assert his freedom and individuality against the forces of conformity and tradition. In the introduction Villarreal acknowledges Joyce as a major literary influence, along with the U.S. writer William Faulkner (1897–1962).

Controversial subject

Villarreal took the name of his novel, *Pocho*, from a Mexican slang word. A pocho is a person born in the United States of Mexican parents. In Mexico it is used as a pejorative term. It implies that the person is uneducated and unsophisticated and has turned his back on his Mexican heritage in preference for gringo (Anglo) culture.

The word originally meant "discolored," and Villarreal chose it deliberately to contrast it with more neutral terms such as *mestizo* and *Chicano*. Chicano also originated as a negative term until the 1960s, when politically aware Mexican Americans began to apply it to themselves. In that way, they made the word a label for their cultural pride.

During the 1960s, Villarreal continued to work as a technical writer and editor, first in California and then in Boulder, Colorado. When *Pocho* was reissued in 1970, the book became highly controversial. The 1970 edition included an introduction by Hispanic American history professor Ramón Eduardo Ruiz that suggested the book had particular political and socioeconomic value.

The new edition led to considerable criticism from Chicano activists. Villarreal refused to see himself as a Chicano, and questioned whether Chicano literature existed as a body of work. He claimed that, like him, most Chicano writers were influenced by English-language works rather than those by Spanish writers. However much Villarreal disagreed with the growing Chicano movement, he was also very grateful to it. It was the reason his book had been rescued from obscurity. In 1980 another reprinting of *Pocho* dropped the introduction that paid tribute to Joyce.

Professional writer

Since 1971 Villarreal has taught at many different universities while still pursuing a career as a freelance writer. In 1973 he took Mexican citizenship, because he was spending more time in the country teaching at different institutions.

Villarreal also continued to write novels. In 1974, he published his second novel, *The Fifth Horseman: A Novel of the Mexican Revolution*. It went back in time and filled in the background to *Pocho*. Villarreal's intention was to show the events that led up to the Mexican Revolution of 1910, and why Richard Rubio's parents fled Mexico. His third novel, *Clemente Chacón* (1984), follows a young Mexican who has become a successful businessman in the United States. The events of the novel were set in El Paso, Texas, during a single day in September 1972. The three novels were intended to form parts of a tetralogy. However, the fourth and final installment has yet to be written.

In 1994, to coincide with Villarreal's 70th birthday, his publishers put out a Spanish translation of *Pocho*. Villarreal has continued to work as a freelance writer, but no new major work has appeared. However, his reputation in the Mexican American community is assured because of *Pocho*. As Ruiz stated in the 1970 introduction to the novel, Villarreal will always be an important Chicano literary figure because he was "the first man of Mexican parents to produce a novel about the millions of Mexicans who left their fatherland to settle in the United States."

Further reading: Villarreal, José Antonio. *Pocho*. New York, NY: Anchor Books, 1989.

http://www.scu.edu/diversity/jose.html (biography).

VILLARREAL, Luis
Scientist

Luis Perez Villarreal is a pioneering scientist in the fields of virology and biochemical research. A professor of molecular biology and biochemistry at the University of California, Irvine (UCI), Villareal is also director of the Center for Virus Research at UCI.

Committed to providing good science education to students, Villarreal established the "Bridges to the PhD Program," which enables talented students from California State University at Los Angeles to become postgraduate students at UCI. He also set up the Kids in Science program for elementary school students. Villarreal oversees part of the minority science program in the School of Biological Sciences, which aims to increase the number of underrepresented groups in biomedical research. In recognition of his work in the field, UCI created the Luis P. Villarreal Scholarship.

Early life
The youngest of four brothers, Villarreal was born in East Los Angeles, California. His mother and father met in northern Mexico during the 1930s, and moved to Los Angeles after the Great Depression. His father worked as a property developer. The job involved a lot of moving around, and the young Villarreal attended three different junior high schools and five different high schools.

▼ *Luis Villarreal wants young people to share his love of science. He has dedicated much of his time to providing accessible science education for students.*

KEY DATES	
1971	Receives degree from California State University at Los Angeles.
1976	Earns doctorate in virology from the University of California, San Diego.
1997	Wins SACNAS Distinguished Scientist award.
2003	Elected Fellow of the American Society of Microbiology.

An interest in science
Villarreal took an early interest in science and quickly realized he would like to pursue an academic career. After graduating from high school, he decided to attend the local community college before starting his degree in biochemistry at California State University at Los Angeles. He earned a bachelor of science degree in 1971. Funded by a Ford Foundation Fellowship, he earned his doctorate in virology from the University of California, San Diego, in 1976. He then won a two-year Helen Hay Whitney Postdoctoral Fellowship, which he undertook at Stanford University, working under the Nobel Laureate Paul Berg.

Achieving recognition
A talented scientist, Villarreal's research centers on the evolution of viruses and their use as vectors in gene therapy and for cancer treatment. He has also worked with federal agencies to develop defense systems against bioterrorism threats.

Villarreal has received several awards for his work and commitment to improving science education, including the prestigious Career Development Award from the National Institute of Health (NIH) and a National Science Foundation Presidential Award for mentoring. In 1997 he was honored with a Distinguished Alumnus Award by California State University. In that same year, Villarreal won a Distinguished Scientist award from the Society for Advancement of Chicanos and Native Americans (SACNAS). In June 2003 Villarreal was elected a fellow of the American Society of Microbiology.

Further reading: www.uvm.edu/~biology/Classes/011/alive.pdf (accessible discussion by Villarreal of the question: "Are Viruses Alive?").

VILLASEÑOR, Victor
Writer

A popular Chicano author, Victor Villaseñor is best known for *Rain of Gold*, published in 1991. The book is a sprawling, colorful account of his Mexican and Mexican American family history, including his parents' struggles with discrimination as they sought to make a new life for themselves in the United States. Villaseñor's direct style and compassionate, powerful portrayal of ordinary lives have helped bring the everyday experiences of Hispanic immigrants to a broad, mainstream audience.

Overcoming barriers

Victor Edmundo Villaseñor was born in 1940 in Carlsbad, California, where his immigrant parents owned a pool hall. Soon after his birth, his family moved to a ranch in nearby Oceanside, California, where Villaseñor was raised. Despite international success and a lifetime of travel, Villaseñor still lives on the land today.

Until the age of five Villaseñor spoke only Spanish. Like all Latinos of his age, he was forbidden from speaking Spanish at school. Even at that young age, Villaseñor felt a sense of anger and shame at this discrimination. The discrimination he suffered as a Latino was complicated by a severe form of dyslexia, which for a long time went undiagnosed. Eventually he dropped out of high school in his junior year, unable to read or write.

KEY DATES

1940 Born in Carlsbad, San Diego County, California, on May 11.

1959 Drops out of school and visits Mexico, where he begins to explore his Hispanic roots.

1973 Publishes first novel, *Macho!*

1991 Publishes *Rain of Gold*, an account of his family's history.

1992 Founds the peace movement Snow Goose Global Thanksgiving.

1997 *Wild Steps of Heaven* is published.

2002 Publishes *Thirteen Senses*.

2004 Publishes the autobiographical *Burro Genius*.

Discovering his roots

At the age of 19 Villaseñor went to stay with relatives in Mexico. There he became aware of the richness and vitality of Hispanic culture. Returning to the United States, he taught himself to read, immersed himself in both Spanish and English literature, and began to write.

His earliest novels and short stories, however, were all rejected by publishers, and it was not until 1973 that he was able to publish his first novel, *Macho!* This was the story of a young Mexican of Native American descent who moves to the United States. Other novels, short stories, and nonfiction books followed, but while they often received good reviews, none of them won Villaseñor popular or commercial success.

Popular success

In the mid-1970s Villaseñor began to collect family stories from relatives living in both California and Mexico. Over time he wove these histories together into a family narrative, eventually published as *Rain of Gold* in 1991. His mainstream publisher in New York City refused to publish the work as it stood, and Villaseñor resold the work, at a fraction of the original fee, to Arte Público—the Houston-based publisher of Hispanic American literature founded by academic and writer Nicolás Kanellos.

Rain of Gold proved to be the popular success that Villaseñor had dreamed of. It was followed by two other family epics—*Wild Steps of Heaven* (1997) and *Thirteen Senses* (2002). The latter was a tribute to his parents' long marriage. In 2004 he published *Burro Genius*, the first volume of an autobiographical trilogy, in which he writes movingly of his struggles at school. Of his motivation in becoming a writer, Villaseñor has written that he wanted to "supply to others the heroes I never had growing up. Heroes my children and other Latinos can be proud of."

In 1992 Villaseñor set up the Snow Goose Global Thanksgiving peace organization. This group campaigns for a secular international festival so all people from around the world can celebrate on the same day.

See also: Kanellos, Nicolás

Further reading: Villaseñor, Victor. *Burro Genius: A Memoir.* New York, NY: Rayo, 2004.
www.victorvillasenor.com (Villaseñor's Web site.)

VIRAMONTES, Helena Maria
Writer

Helena Maria Viramontes is an influential Latina writer. She is also an associate professor of English at Cornell University in Ithaca, New York.

Early life
Viramontes was born on February 26, 1954, in East Los Angeles, California. She was one of the nine children of a Chicano construction worker and a homemaker. After graduating from Garfield High School in Los Angeles, Viramontes went on to Immaculate Heart College. She graduated with a BA in English literature in 1975. Viramontes began writing short stories. In 1977 she won first prize in a literary contest sponsored by *Statement* magazine for her story "Requiem for the Poor." Viramontes also won the *Statement* prize in 1978 for the short story "The Broken Web." In 1979 she was awarded the fiction prize in the University of California at Irvine Chicano Literary Contest for the short story "Birthday."

In 1981 Viramontes enrolled in the University of California at Irvine's MFA creative writing program. She quit later that year but completed the program in 1994.

▼ *Viramontes's influences include the Hispanic authors Sandra Cisneros and Gabriel García Márquez.*

KEY DATES

1954   Born in East Los Angeles, California, on February 26.

1977   Wins *Statement* magazine's literary prize for "Requiem for the Poor."

1985   Publishes her first book, *The Moths and Other Stories*.

1995   Publishes *Under the Feet of Jesus*.

1996   Publishes *Their Dogs Came with Them*.

Into print
Viramontes published her first book, *The Moths and Other Stories*, in 1985. It contained the stories "The Moth" and "The Cariboo Café," which have since been anthologized in several collections of contemporary Chicana fiction. In 1993 Viramontes published her second collection of short stories, *Paris Rats in ELA*. Viramontes examines the difficulties that Latino and Latina immigrants face in the United States. She also addresses gender in Chicano society and the different roles that men and women are expected to fill.

In 1995 Viramontes published her first novel, *Under the Feet of Jesus*, a moving and powerful story that follows a young girl, Estrella, and her family of Chicano migrant workers. Using elements of the stream-of-consciousness writing style, Viramontes shows the reader the uncertain life of farmworkers. The novel's ending is pessimistic, and Estrella learns the painful lesson that, in the end, she must rely on herself if she is to survive. Viramontes's novel exposes the continuing yet often overlooked adversity present in current American agriculture. She dedicated the work to César Chávez, who battled valiantly to advance the rights of migrant workers. Viramontes's other work includes the novel *Their Dogs Came with Them* (1996).

See also: Chávez, César; Cisneros, Sandra

Further reading: Viramontes, Helena Maria. *Under the Feet of Jesus.* New York, NY: Penguin Books, 1995.
http://voices.cla.umn.edu/vg/Bios/entries/viramontes_helena_maria.html (Web site devoted to the artistic works of women of color).

WELCH, Raquel
Actor

In 1966, Raquel Welch appeared clad in an animal-fur skin bikini to promote the movie *One Million Years B.C.*, and a cultural icon was born. Of mixed Bolivian and Irish-American heritage, Welch remained a popular pin-up for many years. Welch has appeared in numerous films over the years, and although well known for playing light, comedic roles, she has also tackled more ambitious and experimental film projects. As a more mature actor, Welch has chosen to embrace her heritage, playing a wide range of Latina characters in such projects as *Tortilla Soup*. Welch also achieved success promoting a popular exercise regime and a range of wigs.

Early life

Born Jo-Raquel Tejada in Chicago, Illinois, on September 5, 1940, Welch traces her Hispanic roots to her father's side of the family. Armand Tejada, an engineer, was raised in La Paz, Bolivia, and immigrated to the United States. Welch and her younger brother and sister grew up on the West Coast. In an interview with the *The New York Times* in 2002, Welch recalled that her father refused to speak Spanish in the home because he wanted his children to grow up speaking perfect English.

Welch developed an early love for the performing arts. "I had memorized all Al Jolson's numbers by the time I was three," she recalled in an *ABC Film Review* interview. As she grew older, Welch sang in the church choir, studied ballet, and appeared in local dramatic productions. Her extreme good looks and fabulous figure also led Welch to enter beauty competitions in and around La Jolla.

In 1958 Welch married boyfriend James Welch, the first of her four husbands. The couple had a son and a daughter before their divorce in the mid-1960s.

Sex symbol

After a stint as a weather girl, Welch began to appear in light-hearted movies such as the Elvis Presley musical *Roustabout* (1964) and *A Swingin' Summer* (1965), a film that had the tag line "Spread Out the Beach Towels … Grab Your Gals … it's gonna be A SWINGIN' SUMMER!"

In 1965 Welch married her second husband, former child star and press agent Patrick Curtis, who helped launch her career. She supplemented her acting career by modeling, appearing in several European magazines. In 1966 her movie career began to take off. Welch appeared

▲ *After sporting an animal-fur bikini in* **One Million Years B.C.,** *Raquel Welch became a cultural icon of the 1970s.*

INFLUENCES AND INSPIRATION

Raquel Welch's career really began to take off in 1966, the year in which she turned from aspiring performer to cultural and sexual icon. Welch is probably best recognized as Loana, the cave woman in *One Million Years B.C.*, but some film commentators consider the science-fiction adventure *The Fantastic Voyage* of greater merit and influence.

The latter movie follows the adventures of a team of medical scientists on a high-tech submarine. They are shrunk, and injected into the bloodstream of a scientist in order to destroy his life-threatening blood clot. Once inside, they discover that the surgical laser rifle needed to destroy the clot has been sabotaged. Welch plays the attractive and intelligent assistant of Dr. Duval.

Although the science in the film is not very accurate, *The Fantastic Voyage* won an Academy Award for best visual effects. Particularly highly praised were the scenes that depicted scuba-diving surgeons battling white blood cells and tapping the lungs in order to replenish the patient's oxygen supply. The makers also found ample opportunity to promote Welch's appearance, notably in the scene in which she strips off to swim in a wetsuit in the dying man's bloodstream. Welch thus became a model of the beautiful and brainy movie heroine.

in several European movies, including the Italian sex comedy *La Fate*. Her big break came when she appeared in the movies *The Fantastic Voyage* (*see box*) and *One Million Years B.C.*

A prehistoric adventure made by Britain's legendary Hammer Studio, *One Million Years B.C.* follows caveman Tumak (John Richardson), cast out of the Rock tribe into the wilderness. He is taken in by the Shell tribe and meets the cave girl Loana (Welch). Featuring an army of animated dinosaurs devised by stop-motion special-effects man Ray Harryhausen, the film boasted that its story erupted on the screen with "volcanic excitement," and Welch's status similarly exploded with the release of publicity shots showing her in a skimpy cavewoman outfit, one of the best-known images in film history.

Welch's appearance as Lust in the comedy *Bedazzled* (1967) played on her image as a fantasy figure for men. In the following year Welch played her first Hispanic character in *Bandolero!*, as a Mexican woman spirited away by brothers James Stewart and Dean Martin.

KEY DATES

1940	Born in Chicago, Illinois, on September 5.
1966	Stars in *The Fantastic Voyage* and *One Million Years B.C.*
1970	Stars in *Myra Breckinridge*, opposite Mae West.
1995	Listed one of the 100 sexiest stars by *Empire* magazine.
2001	Cast as Hortensia in the film *Tortilla Soup.*
2002	Appears in the Latino TV series *American Family.*

Branching out

In the 1970s, Welch starred in a variety of films. She appeared in two adaptations of satirical novels, the first based on Terry Southern's *The Magic Christian,* along with Peter Sellers, Ringo Starr, and Richard Attenborough. She also took a lead role, opposite screen legends Mae West and John Huston, in *Myra Breckinridge* (1970), adapted from Gore Vidal's tale of a transsexual.

Welch appeared with Richard Burton in *Bluebeard* (1972) and Burt Reynolds in *Fuzz* (1972) before scoring a big hit, and winning a Golden Globe, with *The Three Musketeers* (1973), Richard Lester's entertaining adaptation of Alexandre Dumas's novel. She also appeared in the film's 1974 sequel.

Welch toured with her own nightclub show and began to take more challenging roles, playing, for example, a Native American woman in *The Legend of Walks Far Woman* (1979). She also appeared in popular TV shows such as *Spin City*. Welch also took on two Latina roles in quick succession, playing a fiery widow in the comical melodrama *Tortilla Soup* (2001) and joining a talented Latino ensemble for the TV series *American Family.*

In 2002, urged by her friend, the producer Moctesuma Esparza, Welch traveled to Bolivia to try to understand her Hispanic identity and culture.

See also: Esparza, Moctesuma

Further reading: Haining, Peter. *Raquel Welch.* New York, NY: St. Martin's Press, 1985.
http://www.hispaniconline.com/magazine/2003/april/CoverStory (interview with the star about her father and Latina roles).

WILLIAMS, William Carlos
Writer

A long with Walt Whitman, William Carlos Williams is considered one of the most distinctively American poets in U.S. history. Many critics regard Williams's experiments in his use of language with "the American grain" as the most sustained, and most successful, effort to speak in a uniquely American voice.

Early life

William Carlos Williams was born in 1883, in Rutherford, New Jersey. His father, William George, was a British immigrant who remained a British citizen all his life. His mother, Raquel Hélène Williams, was born in Puerto Rico. Williams was strongly influenced by his mother, familiarly called "Elena," especially her love of European culture (she had studied art for three years in Paris, France, as a young woman).

The Williams household was often filled with Elena's family visiting from Puerto Rico or Martinique. The Caribbean influence had an effect on the young poet, but Williams did not engage his Hispanic ancestry in his work except in occasional passing allusions. In later years, however, he has been considered increasingly within the context of Hispanic American writers.

Williams attended public school in Rutherford until 1897. His mother then took him and his brother to be schooled in Switzerland and France. After two years the family returned to the United States, and Williams attended Horace Mann High School in New York City. At Horace Mann, Williams began to show an aptitude for science as well as language. He began to write in his spare time.

Medical training

In 1902 Williams entered medical school at the University of Pennsylvania (Penn) in Philadelphia. Determined to become a doctor, Williams also continued his commitment to poetry and art. He formed an important friendship with the poet Ezra Pound at Penn, as well as with the poet Hilda Doolittle and the painter Charles Demuth. His relationships with these figures, along with his frequent trips to New York to experience that city's art scene, cemented Williams's decision to pursue his passion for poetry while establishing himself as a medical doctor.

After receiving his M.D. from Penn in 1906, Williams spent the next four years interning in New York as well as pursuing postgraduate studies in pediatrics at the

▲ *William Carlos Williams was a practicing doctor throughout his life. In his spare time he wrote award-winning poetry.*

University of Leipzig in Germany. He traveled in France, England, Spain, and the Netherlands. In 1910 Williams returned to his native Rutherford and established his own medical practice, which he maintained there until 1951.

Family life

In 1912 Williams married Florence "Flossie" Herman; the couple would produce two sons. Flossie would appear in many of Williams's finest poems over the years.

Williams's first book of poems, entitled simply *Poems*, appeared in 1909, but he first gained notice with "The Tempers," which Ezra Pound's London publisher Elkin Mathews brought out in 1913.

At the same time Williams established himself as a family doctor among his mostly middle-class community in Rutherford and its surrounding area. Over his 40 years as a doctor, Williams estimated that he had delivered more than 2,000 babies. Even as his writings began to

INFLUENCES AND INSPIRATION

At Horace Mann High School on Manhattan's Upper West Side, William Carlos Williams encountered a teacher, William Abbott, who introduced the young student to the poets who would most influence his own writing career: John Keats and, especially, Walt Whitman. In Whitman, Williams found a true American forefather who celebrated the nation in expansive poetic forms in a manner highly formative for the younger poet. While Whitman was perhaps the most important influence on his poetry, Williams did not forget the teacher who introduced him to these poets: Williams dedicated his *Selected Essays* (1954) to the memory of "Uncle Billy" Abbott.

Another important influence on Williams was his Puerto Rican mother. Elena Williams loved art and passed on that love to her son. Having studied art in Paris, she introduced Williams to the European art world while a young boy. Williams would continue to be heavily influenced by visual art through his entire writing career. Many have considered his precision with language, such as in the well-known "The Red Wheelbarrow," to be an extension of his highly developed visual sense.

Williams's mother lived in his Rutherford home from 1918 until her death in 1949 at the age of 102. Together they translated several Spanish- and French-language works. Williams's *Yes, Mrs. Williams* (1959) is the son's account of her life that contains passages in Elena's own voice.

gain him wider recognition, Williams's literary career was unknown to most of his patients, who saw him simply as a family doctor.

Fiction writer

Although thought of today primarily as a poet, during his own lifetime Williams was known as much for his fiction as for his poetry. He wrote a trilogy of novels—the Stecher trilogy—between 1937 and 1952, based on the lives of his wife's immigrant family.

Williams also drew on his experience as a doctor in several outstanding short stories. Many of them, such as "The Use of Force," have been widely anthologized. His autobiography, published in 1951, contains details of Williams's early life with his mother's Puerto Rican family.

KEY DATES	
1883	Born in Rutherford, New Jersey, on September 17.
1906	Receives M.D. from University of Pennsylvania.
1910	Establishes medical practice in Rutherford.
1912	Marries Florence Herman on December 12.
1951	Retires from medical practice and publishes his autobiography.
1958	*Paterson* first published in complete book form.
1962	*Pictures from Brueghel and Other Poems* is published, which wins the Pulitzer Prize.
1963	Dies in Rutherford, New Jersey, on March 4.

Poetry

As a poet, Williams remains one of the most innovative and important voices in U.S. literature. His experiments with American idioms and rhythms have resulted in such well-known poems as "This Is Just to Say" and the late work "Asphodel, That Greeny Flower," a long love poem to his wife that some critics regard as among the most beautiful poems in the language. Williams's commitment to American subjects and American speech patterns influenced countless subsequent poets into the 21st century.

Williams's masterpiece, *Paterson*, is a book-length poem that was originally published in five separate books from 1946 to 1958. In it, Williams presents a doctor and poet persona named Paterson, who also lives in the town of Paterson, a town near Rutherford. Paterson personifies Williams's preoccupation with language and dedication to everyday, ordinary detail. In *Paterson* appears the slogan often associated with Williams's poetic works, "No ideas but in things."

Williams's later years were complicated by illness, including a series of strokes that left him increasingly unable to work. He died in Rutherford on March 4, 1963. Later that year Williams was awarded a posthumous Pulitzer Prize in poetry for his *Pictures from Brueghel and Other Poems* (1962).

Further reading: Mariani, Paul. *William Carlos Williams: A New World Naked.* New York, NY: McGraw Hill, 1981.
http://www.english.uiuc.edu/maps/poets/s_z/williams/bio.htm (biography).

XIMENES, Vicente
Activist

Vicente Ximenes was an influential Chicano civil rights activist. He dedicated his life to improving the opportunities available to U.S. Latinos and Latinas.

Early life

Born on December 5, 1919, Ximenes was the son of José Jesus Ximenes and Herlinda Trevino. Raised in Floresville, Texas, Ximines went from a segregated elementary school to an integrated high school. He refused to attend his graduation ceremony in protest against the discrimination that Hispanic students had experienced at the school.

Ximenes went to work for the Civilian Conservation Corps (CCC), first as a field worker and later as chief clerk. By 1940 he had earned enough money to begin studying at the University of Texas at Austin, where he met Héctor P. García.

From war to the AGIF

After the United States entered World War II (1939–1945) in 1941, Ximenes joined the U.S. Air Force as a cadet in San Antonio, Texas. Promoted to bombardier on a B–17, he flew combat missions in North Africa and Italy and was awarded the Distinguished Flying Cross and Air Medal. In 1943 Ximenes instructed bombardier cadets at the San Angelo base in Texas. He retired four years later as a major.

Ximenes returned to study, earning a degree in economics in 1950 and a master's degree a year later. In 1952 he joined the American GI Forum (AGIF), the organization set up by his friend, Héctor P. García, in 1948. Ximenes organized new chapters in the Southwest, and eventually became the AGIF's national president.

▲ **Vicente Ximenes headed the Equal Employment Opportunity Commission between 1967 and 1972.**

Leading force

In the 1960s President Lyndon B. Johnson named Ximenes to several key posts. He was appointed chair of the president's Cabinet Committee on Mexican American Affairs (1967), and with García's support became the first Hispanic commissioner of the Equal Employment Opportunity Commission in 1967. He was also vice-president for field operations of the National Urban Coalition and helped improve housing for millions of Hispanics.

The recipient of several awards and honors, Ximenes received an honorary PhD from Highlands University of New Mexico in 1984. After his retirement Ximenes moved to New Mexico.

See also: García, Héctor P.

Further reading: http://utopia.utexas.edu/explore/latino/narratives/05Ximenes_Vincente.html (interview with Ximenes).

KEY DATES	
1919	Born in Floresville, Texas, on December 5.
1941	Becomes U.S. Air Corps cadet.
1947	Discharged from U.S. Air Corps with rank of major.
1950	Receives BA at University of Texas at Austin.
1952	Elected national president, American GI Forum.
1967	Becomes commissioner, Equal Employment Opportunity Commission (until 1972).

Y'BARBO, Antonio Gil
Colonizer

Antonio Gil Y'Barbo (also known as Ybarbo, Ibarvo, Ebarbo, Ibarbo, y Barvo, and y Barbo) was a lieutenant governor in colonial East Texas. He championed the rights of displaced settlers following colonial redistricting. He is best known as the founding father of Nacogdoches, Texas.

Early life
Y'Barbo was born in 1729 in Los Adaes, Louisiana, then the capital of Texas. Y'Barbo's parents, Mathieu Antonio and Juana, originally came from Andalusia in southern Spain. They settled in Los Adaes in 1725. Y'Barbo became a successful trader. He also built a ranch in Texas's present-day Sabine County, near the Louisiana border.

Resettlement
In 1763, the Treaty of Paris, signed by Great Britain, Spain, and France, ended the Seven Years' War and its American counterpart, the French and Indian War (both 1754–1763). France ceded Canada and its territory east of the Mississippi to Britain, and Spain gave up Florida to Britain. In 1764, King Carlos of Spain ordered a complete review of fortress locations in Texas. Six years later he ordered all missions and settlers in East Texas to relocate to the San Antonio area. The order ruined the lives of many Spanish settlers; they were forced to move hundreds of miles from their homes.

In 1773, Y'Barbo emerged as a champion of these displaced people's rights. He petitioned the Spanish government to allow settlers to return to their homes. In 1774 he negotiated with the Spanish government to resettle areas as far east as the Trinity River, where he founded a settlement called Bucareli. The settlers there had to endure much hardship, including flooding and attacks by local native peoples.

By 1779 Y'Barbo had been authorized to proceed even farther east. Early that year he led a group of settlers to Nuestra Senora de Guadalupe de los Nacogdoches (Our Lady of Guadalupe of the Nacogdoches), a Spanish mission that had been established in 1716. The group settled there: In the summer of 1779 Nacogdoches was granted the distinction of becoming a pueblo (town), the first in Texas.

Gateway to Texas
Y'Barbo parceled off land and granted it to settlers. He designed the town's street plan; he also established Nacogdoches's rules of governance. He built his home, a stone house known as Casa Piedras, or the Old Stone Fort, at the town's main intersection. His home served as a trading post and the location for town meetings, and became the center of Nacogdoches's government.

Nacogdoches was considered the gateway to the Texas frontier. Its location on the well-traveled Old San Antonio Road meant that it became a popular place for smugglers operating across state lines. The Spanish government appointed Y'Barbo lieutenant governor of the region and judge of contraband, in the hope that he might combat the smuggling problem. However, in 1790 Y'Barbo himself was accused of smuggling, although nothing was proved. He resigned as lieutenant governor later that year.

In 1802 Y'Barbo was forced to leave Nacogdoches (now the second largest settlement in Texas) in disgrace. After several years of trying to prove his innocence, Y'Barbo was finally cleared of all charges and he was allowed to return home to the town that he had established. In 1809 Y'Barbo died peacefully at the Rancho La Lucana on the Attoyac River. The Old Stone Fort is today a historical attraction, and Y'Barbo is recognized as the founding father of the oldest town in Texas.

Further reading: McDonald, Archie P. *The Old Stone Fort.* Austin, TX: Texas State Historical Association, 1981. http://www.tsha.utexas.edu/publications/journals/shq/online/v009/n2/article_1.html (*Southwestern Historical Quarterly* article on Y'Barbo).

KEY DATES	
1729	Born in Los Adaes, Louisiana (then capital of Texas).
1773	Becomes a champion of displaced settlers.
1774	Travels to the Trinity River, where he founds Bucareli.
1779	Founds the pueblo (town) of Nacogdoches, Texas.
1780s	Is appointed lieutenant governor of Texas.
1790	Resigns as lieutenant governor of Texas, after being accused of smuggling.
1809	Dies at the Rancho La Lucana, Texas.

YGLESIAS, José
Writer

José Yglesias was a bilingual writer of mixed Cuban and Spanish origin. In addition to his many novels, he also wrote four nonfiction books, as well as numerous reviews, articles, and short stories. Yglesias's work examined the experience of Hispanic Americans living in the United States.

Early life
Born in Ybor City, Florida, a Hispanic neighborhood of Tampa, in 1919, Yglesias was the son of a Spanish-born father and Cuban mother. His father had moved from his native Galicia, Spain, to Cuba, before immigrating to the United States.

From 1937 Yglesias worked in a variety of jobs, including as a dishwasher, stock clerk, assembly-line worker, and typist-correspondent. In 1942 Yglesias joined the U.S. Navy, serving in World War II (1939–1945). He received the Naval Citation of Merit.

Becoming a writer of some repute
At the end of the war, Yglesias returned to civilian life. Between 1948 and 1950, he was a film critic at the *Daily Worker* in New York. While he worked on his first novel, Yglesias earned a living as the assistant to the vice president of the pharmaceutical company Merck, Sharp, & Dohme International. He resigned in 1963, when his first novel, *A Wake in Ybor City*, was published.

From 1963 until his death in 1995 Yglesias was a prolific writer. In 1964 he traveled with his wife, the novelist Helen Bassine, and their son to Galicia, Spain. He wanted to discover more about his father, who had returned to live there before his own death. Yglesias's account of the journey appeared as *The Goodbye Land* (1967), excerpts of which were first published in the *New*

▲ *José Yglesias received several awards for his writing, including a National Endowment for the Arts fellowship and two Guggenheim fellowships.*

Yorker magazine. Critics praised the book and Yglesias's ability to convey the flavor of a remote region of Spain.

In his subsequent nonfiction and fiction, Yglesias explored the lives of individuals in Latin America. In 1967 he published *In the Fist of the Revolution*, a study of the Cuban Revolution and its effect on the lives of ordinary Cubans. *Down There* (1970) was a study of young revolutionaries in Brazil, Chile, Cuba, and Peru.

Yglesias's novels include *The Truth about Them* (1971), focusing on a Cuban American family settling in Florida. His 1987 novel *Home Again* (1987) looked at an elderly Cuban American returning to his family in Florida. He also published many articles and short stories in such publications as the *New Yorker* and the *New York Times*.

Yglesias died of cancer in New York in 1995. His work continues to be of interest to readers interested in the history and culture of ordinary Hispanic Americans. The Arte Público Press has reissued several of his novels.

Further reading: Yglesias, José. *Home Again.* Houston, TX: Arte Público Press, 2002.
www.britannica.com/eb/article-9112365 (short biography of José Yglesias).

KEY DATES	
1919	Born in Ybor City, Tampa, Florida, on November 29.
1942	Enlists in U.S. Navy.
1963	Publishes first novel, *A Wake in Ybor City*.
1995	Dies in New York City on November 7.
1996	Arte Público republishes his fiction, beginning with *Break-In*.

YZAGUIRRE, Raúl
Activist

Mexican American Raúl Yzaguirre is among the most prominent activists working for the economic, political, and social empowerment of Latinos in the United States. For more than 30 years—from 1974 to 2005—he served as director of the Washington, D.C.-based National Council of La Raza (NCLR), helping make it one of the United States's largest and most influential Hispanic civil rights and advocacy organizations. While Yzaguirre has addressed a broad range of problems affecting the Latino community during his career, he has been especially concerned with combating poverty and economic inequality. Yzaguirre later became director of the Center for Community Development and Civil Rights at Arizona State University in Phoenix.

Young activist

Yzaguirre was born in 1939 in San Juan, a small town in south Texas, close to the U.S. border with Mexico. At that time, Mexican Americans suffered routine discrimination, and many public services were segregated along racial lines. Yzaguirre began working as a civil rights activist as a teenager. When he was only 15 years old, he helped organize the first junior affiliate of the GI Forum, a key Chicano civil rights organization of the post-World War II period. Chapters of GI Forum Juniors were soon set up across Texas.

After graduating from high school in 1958, Yzaguirre enrolled in the U.S. Air Force. For the next four years, he was stationed at Andrews Air Force Base in Maryland. During his service he also studied part time at the

▲ *A tireless campaigner for Latino rights, Raúl Yzaguirre is an active marcher as well as an innovative administrator.*

INFLUENCES AND INSPIRATION

At the age of 13, Raúl Yzaguirre ran away from home and took a job on board a merchant ship working out of the Texas port of Corpus Christi. Like many other young Chicanos of the early 1950s, he felt a deep sense of alienation from his society and from the education system, both of which treated Mexican Americans as second-class citizens.

As he traveled from port to port, Yzaguirre often heard stories about the work of the Mexican American civil rights activist Héctor Pérez García and the organization he had founded in 1948, the GI Forum. García's high-profile assault on anti-Mexican racism made Yzaguirre conscious of how discrimination had impacted on his own life, and

showed him that something could be done about it, both at a personal level and through community action. Fired with enthusiasm, Yzaguirre returned to his hometown, reenrolled in high school, and helped set up the junior wing of the GI Forum. Running away from discrimination was not the answer, he realized; challenging it head-on was.

University of Maryland. After leaving the Air Force, he completed his bachelor's degree at George Washington University in Washington, D.C. In the U.S. capital, Yzaguirre became involved in the rapidly emerging Chicano civil rights movement. In 1964, he was one of the founding members of the National Organization for Mexican American Services (NOMAS), which offered support to Mexican American community groups.

Unified voice

During the 1960s, most such grassroots groups worked in isolation. Their lack of unity, together with a shortage of funding, often severely weakened their effectiveness. Unlike the African American civil rights movement, which enjoyed the support of nationwide organizations such as the National Association for the Advancement of Colored People (NAACP), Chicano groups could not look to a central organization either for technical support or to act as an advocate at national level. Yzaguirre and his fellow activists realized that, if there was to be progress in the struggle against discrimination, the movement needed a much larger and better-funded national body than NOMAS.

The NOMAS activists took their idea to the Ford Foundation, which in 1968 gave funding for the establishment of the Southwest Council of La Raza (SWCLR), with headquarters in Phoenix, Arizona. Initially, the organization focused its activities in the Southwest, but in 1973 it moved its headquarters to Washington, D.C., and changed its name to the National Council of La Raza (NCLR). However, the organization was still very small, and its future was constantly threatened by disagreements between its leaders. In 1974, NCLR director Henry Santiestevan stepped down, and the board selected Raúl Yzaguirre as the organization's new leader.

Strength of purpose

Over the following three decades, Yzaguirre's strong personality, commitment, and firm leadership enabled him to transform the NCLR into a truly national force. At the time of his appointment, the organization had a staff of just nine people, and a total budget of half a million dollars. By 1981, NCLR had funding approaching $5 million, employed almost 100 staff, and had affiliates in the majority of U.S. states. Yzaguirre's leadership proved especially crucial during the 1980s, when the administration of President Ronald Reagan cut the NCLR's federal funding, forcing the organization to downsize. By the 1990s, however, a drive for both private and corporate funding had enabled the organization to flourish once more. By the start of the 21st century, more than 300 NCLR affiliates were in operation.

KEY DATES	
1939	Born in San Juan, Texas, on July 22.
1968	Foundation of the Southwest Council of La Raza (SWCLR).
1974	Appointed president of the NCLR.
1993	Awarded the Order of the Aztec Eagle by the Mexican government.
2005	Retires as NCLR director; becomes professor at Arizona State University.

Yzaguirre expanded the NCLR's focus from purely Mexican American to "pan-Hispanic." During the 1960s and 1970s, Hispanic civil rights groups were largely confined within ethnic and geographical boundaries: Chicanos in the Southwest, Cuban Americans in the Southeast, and Puerto Ricans in the Northeast all operated independently. Yzaguirre believed that opposition to discrimination could be made much more effective through the creation of a united Hispanic front. That became official NCLR policy in 1979; five years later, representation of all the major Hispanic groups on the NCLR board was made obligatory.

Ongoing service

Yzaguirre's contribution to the development of the U.S. Hispanic community has received wide recognition. In 1979, he became the first Latino to receive a Rockefeller Public Service Award, while in 1993 he was awarded the Order of the Aztec Eagle, the highest honor given by the government of Mexico to noncitizens. In 1994, his national profile won him an appointment as chairman of President Bill Clinton's Advisory Commission on Educational Excellence for Hispanic Americans.

In 2005, Yzaguirre stepped down as director of the NCLR, a decision that was influenced in part by his diagnosis with early-stage Parkinson's disease. That same year, however, he joined the faculty of Arizona State University, where he was charged with the development of the university's links with the Hispanic community.

See also: García, Héctor P.

Further reading: McKay, Emily Gantz, and Raúl Yzaguirre. *The Forgotten Half: Two Thirds: An Hispanic Perspective on Apprenticeship, European Style: Report of the National Council of La Raza Consultation on Apprenticeship.* Washington, D.C.: National Council of La Raza, 1993.
www.nclr.org (NCLR Web site that includes work by Yzaguirre).

ZAMORA, Bernice
Poet

Bernice Zamora is a Latina poet whose first collection of verse, *Restless Serpents*, had a profound effect on Chicano literature. Her literary output has been small but significant.

Early life

Zamora was born Bernice Ortiz in Aguilar, Colorado, in 1938. Her family—of mixed Spanish and Taos Pueblo descent—had farmed around Aguilar for six generations, but in 1950 the deteriorating condition of the land forced her father to move the family to Pueblo, Colorado, where he worked as a coal miner. Throughout her childhood, the family insisted that only Spanish be spoken in the home; Bernice learned to write and speak English at high school in Pueblo. On graduating, she married a man named Zamora; they had two daughters, and Bernice stayed home to raise them.

Emerging art

In 1966, Bernice Zamora resumed her education, inspired by a female acquaintance who had eight children but studied philosophy at night school. Three years later, Zamora graduated from Southern Colorado University with a BA in French and English. She then commuted from Pueblo to Colorado State University in Fort Collins for two years while she studied for a master's degree.

On completing her MA in 1972, Zamora began work on a doctorate, which she was eventually awarded by Stanford University, California, in 1986. She made a particular study of the different ways in which literature was approached and represented in English and French. Among her major influences were the works of the mid-20th-century French existential philosophers, particularly Jean-Paul Sartre (1905–1980).

KEY DATES

1938	Born in Aguilar, Colorado, on January 20.
1976	Publishes seminal poetry collection, *Restless Serpents*.
1980	Becomes seriously ill.
1994	Publishes second poetry collection, *Releasing Serpents*.

Following the breakdown of her marriage in 1974, Zamora moved to California to study at Stanford. While there, she published *Restless Serpents*, a volume of her own poems, together with some by José Antonio Burciaga. Zamora's poetry examined Chicano cultural traditions, and particularly the experience of women. The power of poetry was also an important theme. Zamora's criticism of oppression, together with her nostalgia for the traditions and values of the barrio, were important in all the works. The book, initially published in a print run of just 2,000 copies, became a seminal text in Chicano poetry.

Growing reputation

Poems from *Restless Serpents* have been anthologized widely. Following the success of the volume, it was expected that Zamora would publish further works. However, she became seriously ill in 1980, and was unable to work for some time. She recovered slowly, and although she was eventually strong enough to resume her work, most of her subsequent poetry was written for private circulation rather than publication. She did not produce anything further in print until 1994.

That year saw the publication of *Releasing Serpents*, her second volume of poetry. The first part of the new volume was a reproduction of her *Restless Serpents* poems; the second half of the book comprised her post-1976 output. Many of the later works reexamined her earlier verse from the perspective of the 1990s.

Cultural impact

Bernice Zamora has been one of the least productive of modern poets, but the cultural impact of her work has been much greater than its volume. At a time when Latinas were underrepresented in U.S. literature, her poetry provided an eloquent expression of the complexity of the human condition as a whole and, particularly, of being a Chicana, an experience she describes as a "cultural limbo": neither Mexican nor American.

See also: Burciaga, José Antonio

Further reading: Zamora, Bernice. *Releasing Serpents*. Tempe, AZ: Bilingual Review Press, 1994.
www.voices.cla.umn.edu/vg/Bios/entries/zamora_bernice.html (biography).

ZAPATA, Carmen
Actress

Carmen Zapata is a leading actress and singer. She was born in 1927 in New York City, and raised in Spanish Harlem. Her parents spoke only Spanish at home.

Broadway to Hollywood

At age 18, Zapata won a part in a new Broadway production of the Rogers and Hammerstein musical *Oklahoma!* That role led to work in other plays and movies; in the meantime, she appeared as a stand-up comic in clubs and hotels. Her credits in film and television are extensive. Her longer-running series include the Public Broadcasting Service (PBS) children's show *Villa Allegre* (1973), *Viva Valdez* (1976), the daytime soap opera *Santa Barbara* (1984–1991), *Hagen* (1980), and *Fidel* (2002). Her feature film credits include *Boulevard Nights* (1979), *The Sleepy Time Gal* (2001), *Sister Act* (1992), *Sister Act II* (1993), and the remake of *A Streetcar Named Desire* (1995). On the Los Angeles Theatre Center stage, she starred in *The House of the Spirits* and *The House of Bernarda Alba*.

Teacher and producer

Having made her name as an actress, Zapata set up the Bilingual Foundation of the Arts, an organization devoted to training her fellow Latinas and Latinos in theater, television, and film. She produced more than 80 plays for the company, and helped establish a children's theater. Several of the foundation's shows went on tour to many parts of the United States and abroad.

Zapata taught theater and cinema arts, and lectured on the subject at colleges across the country. She also worked to make Spanish literature accessible to English speakers. Her most effective innovation in that area was the Outstanding Translations Program, which commissions English versions of classic Spanish plays and more recent

▲ **Carmen Zapata receives a star on the Hollywood Walk of Fame in 2003. She is also well known as a popularizer of Spanish literature in English translation.**

dramatic works from Latin America. Among numerous successes, the most memorable were translations of five plays by Federico Garcia Lorca (1898–1936), including *Yerma*, which won a Drama-Logue Award in 1980.

Later in her career, Zapata provided the voiceovers for several documentaries. Her narration of *Las Madres de la Plaza Mayo* (1985)—a study of the victims of the Argentine military dictatorship, directed by Susana Blaustein Muñoz and Lourdes Portillo—earned her a Grammy nomination.

Further reading: García Lorca, Federico, and Michael Dewell and Carmen Zapata (trans.). *Three Plays: Blood Wedding, Yerma, The House of Bernarda Alba*. New York, NY: Farrar, Straus, and Giroux, 1993.
http://www.bfatheatre.org/pages/program_folder/zapata_bio.htm (biography).

KEY DATES	
1927	Born in New York City on July 15.
1935	Appears in Broadway production of *Oklahoma!*; a range of stage and screen parts follow.
1985	Provides voiceover for documentary film *Las Madres de la Plaza Mayo*.
1992	Plays a nun in *Sister Act*, a movie starring Whoopi Goldberg.

ZARAGOZA, Ignacio
War Hero

Ignacio Seguín Zaragoza was a war hero and Mexican general. He died early at the age of 33. Zaragoza's achievements are still honored in the Mexican and Chicano communities on El Cinco de Mayo (May 5) (*see box on page 132*).

Early life
Born on March 24, 1829, in Bahía del Espíritu Santo (modern Goliad, Texas), Zaragoza was the son of Miguel G. Zaragoza and María de Jesús Seguín, who was related to the renowned politican Juan Seguín. Zaragoza's father was a commissioned officer in the Mexican army and he traveled constantly, leading him to be separated from his family for long periods of time. After the separation of Texas from Mexico in 1836, Zaragoza's father moved his family to the city of Monterrey in the state of Nuevo León.

Becoming a soldier
Zaragoza enrolled in the Seminario de Monterrey, but he showed very little interest in pursuing a religious career. He dropped out of the seminary when the family moved to the state of Zacatecas, where his father had a new military assignment. This geographic change gave Zaragoza the opportunity to experience at first hand the desperate state in which the majority of Mexicans lived. He also witnessed the strict discipline required of his father as a military man. Both observations instilled in Zaragoza a strong sense of patriotism. When the United States invaded Mexico in 1846, Zaragoza tried to enlist in the army but he was rejected.

After his father's death in 1851, Zaragoza became a sergeant in the militias that were being formed around the country to establish peace in local communities. When the militia was incorporated into the Mexican Army, he quickly rose through the ranks, becoming a captain.

A liberal and a patriot
Mexico's political situation in the 1850s was unstable. Antonio López de Santa Anna, whom many blamed for losing more than half of Mexico's territory to the United

◀ Ignacio Seguín Zaragoza was related to the Tejano hero Juan Seguín, who fought to help Texas gain independence from Mexico in the 1830s.

States in 1848, had returned to power as president of Mexico in 1853. He expelled several liberals from the country and alienated many Mexicans, including the liberal Zaragoza, by his oppressive policies.

In March 1854, the liberal general Juan Alvarez and other activists proclaimed the Plan de Ayutla, a manifesto calling for the overthrow of Santa Anna. Zaragoza supported the move. Santa Anna eventually fled into exile in 1854, and Alvarez became president, naming Benito Juárez as his minister of justice. In December 1855 Alvarez stepped down in favor of the moderate Ignacio Comonfort. Two years later Comonfort supported a new constitution that restricted the powers of the church. He also made Juárez minister of the interior and then chief justice of the Supreme Court, the person next in line to the presidency in the event of the president's death or removal from office.

The new constitution was not universally supported, however. Two distinct parties, the liberals and conservatives, emerged. The former supported a constitutional and democratic government, while the latter endorsed a monarchy influenced by the church and the military. Zaragoza sided with the liberals.

In December 1857, a right-wing general, Félix Zuloaga, led a coup in which Congress was dissolved. He deposed Comonfort, assuming the presidency. Juárez proclaimed himself president under the constitution, but the conservatives refused to recognize him. In 1858 Mexico was again plunged into conflict, the War of the Reform, which lasted three turbulent years.

A man of distinction
During the war Zaragoza distinguished himself in battle. In 1860 he was named commander of military forces at Guadalajara, and he succeeded in defeating the troops of Leandro Marquez. At the end of the year, serving as field marshal under Gonzalez Ortega, Zaragoza took part in the final battle of the War of the Reform at Calpulapan. After three years of intense fighting between the two factions,

LEGACY

War hero Ignacio Zaragoza's name lives on in Mexico and the United States: There are numerous schools in Mexico named after him, and many municipalities have plazas, streets, and stadiums that carry Zaragoza's name.

Zaragoza and the Mexican victory over the French at the Battle of Puebla on May 5, 1862, are honored by the holiday Cinco de Mayo (May 5).

When the French army began its advance on Mexico City in 1862, Zaragoza led the Mexican forces to stop them. His army was ill-equipped and was made up of about 5,000 Mestizo and Zapotec Indians. Despite this, Zaragoza and his forces defeated the French.

Although the Mexican army was eventually defeated, the Battle of Puebla symbolizes for many people, Mexican unity and patriotism.

In the United States, Cinco De Mayo is celebrated in most cities that have a high concentration of people of Mexican descent. More of a fiesta, Chicanos celebrate the day by having parades, mariachi music, and dancing. Many U.S. schools with a multicultural curriculum also celebrate Cinco de Mayo.

the constitutional army marched victoriously to Mexico City, reinstating Juárez as the legitimate president. Zaragoza was placed in charge of the troops during the occupation of the city.

On his return to the capital, Juárez began to try to stabilize Mexico. He expected the members of the conservative party to concede defeat and to allow the liberal party to implement the Reform Constitution of 1857. Juárez invited the rebels to join him in developing a government representative of all Mexicans. He expected that the conservatives would participate in the new government in good faith, but it was not to be.

On April 13, 1861, Juárez appointed Zaragoza secretary of war and the navy, an honor Juárez claimed that he deserved for his patriotism and heroism. Juárez himself was constitutionally elected president in June 1861. As soon as Zaragoza took up his new roles, he set about retraining the military. He reinstated the Military College to train officers and reorganized the medical corps. He also helped pass a law mandating military service for young men.

The war had left Mexico in severe financial difficulties. After several unsuccessful attempts to deal with the national debt, Juárez declared a two-year moratorium on debt payments to European countries. England, Spain, and France did not approve of the move, however, and took military action against Mexico to recover their debts.

French intervention

On November 21, 1861, Zaragoza resigned his position as secretary of war to become general in the Mexican military forces. The armies of Spain, France, and England landed at Vera Cruz and began making preparations to march on Mexico City. The Juárez government entered into negotiations with representatives of the European powers.

While Spain and England decided to withdraw their troops, on April 14, 1862, the French army began marching toward the Mexican capital. Zaragoza decided to meet the French army in the city of Puebla. On the morning of May 5, 1862, the Mexican army, led by Zaragoza, defeated the French. Following the victory, Zaragoza began to plan his next battle, but his health deteriorated rapidly. On September 8, 1862, at the age of 33, Zaragoza died of typhoid fever.

KEY DATES	
1829	Born in Bahía del Espíritu Santo, Texas, on March 24.
1853	Begins military career as a captain.
1857	Supports liberal Benito Juárez's claim to presidency.
1858	War of Reform begins.
1859	Promoted to general in War of Reform (1858–1861).
1861	Appointed secretary of war on April 13.
1861 July 17.	President Juárez suspends the national debt on July 17.
1861 November 21;	Resigns his position as secretary of war on November 21; reinstated as general in army.
1862	Defeats the French army on May 5 (Cinco de Mayo); dies at the age of 33 on September 8.

See also: Seguín, Juan N.

Further reading: http://www.presidiolabahia.org/zaragosa.htm (article on Zaragoza).

ZENO GANDÍA, Manuel
Writer, Politician

Manuel Zeno Gandía was a distinguished writer, physician, politician, and journalist. Born in Puerto Rico in 1855 and raised in the city of Arecibo, he later traveled to Spain, where he took a degree in medicine at Madrid Central University, and then completed his internship in France. During his medical studies, Zeno Gandía developed a passion for literature, and began writing poems and theater pieces. In 1876 he returned to Puerto Rico, where he established his own medical practice in the town of Ponce.

While practicing as a doctor, Zeno Gandía also wrote prolifically. He was the author of numerous critical studies of poetry, as well as chronicles of his European travels, and essays on a range of subjects including colonialism and the philosophy of science and medicine. In 1886 he was appointed editor of the *Revista de Puerto Rico*, a position he held until 1888. He also collaborated on other magazines, such as *Azucena* (1877), edited by Alejandro Tapia y Rivera, *Revista Puertorriqueña* (1877), edited by Manuel Fernández Juncos, *La Página* (1879), and *El Estudio* (1883). In addition, he became owner and editor of two newspapers: *La Correspondencia* (1890) and Ponce's *La Opinión* (1900–1901).

Puerto Rico independence movement
After the Spanish–American War of 1898 Zeno Gandía joined a group of political activists who attempted to convince U.S. president William McKinley that Puerto Ricans should be granted the right to decide their own political destiny. Although the lobbyists were powerful and influential—they included Eugenio María de Hostos and Julio J. Henna—the U.S. government rejected their proposals, and decided to give the island territory status rather than independence or statehood. Zeno Gandía was deeply disappointed by the decision, and consequently allied himself with Matienzo Cintrón, Rafael del Valle, and others to found the Union Party of Puerto Rico. Having been elected to the national assembly in 1902 as member for his native Arecibo, Zeno Gandía gave up his medical practice to concentrate on politics. He was a major influence in the creation of the Puerto Rican Independence Party.

Literary output
Throughout the period Zeno Gandía maintained a prolific literary output in verse and prose. He produced six volumes of poetry: *La señora Duquesa*, *La palmada*, *El microscopio*, *Tras de la tumba*, *La flor y el lodo*, and *Madrigal*. The work on which his posthumous reputation is based, however, was a sequence of five novels collectively entitled *Crónicas de un mundo enfermo*. The individual volumes were *La charca* (1894), *Garduña* (1896), *El negocio* (1922), and *Redentores* (1925). *La charca* has become a classic. It was the first Puerto Rican novel to describe the rough life in the rural coffee regions of the island and the difficulties that poor land workers encountered with their affluent landowners. In 1873 Zeno Gandía published in Madrid an important scientific work about the influence of climate on human illnesses.

Zeno Gandía was an outstanding linguist. In addition to his native Spanish he spoke fluent French, English, Italian, and Hebrew. During the final years of his life he became prominent as a lecturer on native Antillean prehistory and language. He also wrote a book on the subject, *Resumptia indoantillana*, but it remained unpublished at his death in 1930 at the age of 75. Today Manuel Zeno Gandía is widely commemorated in Puerto Rico, where avenues, a school, an industrial park, and a credit cooperative in Arecibo are all named for him.

KEY DATES

1855	Born in Arecibo, Puerto Rico, on January 10.
1886	Appointed editor of *Revista de Puerto Rico*.
1894	Publishes the Puerto Rican classic *La charca*.
1902	Is elected member of the Chamber of Representatives for his hometown Arecibo.
1930	Dies in Santurce, Puerto Rico, on January 30.

See also: Hostos, Eugenio María de; Juncos, Manuel Fernández; Tapia y Rivera, Alejandro

---

Further reading: Rivera de Álvarez, Josefina. *Diccionario de literatura puertorriqueña* (Dictionary of Puerto Rican Literature). San Juan, Puerto Rico: Instituto de Cultura Puertorriqueña, 1985.

ZÚÑIGA, Martha
Biologist

Martha Zúñiga is a distinguished Mexican American biologist who specializes in the fields of immunology and virology.

Early life

The second of 10 children, Martha Cecilia Zúñiga was born in 1950 in Laredo, Texas. Her early interest in mathematics and science was originally inspired by a school visit from NASA education officers, and later encouraged by her parents. Zúñiga traces her particular interest in biology to an event that took place when she was 11. One day, her father, who hunted wild rabbit for meat, killed a pregnant female, and she became fascinated by the perfectly formed fetuses inside the animal's uterus.

When Zúñiga was 16, she attended a National Science Foundation summer program at Loyola University in New Orleans, Louisiana. After high school, she went to the

▼ *The work of Martha Zúñiga has contributed greatly to medical research; her life has been an example to other Mexican American scientists.*

KEY DATES	
1950	Born in Laredo, Texas.
1968	Attends the University of St. Thomas, Houston, Texas.
1975	Receives master's degree in biology from Yale University.
1977	Receives doctorate from Yale.
1989	Receives Presidential Young Investigator Award.
1990	Joins University of California, Santa Cruz
2004	Begins service as lecturer for Sigma Xi.

University of St. Thomas, Houston, on a scholarship, and then moved to the University of Texas at Austin. She graduated with a BA in zoology, and decided to pursue postgraduate studies in biology rather than attend medical school, as her parents had hoped. With funding from a Ford Foundation Fellowship, Zúñiga accepted a place in the PhD program at Yale University. She earned a master's degree in 1975 and a doctorate in 1977. She then attended Yale University School of Medicine, before completing her postdoctoral training at the California Institute of Technology (Caltech).

Career in California

In 1989, Zúñiga won the Presidential Young Investigator Award. A year later, she joined the University of California, Santa Cruz, as professor of molecular, cell, and developmental biology. Her research examines the ways in which bacteria and viruses interact with the immune system, and how those interactions can be modified and used to treat autoimmune diseases, cancer, and organ transplant rejection. Zúñiga also teaches undergraduate and graduate courses in immunology, virology, and advanced cell biology.

Zúñiga has been acknowledged by the science and engineering honors society Sigma Xi, serving as a distinguished lecturer between 2004 and 2006. She is also an active member of the Society for Advancement of Chicanos and Native Americans (SACNAS).

Further reading: http://www.sacnas.org/beta/pdf/zuniga_martha_H.pdf (brief autobiography on the SACNAS Web site).

SET INDEX

Volume numbers are in **bold** type. Page numbers in *italics* refer to captions.

A

9/11 attacks *see* September 11th terrorist attacks
10 Years' War, Fernández Cavada and **3**:*112*
20/20 (news program) **8**:89
21 Grams (film) **3**:46
500 Years of Chicano History in Pictures (book) **5**:69
"Abaniquito" (song) **6**:39
Abbott, William **8**:123
Abraxas (album) **7**:120
Abu Ghraib Prison torture scandal **4**:42, **7**:113
acculturation **1**:79–82
Acevedo-Vilá, Aníbal **1**:*4*
Acosta, José Julián **1**:5
Acosta, Juan **1**:6
Acosta, Oscar Zeta **1**:*7–8*
activism **1**:9–14
actos **1**:10
Acuña, Rodolfo **1**:15, **6**:48
Ada, Alma Flor **1**:*16*
Adolfo **1**:*17*
advocacy groups **8**:46
Advocates, The **6**:107
affirmative action **8**:34
Affleck, Ben **5**:39
Agreda, María de Jesús de **3**:25; **7**:34
AFL-CIO, Linda Chavez-Thompson and **2**:96–97
Afro-Cuban Jazz Moods (album) **6**:77
Afro-Cuban Jazz Suite, The (album) **6**:77
Afro-Cubans, The **5**:*50*, 51
Agosín, Marjorie **1**:*18*
Agricultural Labor Relations Act (ALRA; 1975) **5**:13
Agricultural Workers Organizing Committee (AWOC) **5**:13
agriculture and migrant labor **1**:*19–24*
   see also labor organizations
Aguilera, Christina **1**:25, 129–130, **4**:105, **6**:35
Airto **1**:*26*
Alamo, the **3**:24, **7**:133, 134, **8**:*42–43*, 48, 80
Alamo, The (film) **3**:*11*
Alarcón, Francisco X. **1**:*27*
Alarcón, Martín de **3**:23–24
Alba, Jessica **1**:*28*
Albino, Johnny **1**:*29*
Albita (Albita Rodríguez) **7**:*51*
Albizu, Olga **1**:*30*
Albizu Campos, Pedro **1**:*31–32*, **2**:109, **5**:23, 24, **8**:16
Alcalá, Kathleen **1**:*33*
Alcaraz, Lalo **1**:*34–35*
Alegría, Fernando **1**:*36*
Alers, Rafael **1**:6
Alfaro, Luis **1**:*37*
Algarín, Miguel **1**:*38–39*
Alianza Americana **6**:42
Alianza Federal de Mercédes (Federal Land Grant Alliance) **1**:12, **2**:108, **6**:*125–126*, **8**:59

Alianza Federal de Pueblos Libres (Federal Alliance of Free Towns) **8**:60
Alien Registration Act (Smith Act; 1940) **5**:98–99
Allende, Isabel **1**:*40–41*
Allende, Salvador **3**:77
almanaques **4**:109
Almaraz, Carlos **1**:*42*
Almeida, Santiago **5**:78, **6**:37, **8**:49
Alomar, Roberto **1**:*43*
Alonso, Alicia **1**:*44–45*
Alou, Felipe **1**:46
altarcitos **7**:37
Alurista **1**:*47–48*, **4**:49
Alvarado, Juan Bautista **1**:*49–50*, 100, **2**:69–70
Alvarado, Linda **1**:*51*
Alvarado, Pablo **1**:*52*
Alvarez, Julia **1**:*53*
Alvarez, Luis Walter **1**:*54–55*
Alvarez, Paulina **3**:13
Alvárez de Piñeda, Alonso **1**:*56*
Alvariño de Leira, Angeles **1**:*57*
American Civil Liberties Union (ACLU), Anthony D. Romero and **7**:*78–79*
American Communist Party (ACP), leaders on trial (1949) **5**:98–99
American Educator (magazine) **2**:95
American Family (TV series) **6**:*46–47*
American Federation of Labor (AFL) **5**:9–10
   see also AFL-CIO
American GI Forum (AGIF) **1**:11, *12*, **4**:10, 11, **5**:113, **6**:*42*, 43, **8**:32
   Raúl Yzaguirre and **8**:127
American Revolution
   Bernardo de Gálvez and **3**:*134*
   Esteban Rodríguez Miró and **5**:119
Amor Prohibido (album) **8**:5
Anaya, Rudolfo Alfonso **1**:*58–59*, **2**:91, **4**:103
Anaya, Toney **1**:*60*
Angelico, Fray *see* Chávez, Angélico
Anguiano, Lupe **1**:*61*
Anthony, Marc *see* Marc Anthony
Antonio Maceo Brigade **2**:56
Anzaldúa, Gloria Evangelina **1**:14, *62*, **6**:10
Aparicio, Luis **1**:*63*
Apodaca, Jerry **1**:*64*
Aponte-Martínez, Luis **1**:*65*
Arana, Marie **1**:*66*
Archuleta, Diego **1**:*67*
"Ardillitas, Las" **4**:*71*
Arenas, Reinaldo **1**:*68*
Areu, José **6**:59
Arias, Ron **1**:*69*
Arista, Mariano **8**:44
Arizona, and bilingual education **5**:92
Armes, Jay J. **1**:*70*
Armstrong, Louis **1**:113
Arnaz, Desi **1**:*71–72*, **4**:98, 106, *107*, 108–109, **6**:38

Arnaz, Desi, Jr. **1**:*73*
Arpa School of Painting **4**:64
Arrau, Claudio **1**:*74–75*
Arreguín, Alfredo **1**:*76*
Arrillaga, Mariano Paredes y **8**:43
Arriola, Gus **1**:35
Arroyo, Martina **1**:*77*
Arvizu, Steven **1**:*78*
Asco (art group) **4**:4
Asociación Nacional Mexico-Americana (ANMA) **2**:108, 127
Asociación Protectora de Madres **4**:87
Aspira **6**:101
assimilation **1**:*79–82*
   José T. Canales and **2**:32
Astaire, Fred **4**:80
At War with Diversity (book) **1**:129
atomic particles **4**:12
Atracciones Noloesca **6**:59
Austin, Moses **7**:132
Austin, Stephen Fuller **8**:24, 42
Autobiography of a Brown Buffalo (book) **1**:8
Avila, Carlos **1**:*83*
Avila, Marcus **7**:127
Ayala, Francisco J. **1**:*84*
Azpiazu, Don **1**:*85*
Azteca (group) **3**:88
Aztecs, music **6**:35
Aztec people **4**:107
Aztlán **1**:13, 47
Aztlán: Chicano Journal of the Social Sciences and Arts **4**:40

B

Baca, Elfego **1**:*86*
Baca, Jimmy Santiago **1**:*87–88*
Baca, Judith Francisca **1**:*89–90*, **4**:38
Baca, Polly **1**:*91*
Badillo, Herman **1**:*92*
Baez, Joan **1**:*93–94*, **4**:107
baianas **5**:118
Baird, Lourdes G. **1**:95
Bakhunin, Mikhail **3**:125
Bakke case **8**:34
Balboa, Marcelo **1**:*96*
"Ballad of Gregorio Cortez" (song) **2**:9
Ballad of Gregorio Cortez, The (film) **6**:81
Ball, Lucille **1**:*71*, 72, 73, **4**:*107*, 108–109
Balmaseda, Liz **1**:*97*
Baloyra, Enrique A. **1**:*98*
Bamba, La (album) **5**:46
Bamba, La (film) **8**:82, 84
"Bamba, La" (song) **6**:38, **8**:*83*, 84
Banderos, Antonio **4**:98
Bandini, José **1**:*99*, 100
Bandini, Juan **1**:*99–100*
Bañuelos, Ramona Acosta **1**:*101*, **6**:87
Barceló, Antonio R. **6**:30
Barceló, María Gertrudes **1**:*102*
Barela, Casimiro **1**:*103–104*
Barela, Patrocino **1**:*105*
Barenboim, Enrique **7**:129

Barkley, David Bennes **1**:*106*, **5**:112
Barraza, Santa **1**:*107*
Barrera, Aida **1**:*108*
Barretto, Ray **1**:*109*, 132, **6**:38, 39
barrios **3**:74
Barrymore, Drew **3**:60
Batista, Tomás **1**:*110*
Batiz, Xavier **7**:121
Bautista de Anza, Juan **1**:111
Bauzá, Mario **1**:*112–113*, **5**:50, **6**:38
Bay of Pigs crisis **4**:122, **5**:88
Bazar, Philip **5**:112
Bazooka: the Battles of Wilfredo Gomez (documentary) **4**:37
Bear Flag Republic **2**:70
Beaubien, Carlos **1**:*114*
Beltran, Carlos **5**:115
Benavides, Alonso de **3**:25
Benavides, Cristóbal **1**:*115*
Benavides, Placido **1**:116
Benavides, Refugio **1**:115, *117*
Benavidez, Roy P. **1**:*118*
Benes, Bernardo **1**:119
Benítez, John "Jellybean" **1**:*120*
Benítez, José Gautier **1**:121
Benítez, Sandra **1**:*122*
Benítez, Wilfred **1**:*123*, **6**:100
Bennett, William **5**:71
Berrios, Steve **1**:*124*
Bert, Guillermo **1**:*125*
big bands **6**:38
Big Pun **1**:*126*, **3**:102, **4**:107, **6**:40
bilingualism **1**:*127–130*, **3**:72–73
   Bilingual Education Act (1968) **1**:128
   Carrascolendas (TV series) and **1**:*108*
   code switching **3**:28
Biltmore Six **1**:*7–8*
Birth of a City (mural) **7**:74
Bithorn, Hiram **1**:*131*
Blades, Rubén **1**:*132–133*, **2**:120
Bless Me, Ultima (book) **1**:58, 59, **4**:50
blowouts, in Los Angeles (1968) **3**:90, **4**:4
Bobo, Eric **3**:20
Bocanegra, Carlos **1**:*134*
Bohemia (magazine) **7**:127
boleros **5**:130
   Daniel Santos and **7**:*125*
Bonilla, Tony **2**:*4*
boogaloo **3**:16
border, Mexico-United States **2**:*5–10*, **8**:*46*
   Catarino E. Garza and **4**:22
   cross-border trade **2**:9
   culture **2**:9–10
   illegal immigration across **2**:8–9, **8**:27
   maquiladoras **2**:9, *10*
   suspicious deaths of women along **4**:25, **5**:39
   twin cities **2**:8
Border Arts Workshop/Taller de Arte Fronterizo (BAW/TAF) **6**:75
Border Incident (film) **5**:131
Border Industrialization Program (BIP) **1**:23

Set Index

Border Protection, Antiterrorism, and Illegal Immigration Control Act, amendment (2005) **8**:105
Border Realities (mural) **6**:75
Bordertown (film) **4**:132, **5**:39
Bori, Lucrezia **2**:11
"Borinqueña, La" (song) **5**:4, **7**:73
Borinqueneers **5**:114
Botero, Fernando **2**:12
Botiller v. Dominguez (1899) **8**:32
boveda catalan **4**:68
Boy Without a Flag, The (book) **7**:50
Bracero Experience: Elitelore Versus Folklore, The (book) **4**:96
Bracero Program **1**:21–23, **2**:8, 107, **3**:72, 130, **4**:121, **5**:13, **6**:44, **8**:27, 46
Brando, Marlon **8**:12
Brandon, Jorge **6**:119
Briseno, Rolando **2**:13
Bronx Remembered, El (book) **5**:121
Brooks, Gwendolyn **2**:104
Brown, Lee **5**:71
"browning of the Midwest" **1**:24
Brown v. Board of Education (1954) **2**:106, 107, **6**:126–127
"Bruca Manigua" (song) **7**:54
Buffalo Nickel (book) **7**:98
bugalu **3**:16
Bujones, Fernando **2**:14–15
Bulge, Battle of the **5**:40
Bullock, Sandra **5**:36
Burciaga, José Antonio **2**:16
Bush, George H.W.
   and drug czars **5**:70, 71
   and Lauro F. Cavazos **2**:73–74
Bush, George W.
   Alberto Gonzales and **4**:41–42
   Rosario Marin and **5**:60
Bustamante, Cruz **2**:17

C

Caballero (book) **4**:56
Cabana, Robert Donald **2**:18
Cabeza de Baca, Ezekiel **2**:19
Cabeza de Baca, Fabiola **2**:20
Cabrera, Lydia **2**:21
Caesar, Sid **2**:114, 115
Cahuenga, Treaty of (1847) **6**:116
Cahuenga Pass, Second Battle of **2**:70
Calderón, Alberto **2**:22
Calderón, Gilberto Miguel (Joe Cuba) **3**:16
Calderón, Sila María **1**:4, **2**:23–24
Calendar of Dust (book) **7**:95
calendars **4**:109
California
   affirmative action in **8**:34
   bandits (1800s) **3**:120
   Gold Rush **8**:26
   language **1**:129, **5**:92
   Mariano Guadalupe Vallejo and **8**:88
   Proposition 187 (1994) **4**:82, **6**:58
   Proposition 227 (1998) **8**:33
   state prison **5**:123
   transfer from Mexico to the United States **6**:116, 117

Treaty of Guadalupe Hidalgo and **4**:66
Calleros, Cleofas **2**:25
caló **4**:70
Calvillo, María Del Carmen **2**:26
Camacho, Héctor **2**:27–28
Camillo, Marvin **6**:122
Campaign 3 P.M. **7**:53
Campeche y Jordán, José **2**:29, **7**:49, 74
Campos, Juan Morel **2**:30
Canales, José T. **2**:31–32
Canales, Laura **2**:33, **8**:5
Canales, Nemesio **2**:34
"Canción de invierno" (elegy) **6**:9
"Canción Mexicana" (song) **4**:70, 71
cancións (songs) **6**:36
"Candida" (song) **6**:85
Canícula (book) **2**:37
Cannery and Agricultural Workers Industrial Union (CAWIU) **5**:11
Canseco, Jose **2**:35
Cansino, Rita *see* Hayworth, Rita
Cantor, Andrés **2**:36
Canto y Grito Mi Liberacíon (book) **7**:111
Cantú, Norma Elia **2**:37
Capetillo, Luisa **2**:38
Capirotada (book) **7**:43
Capital Punishment (album) **4**:107
Capobianco, Tito **2**:40
Capó, Bobby **2**:39
Cara, Irene **2**:41
CARA–Chicano Art: Resistance and Affirmation (exhibition) **6**:6, 75
Caramelo (book) **2**:104
Caras Viejas y Vino Nuevo (book) **6**:12
"Caravan" (song) **8**:61
Carbajal, José Maria Jesús **1**:116, **2**:42, **3**:6
Carbajal, Michael **2**:43
Carew, Rod **2**:44
Carey, Mariah **2**:45–46
Carlito's Way (book and film) **8**:63
Carmona, Richard H. **2**:47–48
Carollo, Joe **8**:30
Carpenter, John **7**:72
Carranza, Venustiano **7**:26
Carrasco, Barbara **2**:50
Carrascolendas (TV series) **1**:108
Carrera, Barbara **2**:51
Carreta, La (play) **5**:62
Carreta Made a U-Turn, La (poetry) **5**:19
Carrillo, Elpidia **2**:52
Carrillo, Leo **2**:53
Carrillo, Leopoldo **2**:54
Carr, Vikki **2**:49
Cartéles (magazine) **7**:127
Carter, Lynda **2**:55, **4**:80
Caruso, Enrico **3**:18
CASA (Centro de Acción Social Autónoma) **6**:9
Casal, Lourdes **2**:56
Casals, Jordi **2**:57
Casals, Pablo **2**:58
Casals, Rosemary **2**:59
Casares, Oscar **2**:60
Casas, Juan Bautista de las **2**:61
Casas Revolt **2**:61, **7**:132
Casino de la Playa band **7**:54
Castaneda, Carlos **2**:62–63

Castañeda, Carlos Eduardo **2**:64–65
Castillo, Ana **2**:66
Castillo, Leonel **2**:67
Castro, Fidel **1**:119, **2**:110, **4**:122, **7**:37
   Daniel Santos and **7**:125
   and the Elián González case **4**:123
   and Jorge Mas Canosa **5**:88
   and José Martí **5**:64
Castro, George **2**:68
Castro, José **2**:69–70
Castro, Raúl **2**:71
Catholicism **7**:33–38
   mariachi masses **6**:36
   María Elena Durazo and **3**:82
   Virgilio Elizondo and **3**:84
Caucasian Race Resolution, of Texas **8**:47
Cavazos, Bobby **2**:72
Cavazos, Lauro F. **2**:73–74, 75
Cavazos, Richard E. **2**:75–76, **5**:113
Center for Latino Educational Excellence (CLEE) **7**:47
Centro de Arte Puertorriqueño **7**:85
Cepeda, Orlando **2**:77
Cerro Maravilla incident **7**:83
Cervantes, Lorna Dee **2**:78
Cesar Pelli Associates **6**:106
Chacón, Eusebio **2**:79
Chacón, Felipe Maximiliano **2**:80
Chacón, Iris **2**:81
Chagoya, Enrique **2**:82
Chang-Díaz, Franklin R. **2**:83
Chapa, Francisco A. **2**:84, **3**:14
Chaplin, Charlie **3**:17
Charanga Duboney **6**:98
Charca, La (book) **8**:133
Charlie Brown TV animations **5**:101
Chata, La (La Chata Noloesca) **6**:59
Chaves, J. Francisco **2**:85
Chaves, Manuel Antonio **5**:112
Chávez, Angélico **2**:86–87
Chávez, César **1**:12, 81, **2**:88–89, 108, 121, **6**:44, 124, **8**:81
   and the Delano grape strike **5**:12
   Dolores Huerta and **4**:113, 114
   holiday devoted to **5**:14
   Maria Hinojosa and **4**:99
Chávez, Denise **2**:90–91
Chavez, Dennis **1**:60, **2**:92–93, **6**:7
Chavez, Julio Cesar **3**:32
Chavez, Julz **2**:94
Chavez, Linda **2**:95
Chávez, Thomas E. **2**:87
Chávez Fernández, Alicia **4**:113, 114
Chavez Ravine (play) **4**:71
Chavez-Thompson, Linda **2**:96–97
Cheech and Chong **5**:57–58
Chicanismo (film) **1**:37
Chicano (book) **8**:93
Chicano Art: Resistance and Affirmation *see* CARA
Chicano moratorium **7**:100
Chicano movement **1**:81, **2**:108–109, **4**:104–105, 106, 109, **6**:125–126
   Bert Corona and **2**:127
   bilingual newsletters **5**:93

Corky Gonzales and **4**:49
Gloria Molina and **5**:122
Luis Omar Salinas and **7**:101
Mario Compeán and **2**:121
Martha P. Cotera and **3**:10
Oscar Zeta Acosta and **1**:7–8
Réies López Tijerina and **8**:59, 60
Rodolfo Acuña and **1**:15
Chicanos
   meaning of the term **1**:15
   muralists **1**:89–90, **4**:65, 83, 109
   theater **4**:115
Chicano studies **1**:9–10, 13, 59, **6**:48
   international conference on **4**:96
Chico and the Man (TV series) **7**:13
Chicxulub crater **6**:70
"Child of the Americas" (poem) **5**:27
Chinese Exclusion Act (1882) **4**:120
CHiPs (TV series) **3**:98
Chong, Tommy **5**:57–58
Christian, Linda **2**:98
Chulas Fronteras (documentary) **4**:130
Cibola, Seven Cities of **2**:129–130, **3**:49–50
"Cierra los Ojos" (song) **5**:129
Cinco de Mayo holiday **8**:131, 132
Cintrón, Nitza Margarita **2**:99
Cisneros, Evelyn **2**:100
Cisneros, Henry G. **2**:101–102
Cisneros, Sandra **2**:103–104
Ciudad Juarez murders **5**:39
civil rights **2**:105–110, **6**:42–43
   see also Chicano movement
Civil Rights Act (1964) **2**:107
Civil War **5**:111–112
   Cristóbal Benavides and **1**:115
   Fernández Cavada and **3**:112
   Francisco J. Chaves and **2**:85
   Loreta Janeta Velazquez and **8**:103
   Refugio Benavides and **1**:117
   Texas in **8**:45
Clark, Ellen Riojas **2**:111
Clark, Georgia Neece **6**:87
Clemente, Roberto **2**:112–113, **8**:19
Clinton, Bill **6**:45
   and Bill Richardson **7**:42
   and Federico Peña **6**:110
Clooney, Rosemary **3**:116, 117
Coca, Imogene **2**:114–115
Codex Delilah: a Journey from México to Chicana (artwork) **6**:5
Coca-Cola Company, Roberta Goizueta and **4**:30–31
Colmenares, Margarita **2**:116
colonias **8**:26
Colón, Jesús **2**:117, **8**:98
Colón, Miriam **2**:118
Colón, Willie **1**:132–133, **2**:119–120, **5**:20, 51
Colquitt, Oscar B. **2**:84
comancheros **8**:35
Combs, Sean "Puff Daddy" **5**:38, 39
Coming Home Alive (book) **5**:27
Coming of the Night, The (book) **7**:32

Comisión Femenil Nacional (CFMN) **5**:122
Comité, El **6**:128
communism, trial of American Communist Party leaders **5**:98–99
Community Service Organization (CSO)
  César Chávez and **2**:89
  Dolores Huerta and **4**:113
Comonfort, Ignacio **8**:131
Compeán, Mario **2**:*121*
Confederación de Uniones Oberos Mexicanos (CUOM) **1**:21, **2**:106
conga, the **1**:72
Congreso de Pueblos que Hablan Español, El **6**:21
Congress of Industrial Organizations (CIO) **5**:12
  Luisa Moreno and **6**:21
Congressional Hispanic Caucus (CHC) **6**:132–133
Conjunto La Perfecta **6**:99
conjunto music (*musica norteña*; *norteño*) **5**:46, **6**:35, 37, **8**:49, 50
  Arsenio Rodríguez and **7**:54, 55
  Narciso Martínez and **5**:77, 78
Cooder, Ry **4**:130
Coordinator of Inter-American Affairs (CIIA) **4**:108, **8**:46
Cordero, Angel, Jr. **2**:*122*–123
Cordero, Rafael **1**:5, **8**:38
Córdova, France Anne **2**:*124*
Corea, Chick **1**:26, **2**:*125*–126
Corona, Bert **2**:*127*, **7**:89
Corona, Juan **2**:*128*
Coronado, Francisco Vásquez de **2**:*129*–130, **3**:49, 50, 51, **8**:23, 35
Coronel, Antonio F. **2**:*131*–132
Corpi, Lucha **2**:*133*
Corretjer, Juan Antonio **2**:134, **7**:125
"Corrido de Delano, El" (song) **4**:71
corridos (songs) **2**:9, **6**:36–37, **8**:48, 49
Cortés, Carlos E. **3**:4
Cortés, Hernán **3**:53, 54, **7**:33
Cortez, Gregorio **2**:84, **3**:5, 14
  film about **6**:81
Cortijo, Rafael **4**:126
Cortina, Juan Nepomuceno **3**:6–7
Cortines, Ramón C. **3**:8
Corzine, Jon **5**:106
Coser y Cantar (play) **7**:11
Cota-Cárdenas, Margarita **3**:9
Cotera, Martha P. **3**:10
Crawford, James **1**:129
Cristal, Linda **3**:*11*
Crónica, La (newspaper) **2**:105, **4**:116, 117, **5**:92, **6**:42
Cruz, Carlos **6**:89
Cruz, Celia **3**:*12*–13, 75, 83, **4**:107
Cruz, Pablo **3**:*14*
Cruzada para la Justicia (Crusade for Justice) **2**:108, **4**:49
Cruz González, José **3**:*15*
Cuba
  constitution (1940) **7**:55
  diaspora **4**:53
  mass emigration of children from **5**:75, 76, 102

U.S. trade embargo **5**:89
  see also Cubans
Cuba, Joe **3**:*16*
Cuban Adjustment Act (1966) **4**:123
Cuban American National Council (CNC) **3**:61–62, **6**:129
Cuban American National Foundation (CANF) **5**:89, **6**:129
Cuban Americans, activism **1**:*13*–14
Cuban Liberty and Democratic Solidarity Act (Helms-Burton Act; 1996) **5**:106, **7**:86
Cuban Representation in Exile (RECE) **5**:88
Cubans **2**:*110*
  Elián González case **4**:123
  Freedom Flight and **4**:123
  as immigrants **1**:82, **2**:110, **3**:35–36, **4**:*122*–124, **8**:25
  Mariel Boatlift **3**:35, **4**:123–124
  music **6**:37–38, 40
  and newspapers **5**:93
  political movements **6**:129
  political representation **6**:131–132
Cucaracha, La (cartoon strip) **1**:34, 35
"*cuentó puertorriqueno, el*" **5**:121
Cuentos del hogar (book) **4**:128
Cugat, Xavier **1**:72, **3**:*17*–18, **4**:106, **6**:38
Culture Swing (album) **4**:100
Cunningham, Glenn **5**:106
Cursillo movement **3**:121
Cybrids: La Raza Techno-Crítica, Los **5**:22
Cypress Hill **3**:*19*–20, **4**:107, **6**:40

D

Daddy Yankee **3**:*21*, **4**:107, **6**:40
Dallas (TV series) **7**:*12*
Dallmeier, Francisco **3**:*22*
Dancing with Cuba (book) **4**:72
danzas **2**:30
Danzas Mexicanas **5**:30
danzas puertorriqueñas **1**:6
danzón music **7**:55
Dawn (backing duo) **6**:*85*
Day of the Dead **7**:34, 38
De Alarcón, Martín **3**:*23*–24
Dean, James **8**:12
Death of an Anglo (book) **6**:12
Death and the Maiden (play) **3**:76–77
De Benavides, Alonso **3**:*25*
De Burgos, Julia **3**:*26*–27
Decastro, Joseph H. **5**:112
De Hoyos, Angela **3**:*28*
de la Garza, Carlos **3**:*29*
de la Garza, Eligio "Kika" **3**:*30*
De La Hoya, Oscar **2**:28, **3**:*31*–32, **5**:124, **8**:90
Delano grape strike **4**:114, **5**:*12*, 13
Delano-Sacramento march (1994) **2**:89, **7**:56
de la Renta, Oscar **3**:*33*
de la Rocha, Zack **3**:*34*
del Castillo, Adelaida R. **6**:9
del Castillo, Siro **3**:35–36
de León, Alonso **3**:*37*

de León de Vega, Sonia Marie **3**:*38*
De León family **2**:42, **3**:*39*–40
  Fernando De León **1**:116, **3**:39
  Martin De León **3**:39
  Patricia De La Garza De León **3**:39, 40
  Silvestre De León **3**:39–40
Delgado, Abelardo **3**:*41*
del Olmo, Frank **3**:*42*
del Río, Dolores **3**:*43*–44, **4**:108
Del Toro, Benicio **3**:*45*–46
Del Valle, Ygnacio **3**:*47*
Del Villard, Sylvia **3**:*48*
Democracia, La (newspaper) **6**:32
de Niza, Marcos **3**:*49*–50, **8**:22
de Oñate, Cristóbal **3**:51, 52
de Oñate, Juan **3**:*51*–52
"Deportado, El" (song) **6**:36
Deporting the Divas (play) **7**:39
"descargas" **5**:37
Desert Blood (book) **4**:25
De Soto, Hernando **3**:*53*–54
Desperado (film) **4**:77–78
de Vargas, Diego **3**:*55*, **8**:23
de Varona, Donna **3**:*56*
de Zavala, Lorenzo **3**:*57*–58
de Zavala, Lorenzo, Jr. **3**:58
Día de los Muertos (Day of the Dead) **7**:34, 38
Día Normal, Un (album) **4**:132
Diaz, Cameron **3**:*59*–60, **4**:105
Díaz, Guarioné M. **3**:*61*–62
Díaz, Junot **3**:*63*
Díaz, Justino **3**:*64*
Díaz, Porfirio **4**:22, **8**:45
  Victor L. Ochoa and **6**:76
Díaz Alfaro, Abelardo **3**:*65*
Díaz-Balart, Lincoln **3**:*66*, 67
Díaz-Balart, Mario **3**:*67*
Diaz Dennis, Patricia **3**:*68*
Diddy (Sean Combs) **5**:39
"Diepalismo" **6**:96
Dihigo, Martin **3**:*69*
Dimas, Trent **3**:*70*
Dinos, Los **8**:5
Diputación, Pío Pico and **6**:117, 118
"Discriminación a un Mártir" (song) **6**:37
discrimination **3**:*71*–74
D'León, Oscar **3**:*75*
Dolores Huerta Foundation **4**:114
"Donna" (song) **8**:83, 84
Don Pedro *see* Albizu Campos, Pedro
Dorfman, Ariel **3**:*76*–77
Dreaming in Cuban (book) **4**:9
D'Rivera, Paquito **3**:*78*–79
drug czars **5**:*70*, 71
Duran, Alfredo **3**:*80*
Durazo, María Elena **3**:*81*–82
Dying to Cross (book) **7**:27

E

Eastern Airlines **5**:44
East L.A. 13, the **1**:7
East L.A. Blowouts **3**:90, **4**:4
Echo Amphitheater Park **8**:60
Edición Critica, Eugenio María de Hostos (book) **4**:112
education **3**:*72*–73, **5**:127
  language in **1**:127–128, 129, 130, **3**:73, **5**:92
  Lauro F. Cavazos and **2**:73–74
  multicultural **6**:54

Sara Martinez Tucker and **5**:87
  segregation in *see* segregation in education
Ehkymosis (band) **4**:132
Elektric Band **2**:126
Elephant Butte Dam **2**:7
El General **3**:*83*
Elizondo, Virgilio **3**:*84*
El Mozote massacre **4**:72
El Paso, Texas **2**:6
El Salvador, El Mozote massacre **4**:72
Elvira, Rafael **5**:130
employment **3**:*72*
  see also Bracero Program; labor organizations
enganchistas **1**:20
En Mi Imperio (album) **7**:17
Environmental Protection Agency (EPA) **6**:53
Escalante, Jaime **3**:*85*
Escandón, José de **3**:*86*, **4**:24
Escobar, Eleuterio **4**:88
Escobar, Sixto **3**:*87*
Escovedo, Pete **3**:*88*
Escuela Tlatelolco, La **4**:49
Espada, Martín **3**:*89*
Esparza, Moctesuma **3**:*90*
Espejo, El (book) **7**:77
Espíritu Santo land grant **4**:24
Estampas del valle y otras obras (book) **4**:102–103
Estefan, Emilio **3**:*91*, 92, 93, **6**:40
Estefan, Gloria **3**:91, *92*–93, **4**:107, **7**:131
Estés, Clarissa Pinkola **3**:*94*–95
Estevanico (Esteban) **3**:49–50
Esteves, Sandra María **3**:*96*
Estevez, Emilio **3**:*97*
Estrada, Erik **3**:*98*
Estrada, Miguel **3**:*99*, **8**:31
Estrella de Mora, La (newspaper) **8**:74
evolutionary theory, teaching **1**:84
Executive Order 9981 **5**:113
"Eyes of Father Margil, The" (miracle) **5**:55

F

"Fade Into You" (single) **7**:118
Fairbanks, Douglas **4**:108
Fania All-Stars **3**:*100*–101, **6**:39, 94, **7**:20
Fania Records **6**:94
Farm Labor Organizing Committee (FLOC) **1**:23, **5**:14, **6**:44, **8**:101
Farm Workers Association (FWA) **4**:113
"Father of California" *see* Serra, Junípero
"Father of Modern Puerto Rico" *see* Muñoz Marín, Luis
"Father of Texas" *see* Austin, Stephen Fuller
Fat Joe **3**:*102*, **4**:107, **6**:40
Federal Art Project **1**:105
Federal Land Grant Alliance *see* Alianza Federal de Mercédes
Feliciano, Cheo **3**:*103*
Feliciano, José **3**:*104*–105
Felita (book) **5**:121
Felix Longoria Affair **4**:11
feminists, Latina **1**:14
Fender, Freddy **3**:*106*, **4**:107

Fernández, Emilio **3**:44
Fernandez, Evelina **3**:*107*, **8**:87
Fernández, Gigi **3**:*108*
Fernández, Manny **3**:*109*
Fernández, Mary Joe **3**:108, *110*
Fernández, Ricardo R. **3**:*111*
Fernández Cavada, Federico **3**:*112*
Ferré, Luis A. **3**:*113*–114
Ferré, Maria Luisa **3**:114
Ferré, Rosario **3**:114, 115
Ferrer, José **3**:*116*–117, **4**:108
Ferrer, Mel **3**:118
Ferrer, Miguel **3**:*119*
Flipper (TV series) **1**:28
Flores, Hector **4**:10, **6**:44
Flores, Juan **3**:120, **6**:116
Flores, Patrick F. **3**:*121*, **4**:34
Flores, Pedro **3**:*122*, **7**:125
Flores, Tom **3**:*123*
Flores Magón, Ricardo **3**:*124*–125
Floricanto en Aztlán (poetry) **1**:48
Florida
   Ponce de León and **7**:4, 5
   population (2000) **8**:25
food, Tex-Mex **8**:50–*51*
Foraker Act (Organic Act; 1900) **6**:33
Fornes, Maria Irene **3**:*126*, **6**:11
Foto-Novelas (TV series) **1**:83
Four, Los **7**:81
Fox, Vicente **4**:85
Franklin, Aretha **2**:46
Freak (show) **5**:25
Fredonia, Republic of **2**:5
Freedom Flight **4**:123
Freese, Louis **3**:19
Fremont, John Charles **2**:70
Frida (film) **4**:77, 78, **6**:46
Frisco War **1**:86
Fuente, Ivon **8**:30
Fuentes, Daisy **3**:*127*
FUERZA Inc. **5**:60

G

Gabaldon, Diana **3**:128
Gadsden Purchase **2**:6, **7**:104, **8**:25–26
Galán, Héctor **3**:*129*
Galarza, Ernesto **3**:130
Galindo, Rudy **3**:*131*
Gallegos, Herman **3**:*132*
Gallegos, José Manuel **3**:*133*
galleries **4**:109
Gallo: La Vaz de la Justicia, El (newspaper) **4**:49
Gálvez, Bernardo de **3**:*134*, **5**:119
Gamboa, Harry, Jr. **4**:*4*, 38
Gamio, Manuel **4**:*5*
Gandhi, Mohandas K. **2**:89
Garcia, Andy **1**:129–130, **4**:*6*–7, **5**:37, **7**:*116*
García, Clotilde **4**:*8*
Garcia, Cristina **4**:*9*
García, Gustavo C. **4**:*10*, 17, 94, **7**:29, **8**:*33*, 34
García, Héctor P. **1**:*11*, *12*, **4**:8, *11*, **5**:113
   and the funeral of Felix Longoria **5**:34
   and José Angel Gutiérrez **4**:*73*
García, J.D. **4**:*12*
Garcia, Jeff **4**:*13*
Garcia, Jerry **4**:*14*–15
García, Lionel **4**:*16*
García, Macario **4**:*17*
García, Rupert **4**:*18*

García Lorca, Federico **2**:91
García Márquez, Gabriel **1**:41, **8**:21
Garciaparra, Nomar **4**:*19*, **7**:52
Garza, Ben F. **4**:*20*–21
Garza, Catarino E. **4**:*22*
Garza, Reynaldo G. **4**:*23*
Garza Falcón, María de la **4**:*24*
Garza War **4**:22
Gaspar de Alba, Alicia **4**:*25*
Gauss, Christian **5**:99
Gavin, Christina **4**:*27*
Gavin, John **4**:*26*–27
gay community, Ileana Ros-Lehtinen and **7**:87
Gell-Mann, Murray **1**:55
Geneva Convention, war against terrorism and **4**:42
Gentleman's Agreement (1907) **4**:120
Geographics of Home (book) **6**:112
Geronimo **8**:26
Geronimo (mural) **6**:75
Get Real Girls **2**:94
GI Forum *see* American GI Forum
Gil, Federico **4**:*28*
Gillespie, Dizzy **6**:40, 77
   Arturo Sandoval and **7**:*116*, 117
   Chano Pozo and **7**:9
   Lalo Schifrin and **7**:128
Gioia, Dana **4**:*29*
Giuliani, Rudolf W. **3**:8
Giumarra, John **6**:*124*
Global Change Research Program (GCRP) **6**:53
Going Home (folk duo) **7**:118
Going to the Olympics (mural) **7**:*81*
Goizueta, Roberto **4**:*30*–31
Goizueta Family Foundation **4**:31
Goldemberg, Isaac **4**:*32*
Gold Rush, Californian **8**:26
Gómez, Edward **4**:*33*
Gómez, José H. **4**:*34*
Gomez, Scott **4**:*35*
Gomez, Vernon "Lefty" **4**:*36*
Gomez, Wilfredo **4**:*37*
Gómez-Peña, Guillermo **4**:*38*–39
Gómez-Quinoñes, Juan **4**:40
Gonzales, Alberto **4**:*41*–42, 63
Gonzales, Boyer **4**:*43*
Gonzales, Manuel **4**:44
Gonzales, Manuel C. **4**:*45*
Gonzales, Ricardo **4**:*46*–47
Gonzales, Rodolfo "Corky" **1**:12, 14, 47, **2**:108, 109, **4**:*48*–49, **6**:*126*
Gonzales-Berry, Erlinda **4**:*50*
Gonzalez, Alfredo Cantu **4**:51, **6**:*132*
González, Antonio **4**:*52*
González, Celedonio **4**:53
González, Elián **1**:14, **4**:*123*, 124, **5**:96
González, Henry B. **4**:*54*–55
González, Jovita **4**:*56*
Gonzalez, Juan **4**:*57*, **5**:96
González, Juan D. **4**:*58*
Gonzalez, Kenny "Dope" **4**:*59*, **8**:99
González, Odilio **4**:60
González, Pedro J. **2**:106, **4**:*61*–62, 106, **5**:*94*, 95
González, Raúl **4**:*63*
González, Sila Mari **2**:23

González, Xavier **4**:64
Good Neighbor Commission **8**:46
Good Neighbor Policy **4**:108, 127
Gordo (cartoon strip) **1**:35
Gordon, Milton M. **1**:80
Gráfico (journal) **8**:98
Gran Combo, El (band) **4**:126, **7**:69
Gran Concilio de la Orden Caballeros de Honor **4**:117
Grateful Dead, The (rock band) **4**:14, 15
Great Depression
   anti-Hispanic feelings **8**:15
   Felix H. Morales and **6**:15
   and Mexican workers **1**:21, **2**:7, **4**:62, **5**:11, 94, **6**:48, **8**:27, 46
   and Spanish-language radio **5**:94
Great Wall of Los Angeles, The (mural) **1**:90
Green, Jerome **2**:106–107
Gregorio T. v. Wilson (1997) **1**:658
Grisman, David **4**:15
Grito, El (magazine) **7**:77
Grito de Dolores **2**:61
Grito de Lares, El (play) **8**:66
Grito del Norte, El (newspaper) **5**:69
Gronk **4**:*4*, 65
Guadalupe, the Virgin of **7**:34, *36*
Guadalupe Hidalgo, Treaty of (1848) **1**:9, 10, 12, 47, **2**:6, **3**:71, 120, **4**:*66*–67, 105, **7**:34, **8**:25, 44
   and Mexicans **4**:67, 121, **5**:9, **6**:36, **7**:26, **8**:31, 32, 45, 48–49
   religion after **7**:34–35
   and Texas **8**:44
   and settlement in the Southwest **8**:22, 32
   violations **4**:67, **8**:59
Guadalupe Victoria, Texas **3**:*39*, 40
"Guantanamera" (song) **5**:63
Guantanamo Bay, Cuba, prison camp **4**:42, **5**:76
Guastavino, Rafael **4**:68
Guerra, Manuel **4**:*69*
Guerrero, Eduardo and Concepción **4**:71
Guerrero, Lalo **4**:*70*–71, **6**:38
Guerrero, Vicente **8**:24
Guillermoprieto, Alma **4**:*72*
"Guns for Toys" program **5**:91
Gutiérrez, José Angel **1**:13, **2**:109, **4**:*73*, 74
Gutiérrez, Luz Bazán **4**:*74*
Gutierrez, Theresa **4**:75
Guttierez, José Antonio **5**:114
Guzmán, Ralph **4**:76

H

habanera (musical style) **6**:37
Hamlet (essay) **4**:111
Hardscrub (book) **4**:16
Hayek, Salma **4**:*77*–78, 105
Hays Code **4**:107–108
Hayworth, Rita **3**:18, **4**:*79*–80, 108
Heart That Bleeds, The (book) **4**:72

Helms-Burton Act *see* Cuban Liberty and Democratic Solidarity Act
Henna, Julio J. **8**:133
Hepburn, Audrey **3**:*118*
Hermanos al Rescate **6**:125
Hernández, Adán **4**:*81*
Hernández, Antonia **4**:*82*
Hernandez, Ester **4**:83
Hernández, Gilbert and Jaime **1**:35; **4**:*90*
Hernández, Joseph Marion **4**:*84*
Hernández, Juan **4**:*85*
Hernandez, Keith **4**:*86*–87
Hernández, María Latigo **4**:*87*–88
Hernández, Orlando **4**:*89*
Hernández, Pedro **4**:88
Hernandez, Pete **8**:*33*, 34
Hernandez, Rene **5**:51
Hernández Bros., Los **1**:35; **4**:*90*
Hernández Colón, Rafael **4**:*91*
Hernández Cruz, Victor **4**:*92*
Hernández Mayoral, José **1**:4
Hernandez v. Texas (1954) **4**:10, **6**:43, **8**:33
Herrera, Carolina **4**:*93*
Herrera, John J. **4**:*94*, **8**:*33*
Herrera, Silvestre **4**:*95*
Herrera-Sobek, María **4**:96
Herrera y Tordesillas, Antonio de **7**:4, 5
Herrón, Willie **4**:*4*
Hidalgo, Edward **4**:*97*
High Chapparal, The (TV series) **3**:11
Hijuelos, Oscar **4**:*98*
Hinojosa, Maria **4**:*99*
Hinojosa, Tish **4**:*100*
Hinojosa de Ballí, Rosa María **4**:*101*
Hinojosa-Smith, Rolando **4**:*102*–103
hip-hop **4**:107
Hispanic (magazine) **5**:94
Hispanic Causing Panic (album) **6**:40
Hispanic identity and popular culture **4**:*104*–109
Hispanic National Bar Association **6**:45
Hispanic Scholarship Fund (HSF) **5**:87
Historic Cookery (book) **2**:20
H.O.L.A. (record label) **1**:120
Homar, Lorenzo **4**:110, **7**:85
Hombre Que Le Gustan Las Mujeres (picture) **5**:*72*
Homeland (album) **4**:100
Home Owner Loan Corporation **2**:93
Hostos, Eugenio María de **4**:*111*–112, **8**:133
Hotel Employees and Restaurant Employees (HERE) **3**:81, 82
House on Mango Street, The (book) **2**:103, 104
House of the Spirits, The (book and film) **1**:41
housing, social zoning and **3**:73–74
Houston, Sam **8**:*42*, 43
How the Garcia Girls Lost Their Accents (book) **1**:53
How to Read Donald Duck (book) **3**:76
Huerta, Dolores **1**:81, **4**:*113*–114, **5**:14
   and César Chávez **4**:114

Huerta, Jorge A. **4**:*115*
Huerta, Victoriano **7**:26
human rights, Ileana Ros-Lehtinen and **7**:86
Hunter, Robert **4**:14
Huston, Walter **7**:19

I

Idar, Jovita **4**:*116*, 117
Idar, Nicasio **2**:105, **4**:116, *117*, **5**:*92*, **6**:42
identity and popular culture **4**:*104–109*
"If I Had a Hammer" (song) **5**:42
Iglesias, Enrique **4**:105, *118*, **6**:35
I Love Lucy (TV series) **1**:*71*, 72, 73, **4**:98, *107*, 108–109, **6**:47
Imagine (magazine) **8**:112
immigration and immigration law **1**:82, **2**:8–9, 105, 107–108, **4**:*119–124*, **6**:44–45, **8**:27, 45–46
Immigration Act (1924; National Origins Act) **4**:120, 122
Immigration Act (1965) **4**:124
Immigration Act (1990) **4**:124
Immigration Reform and Control Act (IRCA; 1986) **1**:23, 24, **4**:124
Immigration Reform and Immigrant Responsibility Act (1996) **4**:124
poverty and immigrants **4**:*119–120*
see also assimilation; bilingualism; civil rights; Cubans; Mexicans; Puerto Ricans
"Imparcial, El" (poem) **6**:96
Imperial Valley Workers Union **5**:11
Importancia de Llamarse Daniel Santos, La (book) **7**:109
ImpreMedia **5**:94
Incas, de Soto and **3**:*53*
In the Dark (album) **4**:15
Infante, Pedro **5**:95
Infinito Botánica **5**:128
Initiative on Race **2**:97
Insular Labor Relations Act (ILRA; 1945) **5**:12
International Ladies Garment Workers Union (ILGWU) **2**:106
Irakere **3**:79, **6**:40
Arturo Sandoval and **7**:116
Iraq, war in *see* Persian Gulf War, Second
Irvin, Monte **2**:113
Islas, Arturo **4**:125
Ithier, Rafael **4**:*126*
Iturbi, José **4**:*127*
Iturbide, Agustin de **8**:24

J

Jackson, Helen Hunt **2**:132
Jaramillo, Cleofas M. **4**:*128*
Jaramillo, Mari-Luci **4**:*129*
Jarvel, Dagmar **6**:*98*
Jayuya Uprising **1**:32
jazz
bebop **6**:38
Cubop **6**:77
Latin (Afro-Cuban) **1**:113, **5**:50, 51, **7**:16
Jazz Meets the Symphony (music) **7**:129

Jet Capital Corporation **5**:44
Jeter, Derek **7**:52
Jimenez, Flaco **3**:106, **4**:106, *130*, **8**:49, 50
Jiménez, Jose "Cha Cha" **2**:109
Jiménez, Luis **4**:131
Johnson, Bert "Bobo" **6**:68
Johnson, Lyndon B.
and the Civil Rights Act **2**:107, 108
and the funeral of Dennis Chavez **2**:93
and the funeral of Felix Longoria **5**:34
and Porfirio Salinas **7**:103
Jones-Shafroth Act (Jones Act; 1917) **2**:109, **4**:122, **6**:33
Juanes **4**:*132*
Juárez, Benito **4**:49, **8**:131
Julia, Raul **4**:*133–134*
Juncos, Manuel Fernández **5**:4
Jurado, Katy **5**:*5*

K

Kahlo, Frida **4**:78, **5**:120
Kanellos, Nicolás **5**:6
Kapp, Joe **5**:7
Karatz, Bruce **6**:58
Katenback v. Morgan (1966) **3**:73
Keane, Bob **8**:83, 84
Kennedy, John F. **2**:108, **6**:132
Henry B. González and **8**:55
Kennedy, Ted **4**:124
Kesey, Ken **4**:14
Kid Frost **4**:107, **6**:40
Kid Gavilan **5**:8
King, Martin Luther, Jr. **2**:89, **3**:77, **8**:60
"King of Latin Music" *see* Puente, Tito
Kino, Eusebio Francisco **8**:24
"Klail City Death Trip" (books) **4**:*102–103*
Klail City y sus alrededores (book) **1**:3
KLVL (radio station) **6**:15
KMEX-TV **5**:96
"Knock Three Times" (song) **6**:85
Koch, Frederich H. **6**:55, 56
Korean War **5**:113
the Borinqueneers **5**:114
Edward Gómez and **4**:33
Richard E. Cavazos and **2**:75
Kornberg, Arthur **6**:74
Krause, Martin **1**:75
Kreiten, Karlrobert **1**:75
Kreutzberg, Harald **5**:29, 30

L

"La Bamba" (song) **4**:107
labor, migrant *see* agriculture and migrant labor
labor organizations **2**:106, **5**:*9–14*, **6**:43–44
Ladies LULAC **5**:52
Lagos, Ricardo **4**:28
Laguerre, Enrique **5**:15–16
La India **4**:59, **5**:*17*
Lair, Clara *see* Negrón Muñoz, Mercedes
Lalo y Sus Cinco Lobos **4**:70
laminas **1**:107
Lamy, Jean Baptiste **5**:68
Lane, Abbe **6**:*38*
Langoria, Felix **5**:113
language **1**:79–80, *81*, **5**:*92*
and education **1**:127–128, 129, *130*, **3**:73, **5**:92

Spanglish **8**:48
Spanish-language radio stations **4**:106
of Tejanos **8**:51
and voting **3**:73
see also bilingualism
LaPorte, Juan **4**:37
La Providencia, Battle of **2**:70
La Raza Unida Party *see* Raza Unida Party
Laredo **3**:86
Larrazolo, Octaviano **5**:*18*
Lasater, Edward C. **4**:69
las Casas, Juan Bautista de **2**:*61*
Lassa fever **2**:57
Latina (magazine) **5**:94
Latina Feminist Group **5**:27
Latin American Studies Association (LASA) **4**:28
Latin Business Association (LBA) **6**:45
Latino National Political Survey (LNPS) **6**:131
Latinos and Latinas
feminist Latinas **1**:14
Latinas in World War II **5**:112
population **1**:80
the term 'Latinos' **1**:14
Latino Theater Company (LTC) **8**:87
Latino USA (radio program) **4**:106
Lau v. Nichols (1974) **1**:128, **8**:33
Laviera, Jesús **1**:19, **6**:119
Lavoe, Hector **5**:*20*
Layne, Alfredo **4**:37
League of Mexican Culture **5**:93–94
League of United Latin American Citizens (LULAC) **2**:106, **3**:14, **4**:10, 17, **6**:42–43, 45, 125, **8**:26, 32, 46
Belén Robles and **7**:*48*
Ben F. Garza and **4**:20, 21
conference (2005) **6**:83
Esther N. Machuca and **5**:52
Felix Tijerina and **8**:57
first conference **4**:20
George Isidore Sanchez and **7**:107
John J. Herrera and **4**:94
Ladies LULAC **5**:52
Manuel C. Gonzales and **4**:45
María Latigo Hernández and **4**:87
Pete Tijerina and **8**:58
Vilma Martínez and **5**:85
Leal, Luis **5**:*21*
Leaños, John Jota **5**:*22*
Leaving Home (book) **4**:16
Lebrón, Lolita **1**:11, **5**:23–24
LeClerc, Juan Marco **6**:36
Lee, Wen Ho **7**:42
Leguizamo, John **5**:*25*
Lemon Grove case **1**:127–128, **2**:107, **3**:72, 73, **8**:33
León, Alonso de **3**:37
León, Tania **5**:*26*
Letter From Santa Fe Jail, A **8**:60
Levins Morales, Aurora **5**:27
Lewis and Clark Expedition, Manuel Lisa and **5**:31
libraries **5**:93–94
Lifshitz, Aliza **5**:*28*
Liga Femenil Mexicanista **2**:105, **4**:116, **6**:42
Liga Pro-Defensa Escolar, La **4**:88
"Light My Fire" (song) **3**:104

Lil' Rob **4**:107
Limón, José **5**:*29–30*, **6**:103
Lisa, Manuel **5**:*31*
Little Joe y La Familia **5**:104
"Livin La Vida Loca" (song) **5**:65
Llamarada, La (book) **5**:15
Lockridge, Rocky **4**:37
Lomas Garza, Carmen **5**:32, 72
Longoria, Felix **1**:11, **2**:107, **4**:11, **5**:*33–34*
song about **6**:37
Lopez, Al **5**:35
Lopez, George **1**:129, **5**:*36*
Lopez, Israel "Cachao" **3**:93, **4**:6, 7, **5**:*37*, **7**:55
Lopez, Jennifer **1**:129–130, **4**:*105*, 107, **5**:*38–39*, 54, **6**:113, **8**:4
López, José M. **5**:*40*
Lopez, Nancy **5**:*41*
Lopez, Trini **4**:107, **5**:*42*, **6**:39
López, Yolanda **5**:43
Lopez Portillo, José **6**:*48*
Lorenzo, Frank **5**:44
Los Angeles
Edward Roybal and **6**:132
plans for a prison at Boyle Heights **5**:123
school walkouts (blowouts; 1968) **3**:90, **4**:104
Villaraigosa as mayor **6**:*133*, **8**:*113*, 114
Zoot Suit Riots **4**:104
"Los Angeles 13" **3**:90
Los Angeles Star (newspaper) **5**:92
Los Lobos **4**:107, **5**:*45–46*, **6**:39–40, **8**:50, 84
Love & Rockets (cartoon series) **1**:35, **4**:*90*
Loving Pedro Infante (book) **2**:91
lowriders **4**:105
Lozano, Ignacio **5**:93
Lujan, Manuel Luis **5**:*47*
Luján, Tony **5**:*48*
LULAC *see* League of United Latin American Citizens
Luminarias (film) **8**:87
Luna, Solomon **5**:*49*, **6**:92, 93
"Luv Dancin" (song) **7**:114
Luz de Luna (album) **5**:129
Lymon, Frankie **7**:124

M

MacArthur, Douglas **5**:112
Machito **1**:113, **5**:*50–51*, **6**:39, **7**:9
Macho Camacho's Beat (book) **7**:109
Machuca, Esther N. **5**:52
Machuca, Esther N. **5**:52
Malcolm in the Middle (TV series) **6**:25
MALDEF *see* Mexican American Legal Defense and Education Fund
"Mal Hombre" (song) **5**:104
Malinche, La **1**:107, **3**:28
mambo **5**:51
Arsenio Rodríguez and **7**:54
Pérez Prado and **7**:10
Tito Puente and **7**:15–16
Manhattan Project **1**:54
Manifest Destiny **2**:5–6, **8**:24–25
in Texan history **8**:45
"Manteca" (song) **6**:77

Manzano, Sonia **5**:*53*
maquiladoras **2**:9, *10*
maquilas **1**:23
Maravilla, La (book) **8**:97
Marc Anthony **5**:39, *54*
Marcantonio, Vito **8**:54
Margil de Jésus, Antonio **5**:*55*
Mariachi, El (film) **7**:71
mariachi music **6**:36
Marichal, Juan **5**:*56*
Mariel Boatlift **3**:35, **4**:*123–124*
Marin, Cheech **1**:129, **4**:108,
    5:*57–58*, **8**:87
Marin, Rosario **1**:101, **5**:*59–60*
Marisol **5**:*61*
Marqués, René **5**:62–63
Márquez, Gabriel García **4**:72
Martí, José **1**:10, **4**:106, **5**:*63–64*
Martin, Ricky **1**:129, **5**:*65–66*,
    109
Martinez, A. **5**:*67*
Martínez, Antonio José **5**:*68*
Martinez, Betita **5**:*69*
Martinez, Bob **5**:*70–71*
Martinez, Cesar A. **5**:*72*
Martinez, Felix **5**:*73*
Martínez, Manuel Luis **5**:74
Martinez, Mel (Melquiades)
    3:67, **5**:*75–76*
Martínez, Narciso **5**:*77–78*, **6**:37,
    8:*49*
Martinéz, Oscar **5**:*79*
Martinez, Pedro **5**:*80*, 115
Martinez, Tomas Eloy **5**:*81–82*
Martinez, Victor **5**:*83*
Martinez, Vilma **5**:*84–85*
Martinez, Xavier **5**:*86*
Martinez Tucker, Sara **5**:*87*
Mas Canosa, Jorge **5**:*88–89*
Masters at Work **4**:*59*; **8**:*99*
Mata, Eduardo **5**:*90*
Mateo, Fernando **5**:*91*
Maxwell Land Grant **1**:114
Mazzy Star **7**:118
McCaffrey, Barry **5**:71
McDonnell, Donald **2**:88–89
McKernan, Ron "Pigpen" **4**:14
McLaughlin, John **7**:121
MEChA (Movimiento Estudiantil
    Chicano de Aztlán) **1**:47,
    48, **6**:126–127
Medal of Honor, Congressional
    1:*106*, 118
media, Spanish-language
    5:*92–97*
    see also radio; television
Medina, Battle of **8**:80
Medina, Harold R. **5**:*98–99*
Medina, Pablo **5**:*100*
Medrano v. Allee (1972) **4**:23
Melendez, Bill **5**:*101*, **7**:76
"Memorias de Melgarejo"
    7:6
Mendez v. Westminster (1943)
    6:126–127, **8**:33
Mendieta, Ana **5**:102
Mendoza, Antonio de **2**:130
Mendoza, Leonor Zamarripa
    5:*104*
Mendoza, Lydia **5**:*103–104*
Menéndez, Robert **3**:67,
    5:*105–106*
Menendez de Avilés, Pedro
    5:*107–108*
Menudo **5**:66, *109*
*Men on the Verge of a His-Panic
    Breakdown* (book) **7**:39
Merchant, Jimmy **7**:*124*
Messiaen, Olivier **7**:129

mestizaje **3**:84
mestizajes **4**:105, 106
META Inc. **8**:62
Mexican American Cultural
    Center (MACC) **3**:84
Mexican American Education
    Council (MAEC) **2**:67
Mexican American Legal
    Defense and Education
    Fund (MALDEF) **3**:73, 132,
    6:44, 58, 107, **8**:32, 47
    Antonia Hernández and **4**:82
    Luis G. Nogales and **6**:*57*, 58
    Mario Obledo and **6**:67
    Pete Tijerina and **8**:58
    Vilma Martínez and **5**:*84–85*
Mexican American Political
    Association (MAPA) **7**:89
Mexican Americans
    as activists *see* Chicano
        Movement
    assimilation **1**:*79*
    deported to Mexico (1930s)
        5:11, 94, **6**:48
    and discrimination **3**:71, 72
    feminism **7**:25
    labor organizations and
        5:*9–14*
    in the military **5**:111, 112,
        113
    Treaty of Guadalupe Hidalgo
        and **4**:67, 121, **5**:9
    see also Mexicans
Mexican American Unity Council
    8:102
Mexican-American War *see*
    Mexican War
Mexican American Youth
    Organization (MAYO) **3**:10,
    4:73, 74, **8**:47
Mexican Constitution (1824),
    abolished **8**:42
Mexican Federal Union **5**:10
*Mexican Immigrant, His Life
    Story, The* (book) **4**:5
*Mexican Immigration to the
    United States* (book) **4**:5
"Mexican Madonna" *see* Selena
Mexican Revolution, and the
    Plan de San Diego **6**:103,
    7:26
Mexican Robin Hood (Joaquín
    Murrieta) **6**:*34*
Mexicans **4**:120–*121*
    as agricultural or migrant
        workers **1**:*19–24*, **2**:7–8,
        4:*119*
    repatriation (1930s) **4**:121
    see also Mexican Americans
*Mexican Side of the Texas
    Revolution, The* (book)
    2:65
Mexican Village (book) **6**:55, 56
Mexican War (U.S.-Mexico War)
    2:5–6, **4**:66, **5**:92, **7**:94,
    8:25, 43–44, 48
    Los San Patricios **8**:44
    see also Guadalupe Hidalgo,
        Treaty of
Mexico
    area ceded to the United
        States **1**:19, 80, **4**:66, **5**:9,
        92
    the Gadsden Purchase and
        8:25–26
    independence from Spain
        7:34, **8**:24
    see also border, Mexico-
        United States

Mexterminator **4**:38
Meyerhof, Otto **6**:74
Miami Sound Machine **1**:78,
    3:91, 92–93, **6**:40
    Jon Secada and **7**:131
Mickey Mouse comic strips **4**:44
migrant labor *see* agriculture
    and migrant labor
Miguel, Luis **1**:29, **5**:*110*
Milian, Emilio **5**:96
military **5**:*111–114*
    the Borinqueneers **5**:114
    see also American GI Forum;
        Civil War; Korean War;
        Persian Gulf War; Vietnam
        War; World War I; World
        War II
Million to Juan, A (film) **7**:68
Mi mano (painting) **4**:*81*
Minaya, Omar **5**:*115*
miners, labor organizations
    5:10–11
*Minerva Delgado v. Bastrop
    Independent School
    District* (1948) **4**:94
"Minga y Petraca al Nuevo
    Senado" (essay) **7**:109
Minoso, Minnie **5**:*116*
Mi Otro Yo (book) **4**:38
Miranda, Carmen **4**:108,
    5:*117–118*, 134
Miranda, Guadalupe **1**:114
Miranda v. Arizona (1966) **8**:34
Mireles, Edmundo E. **4**:56
Miró, Esteban Rodriguez **5**:*119*
Mislán, Angel **1**:6
missionaries, Spanish **8**:23–24
Mitchell, Arthur **5**:26
Mi Tierra (album) **3**:93
Mohr, Nicholasa **5**:*120–121*
mojados (wetbacks) **2**:107,
    4:121
"Mojado sin Licensia, Un"
    (song) **8**:49
Mojados, Los (book) **7**:*105*
Molina, Gloria **5**:*122–123*
Molina, John John **5**:*124*
Molina, Mario **5**:*125–126*
Moll, Luis **5**:127
Mondini-Ruiz, Franco **5**:*128*
Monge, Yolandita **5**:*129*
Monroe Doctrine **8**:44
Monroig, Gilberto **5**:*26*
Montalban, Ricardo **5**:*131–132*
Monte, El (book) **2**:21
Montero, Mayra **5**:*133*
Montez, Maria **5**:*134*
Montoya, Carlos Garcia **6**:*4*
Montoya, Delilah **6**:*5*
Montoya, José **4**:38, **6**:*6*
Montoya, Joseph **1**:60, **6**:*7*
Montoya, Nestor **6**:*8*
Monument Valley **8**:*22*
Moor's Pavane, The (dance) **5**:30
Mora, Magdalena **6**:9
Moraga, Cherríe **1**:14, 62,
    6:*10–11*
Moraga, Elvira **6**:11
Morales, Alejandro **6**:12
Morales, David **6**:*13*
Morales, Esai **6**:*14*
Morales, Felix H. **6**:*15*
Morales, Noro **5**:51
Morales, Pablo **6**:*16*
Morales Carrión, Arturo **6**:*17*
Moratorium March **3**:90
Morel Campos, Juan **1**:6
Moreno, Antonio **6**:*18–19*
Moreno, Arturo **5**:93, **6**:*20*

Moreno, Luisa **6**:*21*, **8**:15
Moreno, Rita **4**:109, **6**:*22–23*
Morin, Raul **6**:*24*
Mothers of East Los Angeles
    5:123
*Mrs. Vargas and the Dead
    Naturalist* (book) **1**:*33*
Muggerud, Lawrence **3**:19
Mujeres Muralistas, Las **4**:83
Muniz, Frankie **6**:*25*
Muñiz, Ramsey **6**:26
Muñoz, Anthony **6**:*27*
Muñoz, Elías Miguel **6**:*28*
Muñoz, Luis **6**:*29*
Muñoz Marín, Luis **1**:32, **3**:64,
    4:91, **5**:24, **6**:*30–31*, **7**:115
    Jesus T. Piñero and **6**:120,
        121
Muñoz Rivera, Luis **6**:*32–33*
murals **1**:89–90, **2**:16, 50, **4**:64,
    65, 83, 109, **6**:*75*, **7**:*81*,
    8:36
Murrieta, Joaquín **6**:*34*
music **4**:106, **6**:*35–40*
    Aztec **6**:35
    Cuban **6**:*37–38*, 40
    habanera **6**:37
    mariachi **6**:36
    orquestas **6**:37
    Spanish-language musicians
        on the radio **5**:95
    tejano **8**:5
    Tex-Mex **5**:46, **6**:39, **8**:*49–50*
    see also conjunto music; rap;
        salsa
musica norteña see conjunto
    music
Musto, William Vincent **5**:106
mutualistas (mutual aid
    societies) **2**:105, **5**:10,
    6:*42*, **8**:26
My Family (Mi Familia) (film)
    6:46, *47*

N

Nacogdoches, Texas **2**:5, **8**:125
Najera, Eduardo **6**:*41*
Narvaez, Panfilo de **6**:64, 65
National Affordable Housing Act
    (1990) **4**:55
National Association for the
    Advancement of Colored
    People (NAACP), Vilma
    Martínez and **5**:84
National Association of Latino
    Elected Officials (NALEO)
    6:132
National Chicano Moratorium
    6:127
National Chicano Youth
    Liberation Conference
    (1969) **2**:108–109, **6**:126
National Council of La Raza
    (NCLR) **6**:43, 107, **8**:128
National Day Laborer
    Organizing Network
    (NDLON) **1**:52
National Farm Workers
    Association (NFWA) **2**:89,
    4:113, **5**:13, **6**:84
National Hispanic Leadership
    Conference (NHLC) **2**:4
National Hispanic Media
    Coalition **6**:45
National Industrial Recovery Act
    (NIRA; 1933) **5**:12
National Labor Relations Act
    (NLRA; Wagner Act; 1933)
    5:12, 13

National Labor Relations Board (NLRB) **5**:12, 13
National Organization for Mexican American Services (NOMAS) **8**:128
national organizations **6**:*42–45*
National Origins Act (Immigration Act; 1924) **4**:120, 122
Nation of Yahweh **8**:29
Native Americans
the Pueblo Revolt **8**:23
and religion **7**:35, 36, 37
in the Southwest **8**:22, 23, 26
Nava, Gregory **6**:*46–47*
Nava, Julián **6**:*48*
Navarro, José Antonio **6**:*49*
Navarro, Max **6**:*50*
Navas, William A., Jr. **6**:*51*
needle exchanges **5**:71
Negrete, Jorge **5**:95
Negrón Muñoz, Mercedes **6**:52
Neighborhood Youth Corps (NYC), Corky Gonzales and **4**:48–49
Nelson, Eugene **6**:84
Neruda, Pablo **8**:21
New Deal **1**:21, 105
New Faces of 1934 (revue) **2**:114
New Formalism movement **4**:29
New Mexico **2**:80
explored and colonized by de Oñate **3**:*51–52*
Ezekiel Cabeza de Baca and **2**:*19*
Nestor Montoya and **6**:*8*
reconquered by de Vargas **3**:55
newspapers, Spanish-language **1**:*127*, **5**:*92–93*
New World Border, The (book) **4**:38, 39
New York City, the Bronx **7**:50
Nicondra, Glugio *see* Gronk
Niebla, Elvia **6**:53
Nieto, Sonia **6**:54
Niggli, Josefina **6**:*55–56*
Nilda (book) **5**:121
Nineteenth Amendment **6**:93
Nixon, Richard M., Charles Rebozo and **7**:*30*
Niza, Marcos de **3**:*49–50*, **8**:22
Nogales, Luis G. **6**:*57–58*
Noloesca, Beatriz **6**:*59*
nonviolence **1**:*94*
Noriega, Carlos **6**:*60*
Norte, El (film) **6**:46, 83
norteño music *see* conjunto music
North American Free Trade Agreement (NAFTA) **1**:23–24, **5**:9, 14
Nosotros **5**:132
Noticieros (TV program) **7**:27
Noticiero Univision (TV program) **7**:102
Novarro, Ramon **6**:*61*
Novello, Antonia **6**:*62–63*
Nueva Ola, La **5**:129
Nueva York (book) **5**:121
Nuevo Herald, El (newspaper) **5**:*94*
Nuevo Teatro Pobre de América **7**:119
Núñez Cabeza de Vaca, Álvar **3**:49, **6**:*64–65*
Nureyev, Rudolf **2**:15
Nuyorican movement **5**:*17*

Nuyorican Poets Café **3**:96, **6**:*119*, 122
Nuyorican renaissance **1**:38–39
NYPD Blue (TV series) **8**:*14*

O

Obejas, Achy **6**:66
Obledo, Mario **6**:*67*
Obregón, Eugene Arnold **6**:68
O'Brien, Soledad **6**:69
Ocampo, Adriana **6**:70
Occupied America (book) **1**:*15*
Ochoa, Ellen **6**:*71*
Ochoa, Estevan **6**:*72*
Ochoa, Severo **6**:*73–74*
Ochoa, Víctor **6**:*75*
Ochoa, Victor L. **6**:*76*
O'Farrill, Arturo "Chico" **6**:*77*
Ofrenda para Antonio Lomas (artwork) **5**:*32*
Old Spain in Our Southwest (book) **6**:93
Olivas, John **6**:*78*
Oller, Francisco **6**:*79*, **7**:49
Olmos, Edward James **6**:*80–81*
Once Upon a Time in Mexico (film) **7**:72
Ontiveros, Lupe **6**:*82–83*
Operational Technologies Corporation (Optech) **6**:50
Operation Bootstrap **4**:122, **6**:31
Operation Jobs **2**:8, **3**:72
Operation Peter Pan **5**:75, 102
Operation Serenidad (Serenity) **6**:31
Operation Wetback **1**:23, **2**:8, 107–108, **3**:72, **4**:121, **8**:27
Opinión, La (newspaper) **5**:93
Optech (Operational Technologies Corporation) **6**:50
Orden Caballeros de America **4**:87
Orden Hijos de America **2**:106, **4**:87
Order of Sons of America **7**:96
Orendain, Antonio **6**:84
Organic Act (Foraker Act; 1900) **6**:33
Orlando, Tony **6**:*85*
Orozco, Jose Clemente **5**:120
orquesta (*orquesta tejana*) music **6**:37
Orquesta Tropicana **7**:69
Orquestra Cubana de Música Moderna (OCMM) **7**:116
Orquestra Juvenil de Música Moderna **7**:116
Ortega, John **5**:112
Ortega, Katherine **1**:101, **6**:*86–87*
Ortega y Gasca, Felipe de **6**:88
Ortiz, Carlos **3**:87, **6**:*89*
Ortiz Cofer, Judith **6**:*90*
Otero Family **6**:*91–92*
Adelina Otero Warren **6**:92, *93*
Antonio Jose Otero **1**:*67*
Mariano S. Otero **6**:92
Miguel A. Otero I **3**:*133*, **6**:*91*, 92
Miguel A. Otero II **6**:91–92
Miguel A. Otero IV **6**:92
Solomon Luna and **5**:49, **6**:92, 93
Otero Warren, Adelina **6**:92, *93*
Our Catholic Heritage in Texas (book) **2**:65
Outlander (book) **3**:128
Oviedo, Lope de **6**:65

P

P. Diddy *see* Combs, Sean "Puff Daddy"
Pacheco, Johnny **5**:51, **6**:*94*
Pacheco, Romualdo, Jr. **6**:*95*
Pacheco y su Charanga **6**:94
pachucos **4**:70, 104
Palés Matos, Luis **6**:*96*
Palmeiro, Rafael **6**:*97*
Palmieri, Charlie **5**:37, **6**:*98*
Palmieri, Eddie **5**:17, **6**:38, 39, *99*
Palomino, Carlos **6**:*100*
Palooka (film) **8**:107
Pan-American Union **5**:12–13
"Pancho López" (song) **4**:70
Pantín, Leslie **8**:62
Pantoja, Antonia **6**:*101*
Paoli, Antonio **6**:*102*
Papp, Joseph **4**:134
Paredes, Américo **6**:*103*, **8**:67
Paredes y Arrillaga, Mariano **8**:43
Paris, Treaty of (1898) **4**:121
Paris Philharmonic **7**:129
Parker, Gloria **4**:98
Parra, Derek **6**:*104*
Parrot in the Oven: Mi Vida (book) **5**:*83*
Partido del Pueblo (PPD) **7**:115
Partido Liberal **6**:*105*
Partido Liberal Mexicano (PLM) **3**:124, **6**:125
Sara Estela Ramírez and **7**:25
Partido Nuevo Progresista (PNP) **7**:88
Partido Popular Democrático de Puerto Rico (PPD; Popular Democratic Party) **4**:91, **6**:30, 120–121
Paterson (book) **8**:123
Pau-Llosa, Ricardo **6**:*105*
Paz, Juan-Carlos **7**:129
pecan shellers' strike (1938), in San Antonio **5**:11, **8**:15, 41
Pedro J. González and his Madrugadores (radio show) **2**:106, **5**:95
Pelli, Cesar **6**:*106*
Peña, Albert A., Jr. **6**:*107*
Peña, Amado **5**:72, **6**:*108*
Peña, Elizabeth **6**:*109*, **8**:68
Peña, Federico **6**:*110*
Penn, Sean **3**:45, 46
Perales, Alonso S. **5**:84, 85
"Perdido" (song) **8**:61
Pérez, Jorge **6**:*111*
Pérez, Loida Maritza **6**:112
Perez, Rosie **5**:38, **6**:*113*
Pérez, Tony **6**:*114*
Pérez Firmat, Gustavo **6**:*115*
Perfecta, La (band) **7**:20
Perón, Eva **5**:82
Perón, Juan **5**:82
Perón Novel, The **5**:82
Persian Gulf War
First **5**:113, **7**:112
Second **5**:*111*, 114
Pete Henández v. Texas (1954) **4**:*94*
Petronas Towers **6**:106
Phoenix, Arizona **8**:27
Pico, Andrés **6**:*118*
Pico, Pío **1**:100, **2**:70, **6**:116, *117–118*
"Piel Canela" (song) **2**:39
Pierce, Franklin **8**:25
Pietri, Pedro **6**:*119*
Pimentel, George C. **5**:126
Piñero, Jesus T. **1**:32, **6**:*120–121*

Piñero, Miguel **1**:38, **3**:106, **6**:119, *122*
Plan de Ayutla **8**:131
Plan de San Diego **6**:103, **7**:26
Plan de Santa Barbara, El **1**:13, 48, **6**:126, 127
Plan Espiritual de Aztlán, El **1**:47, 48, **2**:109, **4**:*48*, 49, **6**:126
Plan of San Diego **3**:125
Plessy v. Ferguson (1897) **8**:32
Plunkett, Jim **6**:*123*
Plyler v. Doe (1982) **5**:84, 85, **8**:34
Pocho (book) **8**:116
Pocho (magazine) **1**:*34–35*
Political Association of Spanish-speaking Organizations (PASO: *later* PASSO) **6**:132
political movements **6**:*124–129*
see also Chicano movement; MEChA
political representation **6**:*130–133*
Polk, James Knox **2**:6, **4**:67, **8**:25, 43–44, 45
Ponce, Mary Helen **6**:134
Ponce de León, Juan **1**:56, **5**:108, **7**:*4–5*
Ponce de León Troche, Juan **7**:*6*
Ponce Massacre **1**:32
Poor People's March on Washington (1968) **8**:60
Popé **8**:23
popular culture *see* Hispanic identity and popular culture
Popular Democratic Party (PPD), Sila María Calderón and **2**:23–24
population, Hispanic American **1**:80, **4**:104, 119
Latin mix **4**:120
see also Cubans; Mexicans; Puerto Ricans
Portes, Alejandro **7**:*7*
Portillo, Lourdes **4**:109
Portillo Trambley, Estela **7**:*8*
Portrait of the Artist as the Virgin of Guadalupe (painting) **5**:*43*
posters **4**:109
poverty, immigrants and **4**:119–120
Power, Tyrone **2**:98
Poyesis Genetica **4**:38
Pozo, Chano **1**:79, **6**:38, **7**:*9*
Prado, Pérez **7**:*10*
Prensa, La (newspaper) **5**:93
Price of Glory (film) **1**:83
Prida, Dolores **7**:*11*
Prince, Sheila E. and **8**:*13*
Principal, Victoria **7**:*12*
Prinze, Freddie **4**:109, **7**:*13*, 14
Prinze, Freddie, Jr. **7**:*14*
Professional Air Traffic Controllers Organization (PATCO) **5**:14
Protagonist of an Endless Story, The (portrait) **7**:*74*
Proudhon, Pierre-Joseph **3**:125
Public Health Service Commissioned Corps **6**:*62–63*
Puebla, Battle of **8**:132
Pueblo Revolt **8**:23
Puente, Tito **3**:13, *16*, 93, **4**:106, **5**:48, 51, 130, **6**:38, 39, **7**:*15–16*

Set Index

Puente in Percussion (album)
6:39
"Puerto Rican Bombshell" *see*
Chacón, Iris
Puerto Rican Embassy, El (play)
6:119
Puerto Rican Herald (newspaper)
6:33
Puerto Rican Legal Defense and
Education Fund (PRLDF)
3:73, **6**:44
Puerto Ricans **2**:109–110,
4:121–122
as immigrants **1**:82,
4:121–122
in the military **5**:111
nationalism **6**:127–128
political representation **6**:131
Young Lords **2**:109, 110,
6:128, **7**:45
see also Puerto Rico
Puerto Rican Socialist Party
6:128
Puerto Rico
agricultural workers from
1:24
and conservation **5**:16
Father of Modern Puerto Rico
see Muñoz Marín, Luis
labor relations **5**:12
language **5**:92
oral story telling **5**:121
Ponce de León and **7**:4–5
Ponce de León Troche and
7:6
rule by the United States
6:32–33
slavery abolished **1**:5
U.S. commonwealth status
2:110, **4**:91, **6**:30, 31, 121
see also Puerto Ricans
Puff Daddy **5**:39

Q

Queen, Ivy **4**:107, **7**:17
"Queen of Reggaetón" *see*
Queen, Ivy
"Queen of Technicolor" *see*
Montez, Maria
"Queen of Tejano" *see* Selena
"Queen of Tejano Music" *see*
Canales, Laura
Que Pasa, USA? (TV show) **7**:123
Quevedo, Eduardo **7**:89
Quinn, Anthony **7**:18–19
Quintana, Ismael "Pat" **7**:20
Quintana, Leroy V. **7**:21
Quintero, José **7**:22
Quinto Sol Publications **7**:77
Quinto Sol (publishing house)
4:103, **5**:93

R

radio
Radio Martí **6**:129
Spanish-language **4**:106,
5:94–95, **6**:15
Rage Against the Machine **3**:34
railroad, Texas-Mexican **8**:48
Rainbow Coalition **2**:109
Ramirez, Manny **7**:23
Ramírez, Martin **7**:24
Ramírez, Sara Estela **7**:25
Ramona (book) **2**:132, **3**:47
Ramón y Cajal, Santiago **6**:73, 74
Ramos, Basilio **7**:26
Ramos, Jorge **7**:27, 102
Ramos, Tab **7**:28
Rangel, Irma **7**:29

rap
Latin **4**:107
West Coast **6**:40
Raza Unida Party (RUP) **1**:13,
2:109, **3**:10, **4**:73, 74, **6**:127
Corky Gonzales and **4**:49
María Latigo Hernández and
4:88
Ramsey Muñiz and **6**:26
Reagan, Ronald **5**:13–14
Rebirth of Our Nationality, The
(mural) **8**:36
Rebozo, Charles **7**:30
Rechy, John **7**:31–32
"Recovering the Hispanic
Literary Heritage of the
United States" **5**:6
Red Robber of the Rio Grande
see Cortina, Juan
Nepomuceno
Reform, War of **8**:131–132
Regeneración (journal) **3**:124,
125
reggaeton **3**:21, 83, **4**:107, **6**:40
Ivy Queen and **7**:17
Regidor, El (newspaper) **3**:14
Relacion de Cabeza de Vaca, La
(book) **6**:65
Related Group of Florida **6**:111
religion **7**:33–38
mariachi and **6**:36
see also Catholicism
Resaca, La (book) **5**:16
retablos **1**:107, **7**:37
Reto en el Paraíso (book) **6**:12
Return of Felix Nogara, The
(book) **5**:100
Return to Forever (RTF)
2:125–126
Revisita Areíto (magazine) **2**:56
*Revolt of the Cockroach People,
The* (book) **1**:8
"Rey de Bajo, El" *see* Valentín,
Bobby
Reyes, Bernardo **2**:84
Reyes, Guillermo **7**:39
Reyes, Senen **3**:19
Reyna, María Torres **7**:40
Richardson, Bill **7**:41–42
Ride, The (album) **5**:46
Rio Grande **2**:7
Rio Piedras Massacre **1**:31
Rios, Alberto **7**:43
Rivera, Angel **4**:105
Rivera, Chita **7**:44
Rivera, Diego **3**:43, **5**:120
Rivera, Geraldo **7**:45
Rivera, Ismael **4**:126
Rivera, Mon **2**:120
Rivera, Pete **5**:130
Rivera, Tito **3**:79
Rivera, Tomás **4**:103, **7**:46–47
Rivero, Horacio **5**:113
Roback, David **7**:118
Robin Hood of El Dorado
(Joaquín Murrieta) **6**:34
Robles, Belén **7**:48
Roche-Rabell, Arnaldo **7**:49
Rodriguez, Abraham, Jr. **7**:50
Rodríguez, Albita **7**:51
Rodriguez, Alex **7**:52–53
Rodriguez, Arsenio **7**:54–55
Rodriguez, Arturo S. **5**:13, **7**:56
Rodriguez, Chi Chi **7**:57
Rodriguez, Cleto **7**:58
Rodriguez, Eddie **7**:53
Rodriguez, Eloy **7**:59
Rodriguez, Ivan "Pudge" **7**:60
Rodriguez, Jennifer **7**:61

Rodriguez, Johnny **7**:62
Rodriguez, Josefa "Chipita" **7**:63
Rodriguez, Linda Chavez **7**:56
Rodriguez, Luis J. **7**:64–65
Rodriguez, Michelle **7**:66
Rodríguez, Narciso **7**:67
Rodriguez, Paul **1**:83, **7**:68
Rodriguez, Paul, Jr. **7**:68
Rodríguez, Pellín **7**:69
Rodríguez, Richard **7**:70
Rodríguez, Robert **4**:77, 78, 105,
109, **7**:71–72
Cheech Marin and **5**:58
Rodriguez, Tito **3**:103, **5**:51,
6:38, 39
Rodríguez de Tió, Lola **7**:73
Rodríguez-Díaz, Angel **7**:74
Roland, Gilbert **7**:75
Roman, Phil **7**:76
Roman Catholicism *see*
Catholicism
Romano, Octavio **7**:77
Romero, Anthony D. **7**:78–79
Romero, Cesar **7**:80
Romero, Chan **6**:38–39
Romero, Frank **7**:81
Romero, Trinidad **7**:82
Romero-Barceló, Carlos **7**:83
Ronstadt, Linda **7**:84
Roosevelt, Franklin D.
Good Neighbor Policy **4**:108,
127
New Deal **1**:21, 105
Rosado del Valle, Julio **7**:85
Rosa, Robi **5**:66
Ros-Lehtinen, Ileana **3**:67,
7:86–87
Ross, Fred **2**:89, **4**:113, 114
Rosselló, Pedro **2**:24, **7**:88
Rowland, Sherwood **5**:126
Royal Expedition **2**:129–130
Roybal, Edward **6**:132
Roybal-Allard, Lucille **7**:89,
90–91
Rubio, Eurípides **7**:92
Ruiz, John **7**:93
Ruiz de Burton, María Amparo
7:94
Rulfo, Juan **2**:91
rumba **6**:38

S

Sáenz, Ben **7**:95
Sáenz, José de la Luz **7**:96
"Safe and Free" campaign **7**:79
Sagasta, Praxedas Mateo **6**:32
Saint Augustine, Florida, Pedro
Menendez de Avilés and
5:108
Salas, Albert **7**:98
Salas, Eddy **7**:98
Salas, Floyd **7**:97–98
Salazar, Alberto **7**:99
Salazar, Rubén **3**:90, **5**:96,
7:100, **8**:28
Saldívar, Yolanda **8**:5
Salinas, Luis Omar **7**:101
Salinas, María Elena **7**:102
Salinas, Porfirio **7**:103
salsa **3**:100, 101, **6**:39, 98
La India and **5**:17
Machito quoted on **5**:51
Marc Anthony and **5**:54
Salt Lake City, Utah **8**:27
*Salvatierra v. Del Rio
Independent School
District* (1930) **4**:45
Samaniego, Mariano **7**:104
Samba (book) **4**:72

sambas, Carmen Miranda and
5:117, 118
Samora, Julián **7**:105
San Antonio, Texas
founded **3**:24
La Liga Pro-Defensa Escolar
4:88
pecan shellers' strike (1938)
5:11, **8**:15, 41
Tejano-Conjunto festival **8**:50
Sánchez, David **7**:106
Sanchez, George Isidore **7**:107
Sánchez, Loretta and Linda
7:108
Sánchez, Luis Rafael **7**:109
Sanchez, Poncho **7**:110
Sánchez, Ricardo **7**:111
Sanchez, Ricardo S. **5**:111, 114,
7:112–113
Sanchez, Roger **7**:114
Sanchez, Salvador **4**:37, **8**:72
Sánchez Vilella, Roberto **4**:91,
7:115
Sandburg, Carl **2**:104
Sandoval, Arturo **3**:93, **6**:40,
7:116
Sandoval, Hope **7**:118
Sandoval, Humberto **4**:4
San Francisco Poster Workshop
4:18
San Jacinto, Battle of **7**:133, 134,
8:43
San Joaquin Valley, cotton
pickers' strike (1933) **5**:11
San Patricios, Los **8**:44
Santa Anna, Antonio López de
3:58, **6**:49, **7**:132, 133,
134, **8**:24, 26, 43, 131
Santa Evita (book) **5**:82
Santa Fe, New Mexico **8**:23
Santa Fe Expedition **6**:49
Santa Fe Ring **2**:85
Santaliz Avila, Pedro **7**:119
Santamária, Mongo **6**:39
Santana (band) **7**:120
Santana, Carlos **3**:88, **4**:107,
6:39, **7**:16, 120–121
Santayana, George **7**:122
Santeiro, Luis **7**:123
Santería **1**:37
Santiago, Herman **7**:124
Santos, Daniel **7**:125
Santos, Rolando H. **7**:126
Saralegui, Cristina **7**:127
Savage, John **7**:63
Saxon, Johnny **5**:8
Schifrin, Lalo **7**:128–129
Schomburg, Arturo Alfonso
7:130
Schulz, Charles M. **7**:76
Scott, Winfield **4**:66, **8**:25
Secada, Jon **7**:131
segregation in education
2:106–107, **3**:72, 73,
6:107, 126–127, **8**:33
Gustavo C. Garcia and **4**:10,
94
John J. Herrera and **4**:94
Manuel C. Gonzales and **4**:45
see also Lemon Grove case
Seguín, Erasmo **7**:132, 133, **8**:24
Seguín, Juan N. **7**:132, 133–134,
8:24
Selena **5**:38, **8**:4–5, 48
Sen Dog **4**:107
September 11th terrorist attacks
4:124
Serra, Junípero **2**:86, **8**:6, 23
Serra, Richard **8**:7

Serrano, José **8**:*8*
Serrano, Samuel **8**:*9*
Sesame Street (TV show) **5**:*53*, **7**:123
settlement, U.S. *see* Southwest, U.S. settlement in the
Shadow of a Man (play) **6**:11
Shakespeare, William **1**:39
Shaman (album) **7**:*121*
shamans **2**:62, 63
Sheen, Charlie **3**:97, **8**:10, 12
Sheen, Martin **3**:97, **8**:10, *11–12*
Sheila E. **8**:*13*
Short Eyes (play) **6**:122
Show de Cristina, El (TV show) **7**:127
Siembra (album) **1**:133
Silva, France **5**:112
Silvera, Juan **7**:63
Silver Cloud Café, The (book) **8**:97
Sketches of the Valley and Other Works (book) **4**:103
Sleepy Lagoon trial **3**:74
Slidell, John **8**:25, 43
Smits, Jimmy **2**:*52*, **8**:*14*
social zoning **3**:73–74
sociedades mutualistas **4**:22
Solar Montoya (book) **5**:15
Solís Sager, Manuela **8**:15
Somohano, Arturo **8**:16
son, Arsenio Rodríguez and **7**:54, 55
son guaguancó **7**:55
son montuno **7**:55
Sonoma, California **8**:88
Sons of America, Order of **6**:21
Sorting Metaphors (poems) **6**:105
Sosa, Lionel **8**:*17*
Sosa, Sammy **8**:*18–19*
Soto, Gary **7**:101, **8**:*20–21*
Soto, Hernando de **3**:*53–54*
South Texas Agricultural Workers' Union (STAWU) **8**:15
Southwest, settlement in the **8**:*22–27*
Southwest Council of La Raza (SWCLR) **7**:105, **8**:128
Southwest Voter Registration Education Project (SVREP) **4**:52, **5**:85, **8**:102
Spanglish **8**:48
Spanish American League Against Discrimination (SALAD) **3**:*72–73*
Spanish International Network (SIN) **4**:109
Spanish language *see* language
Squatter and the Don, The (book) **7**:94
stereotypes **3**:72, **4**:104, 108, **6**:23, 83
Good Neighbor Policy and **4**:127
Student Nonviolent Coordinating Committee (SNCC) **5**:69
Suárez, Ray **8**:*28*
Suárez, Xavier L. **8**:*29–30*
subatomic particles **1**:54, 55, **4**:12
Sullo, Salvatore **2**:126
Sun Mad (picture) **4**:83
Supernatural (album) **7**:121
Super Orchestra Tropicana **5**:130
Supreme Court **8**:*31–34*

T

Tafoya, José Piedad **8**:35
Taft-Hartley Act (1947) **5**:13
Tanguma, Leo **8**:36
Tan, Luisa **5**:126
Tapia, Luis **8**:*37*
Tapia y Rivera, Alejandro **8**:38
Tavárez, Manuel G. **2**:30
Teachings of Don Juan, The (book) **2**:62
Teatro Campesino, El **8**:*81–82*
Teenagers, The **7**:*124*
Teissonnière, Gerardo **8**:39
tejano music **8**:5
tejanos, culture *see* Tex-Mex culture
Telemundo **4**:109, **5**:97
television
Spanish-language **5**:96–97
TV Martí **6**:129
Telles, Raymond **8**:40
Telling to Live: Latina Feminist Testimonios (book) **5**:27
Tenayuca, Emma **5**:11, **8**:15, *41*
Terrazo (book) **3**:65
Terror Squad **4**:107
Terry, Clark **5**:48
Texas War of Independence **6**:49
Texas
colonias **8**:26
Hispanic population **8**:47
see also Tex-Mex culture
Texas, history of **8**:*42–47*
American settlement (1820s) **2**:5, **8**:42
annexation to the United States **8**:25, 43
Casas Revolt **7**:132
Caucasian Race Resolution **8**:47
in the Civil War **8**:45
Manifest Destiny in **8**:45
Manuel Guerra and **4**:69
Republic of Texas **7**:132, **8**:24, 43
Rosa María Hinojosa de Ballí and **4**:101
see also Texas Revolution
Texas Council on Human Relations **8**:47
Texas Declaration of Independence (1836) **3**:58, **6**:49
Texas Farm Workers Union (TFWU) **6**:84
Texas International Airlines **5**:44
Texas Rangers **8**:49
and Jacinto Treviño **8**:67
Texas Revolution **2**:5, **8**:43
Carlos de la Garza and **3**:29
José Antonio Valdez and **8**:80
José María Jesús Carbajal and **2**:42
Placido Benavides and **1**:116
Texas Tornados **8**:50
Tex-Mex culture **8**:*48–51*
food **8**:*50–51*
music **5**:46, **6**:39, **8**:*49–50*
Thalía **8**:*52*
Thee Midniters **6**:39
thiarubrin **7**:59
Thomas, Piri **8**:*53–54*
Thompson, Hunter S. **1**:8
Thoreau, David **8**:45
Tiant, Luis **8**:*55*
Tico Records **6**:38, 39
Tienda, Marta **8**:*56*
"Tie a Yellow Ribbon Round the Old Oak Tree" (song) **6**:85

Tijerina, Felix **8**:*57*
Tijerina, Pete **8**:*58*
Tijerina, Réies López **1**:12, **2**:108, **6**:125–126, *128*, **8**:*59–60*
Tilted Arc (sculpture) **8**:7
Tizol, Juan **8**:*61*
Tjader, Cal **7**:110
Tomás Rivera Policy Institute (TRPI) **7**:47
Tonatiuh Quinto Sol **7**:77
Tony G **4**:107
Toraño, Maria Elena **8**:62
Torres, Edwin **8**:63
Torres, Esteban E. **8**:*64*
Torres, José **8**:*65*
Torres, Luis Lloréns **2**:34, **8**:66
Tortilla Soup (film) **6**:*109*
Traffic (film) **3**:45, 46
"Tragedia del 29 de Agosto, La" (song) **4**:71
transnationalism **1**:82
treasurers, U.S. **6**:87
Trejo, Ernesto **7**:101
Treviño, Jacinto **8**:67
Treviño, Jesús **8**:68
Trevino, Lee **8**:*69–70*
Trini (book) **7**:8
Trinidad, Felix **3**:32, **8**:*71–72*, 90
Trinidad, Felix, Sr. **8**:72
Trio Imperial **4**:70
Trío Los Panchos **1**:29
Trío San Juan **1**:29
Trist, Nicholas P. **4**:66
Triumph of the Spirit (film) **6**:81
Truan, Carlos **8**:73
Trujillo, Severino **8**:74
Truman, Harry S., assassination attempt on **1**:13
Tucson, Arizona
Leopoldo Carrillo and **2**:*54*
Mariano Samaniego and **7**:104
Tudor, Antony **1**:45
Turlington, Christy **8**:*75*

U

Unanue, Joseph **8**:*76*
Unión de Trabajadores del Valle Imperiale, La **5**:11
Unión Federal Mexicanos **5**:10
Union of Mine, Mill, and Smelter Workers **5**:12
United Cannery Agricultural Packing and Allied Workers of America (UCAPAWA) **2**:106, **6**:21
United Farm Workers (UFW) **1**:12–13, 22, 23, **4**:113, **5**:13, **6**:44
Antonio Orendain and **6**:84
Arturo S. Rodriguez and **7**:56
César Chávez and **2**:88, 89
and Delano grape strike **5**:13
Dolores Huerta and **4**:113
lapel badge **1**:*19*
United Farm Workers Organizing Committee (UFWOC) **5**:13
United Press International (UPI) **6**:57–58
United States, settlement in **8**:*22–27*
United States v. Sandoval (1897) **8**:26
Univision **5**:96–97
Urrea, Luis Alberto **8**:*77*
Urrea, Teresa **8**:*78*
novel about **8**:77
USA PATRIOT Act (2001) **7**:79

U.S. Hispanic Chamber of Commerce (USHCC) **6**:43, 44
U.S. Latino Issues (book) **1**:15
U.S.-Mexico border *see* border, Mexico-United States
U.S.-Mexico War *see* Mexican War

V

Valdés, Gilberto **6**:94
Valdés, Jesús "Chucho" **3**:79
Valdes, Miguelito **7**:9
Valdés, Vicentico **6**:39
Valdes-Rodriguez, Alisa **8**:*79*
Valdez, José Antonio **8**:80
Valdez, Luis M. **4**:*104*, 109, **6**:82, **8**:*81–82*
Valdez, Patssi **4**:4
Valens, Ritchie **4**:107, **6**:38, **8**:82, *83–84*
Valentín, Bobby **8**:85
Valentino, Rudolph **4**:108
Valenzuela, Fernando **8**:86
Valenzuela, José Luis **3**:*107*, **8**:*87*
Vallejo, Mariano Guadalupe **8**:32, 88
Valley of Peace **8**:59
Valverde, Antonio **5**:96
Vanidades (magazine) **7**:127
Varela, Maria **5**:69
Vargas, Diego de **3**:*55*, **8**:23
Vargas, Elizabeth **8**:89
Vargas, Fernando **8**:90
Felix Trinidad and **8**:*71–72*, 90
Vargas, Jay R. **8**:91
Vargas, Kathy **8**:92
Vargas, Miguel "Mike" **4**:109
Vasconcelos, José **4**:21, 106
Vasquez, Richard **8**:93
Vasquez, Tiburcio **3**:120, **8**:*94*
Vasquez Villalpando, Catalina **8**:*95–96*
Vatican, The **7**: 34, 36, 37
Véa, Alfredo, Jr. **8**:97
"Vedette of America" *see* Chacón, Iris
Vega, Bernardo **8**:98
Vega, "Little" Louie **5**:17, **8**:*99*
Vega Yunqué, Edgardo **8**:*100*
Velasco, Treaties of (1836) **7**:132, **8**:43
Velasquez, Baldemar **8**:*101*
Velásquez, Willie **8**:*102*
Velazquez, Loreta Janeta **8**:*103*
Velázquez, Nydia M. **8**:*104–105*
Vélez, Lauren **8**:*106*
Velez, Lupe **8**:*107*
Venegas, Juan E. **8**:108
Victoria, Texas **3**:39, 40
Vieques **2**:24, **6**:128
Vietnam War **5**:113
Alfredo Cantu Gonzalez and **4**:51
Eurípides Rubio and **7**:92
Jay R. Vargas and **8**:*91*
opposition to **1**:94, **4**:76, **7**:100
Richard E. Cavazos and **2**:75
Roy P. Benavidez and **1**:118
Vigil, Donaciano **8**:*109*
Vilar, Irene **5**:24
Villa, Beto **8**:*110*
Villa, Francisco "Pancho" **4**:49
Villalpando, Catalina Vásquez **1**:101
Villanueva, Alma Luz **8**:*111*
Villanueva, Tino **8**:*112*
Villaraigosa, Antonio **6**:*133*, **8**:*113*–114

Set Index

Villaraigosa, Natalia **8**:114
Villarreal, José Antonio **8**:*115*–116
Villarreal, Luis **8**:*117*
Villaseñor, Victor **8**:118
Viramontes, Helena Maria **7**:59, **8**:*119*
Virgil, Donaciano **1**:67
Víspera del Hombre, La (book) **5**:62
Vivir (album) **4**:118
voting **3**:73, **6**:*130*, 131
   see also political representation
Voting Rights Act Amendments (1975) **3**:73, **5**:85
Voz de las Americas (program) **4**:87
Voz del Pueblo, La (newspaper) **5**:73

W

Wagner Act *see* National Labor Relations Act
Walt Disney Productions, Manuel Gonzales and **4**:44
Warren, Earl **8**:33, 34
Washington, Terry **4**:42
Watergate scandal **7**:30
Wedding, The (book) **6**:134

We Fed Them Cactus (book) **2**:20
Weir, Bob **4**:14
Welch, Raquel **8**:*120*–121
Western Federation of Miners (WFM) **5**:10–11
West Side Story (film and stage show) **4**:109, **6**:22, 23, **7**:44
   see also Operation Wetback
Whispering to Fool The Wind (book) **7**:43
white flight **3**:74
Whitney, John Hay **4**:108
"Why Do Fools Fall in Love?" (song) **7**:124
Williams, Elena **8**:122, 123
Williams, William Carlos **8**:*122*–123
With His Pistol in His Hand (book) **6**:103
Woman in Battle, The (book) **8**:103
Women Who Run With the Wolves (book) **3**:94, 95
Wonder Woman **2**:*55*
World News Tonight (TV program) **8**:89
World War I **5**:112
   Latinos in **7**:96

need for agricultural and industrial laborers **4**:122
World War II **2**:107, **5**:112, 113, **8**:46
   Cleto Rodriguez and **7**:58
   Edward Hidalgo and **4**:97
   Felix Longoria and **2**:107, **5**:33–34
   José M. López and **5**:40
   Joseph Unanue and **8**:76
   Macario García and **4**:17
   need for agricultural and industrial laborers **2**:7–8, **4**:121, 122, **5**:12–13, **8**:27, 46
   Raul Morin and **6**:24
   Silvestre Herrera and **4**:95
   Vicente Ximenes and **8**:124

X

Ximenes, Vicente **6**:132, **8**:*124*

Y

Yahweh ben Yahweh **8**:29
Y'Barbo, Antonio Gil **8**:125
Yglesias, José **8**:*126*
Yo Soy Joaquin (film) **4**:109
"Yo Soy Joaquin" (poem) **4**:49
Young, Robert M. **6**:81

Young Citizens for Community Action (YCCA) **3**:90
Young Lords **2**:109, 110, **6**:128, **7**:45
Your Show of Shows (TV series) **2**:114–115
yo-yos **3**:*122*
Yzaguirre, Raúl **8**:*127*–128

Z

Zamora, Bernice **8**:129
Zapata, Carmen **8**:*130*
Zapata, Emiliano **4**:49
Zapatistas **1**:24
Zaragoza, Ignacio **8**:*131*–132
Zeno Gandía, Manuel **8**:133
zoopharmacognosy **7**:59
Zoot Suit (play and film) **3**:107, **4**:71, *104*, **6**:81, 82–83, **8**:*81*, 82
zoot suits **4**:104
Zúñiga, Martha **8**:*134*
Zygmund, Antoni **2**:22